READINGS

in

HER STORY

READINGS

—— *in* ——

HER STORY

Women in Christian Tradition

Barbara J. MacHaffie

FORTRESS PRESS   MINNEAPOLIS

READINGS IN HER STORY
Women in Christian Tradition

Interior design: ediType
Cover design: Lecy Design

Library of Congress Cataloging-in-Publication Data

MacHaffie, Barbara J., 1949
    Readings in her story : women in Christian tradition / Barbara J. MacHaffie.
        p.   cm.
    Includes bibliographical references.
    ISBN 0-8006-2575-7 (alk. paper)
    1. Women in Christianity—History.   2. Women in Christianity—United States—History.   I. Title.
    BV639.W7M25   1992
    270'.082—dc20   92-3693
                                                                CIP

The paper used in this publication meets the minimum requirements of American National Standard for Information Sciences—Permanence of Paper for Printed Library Materials, ANSI Z329.48-1984.   (∞)™

Manufactured in the U.S.A.   AF 1–2575

96   95   94   93   92   1   2   3   4   5   6   7   8   9   10

In Memory of My Mother
Eleanor Katherine Gohrs Zink

CONTENTS

PREFACE

Listening and speaking, hearing and being heard—these are themes woven insistently through the hopes for liberation held by many people in the Christian community. They point out that human beings are alienated from each other in part because they do not pay attention to the voices of others. *Readings in Her Story* is an anthology of historical and contemporary documents dealing with the status of women in the Christian community. It is also a meeting place for those who speak and those who listen. Here you will encounter the voices of men and women arguing persuasively with words of reason and beauty, shouting angrily with words of protest and condemnation, and questioning the way we use words. Here you will discover the mind of sexism and the will to affirm female dignity and equality. Here you will recover some of the voices of women who have been silent for so long and who have much to contribute to our understanding of the past.

I have been guided in my choice of texts by the material covered in *Her Story: Women in Christian Tradition*. Some of the texts themselves are discussed in *Her Story*, while others have been authored by men and women highlighted in that volume. All illustrate important themes and issues in the story of women in Christian history and serve to remind readers that the tradition has both patriarchal and feminist threads running through it. Each document is preceded by a brief introduction and full bibliographic citation. I have tried in the introductions to provide some information on the author of the text, the historical circumstances in which it was written, and its significance for understanding the status of women in Christian traditions. Readers might find it helpful to consult the entire text from which these excerpts have been taken in order to understand fully the development of important arguments. They may also want to supplement this book with other primary source collections, such as Rosemary Radford Ruether's three-volume series *Women and Religion in America*, Joyce Irwin's *Womanhood in Radical Protestantism, 1525–1625*, Alice Rossi's *The Feminist Papers*, and Ann Loades's *Feminist Theology: A Reader*.

Many people have helped to make this collection possible, and to them I owe my thanks. Marietta College and the Lilly Foundation have joined to provide support for this project through the college's program of Professional Improvement Grants. Mrs. Phyllis Zoerkler of Marietta College's library staff has done a superb job of securing material for me on interlibrary loan. Mrs. Linda McLeish and Mrs. Betty June Huck, both on the college's office support staff, and Mrs. Carmen Elswick, a student at Marietta, have helped enormously in the production of the manuscript. Professor Edward Osborne, chairman of the Department of Economics, Management, and Accounting, has graciously provided me with computer facilities. Beverly Zink and Philip Zink have helped to track down elusive sources while my husband, Fraser MacHaffie, offered patient reassurance when I doubted the value of this project.

—Barbara J. MacHaffie

ACKNOWLEDGMENTS

CHAPTER 2

Excerpts from "On the Appointment of Deacons and Deaconesses" are from *Didascalia Apostolorum: The Syriac Version Translated and Accompanied by the Verona Latin Fragments,* with an introduction and notes by R. Hugh Connolly (Oxford: Clarendon Press, 1929). Reprinted by permission.

Excerpts from "The Thunder, Perfect Mind" are from *The Nag Hammadi Library in English,* edited by James M. Robinson. Copyright © 1988 by E. J. Brill, Leiden, The Netherlands. Reprinted by permission of HarperCollins, Publishers, Inc.

Excerpts from Irenaeus, *Against Heresies,* are from *Women's Life in Greece and Rome: A Source Book in Translation,* by Mary B. Lefkowitz and Maureen B. Fant (Baltimore and London: The Johns Hopkins University Press, 1982). Reprinted by permission.

Excerpts from "The Martyrdom of Saints Perpetua and Felicitas" are from *The Acts of the Christian Martyrs,* introduction, texts, and translations by Herbert Musurillo (Oxford: Clarendon Press, 1972). Reprinted by permission.

Excerpts from "The Pilgrimage of Egeria" are from *A Lost Tradition: Women Writers of the Early Church,* by Patricia Wilson-Kastner et al. (Lanham, Md.: University Press of America, 1981). Reprinted by permission of the publisher.

CHAPTER 3

Excerpts from John Chrysostom, "Instruction and Refutation Directed against Those Men Cohabiting with Virgins" are from *Jerome, Chrysostom and Friends: Essays and Translations,* by Elizabeth A. Clark (Studies in Women and Religion, vol. 2) (New York: Edwin Mellen Press, 1979). Reprinted by permission.

Excerpts from *The Life of Melania the Younger,* introduction, translation, and commentary by Elizabeth A. Clark (Studies in Women and Religion, vol. 14) (New York: Edwin Mellen Press, 1985) are reprinted by permission.

Excerpts from *The Life of Christina of Markyate: A Twelfth Century Recluse,* edited and translated by C. H. Talbot (Oxford: Clarendon Press, 1959), are reprinted by permission.

Excerpts from *Malleus Maleficarum,* by Heinrich Institoris and Jakob Sprenger, translated by Montague Summers (New York: Dover Publications, Inc., 1971).

Excerpts from *The Book of the City of Ladies,* by Christine de Pizan, translated by Earl Jeffrey Richards (New York: Persea Books, 1982), are reprinted by permission.

Excerpts from *The Book of Margery Kempe, fourteen hundred & thirty six,* a modern version by W. Butler-Bowden, copyright © 1944 by Devin-Adair, Publishers, Inc., Old Greenwich, CT 06870, are used by permission.

CHAPTER 4

Excerpts from *Commentaries on the First Book of Moses Called Genesis,* by John Calvin, translated by John King, vol. 1 (Edinburgh: Calvin Translation Society, 1947).

Excerpts from *Calvin: Institutes of the Christian Religion,* edited by John T. MacNeill and translated by Ford Lewis Battles, The Library of Christian Classics, vols. 20 and 21, copyright © MCMLX by W. L. Jenkins, are reprinted by permission of Westminster/John Knox Press.

Excerpts from "Concerning Marriage" and "Concerning Adultery" are from *Confession of Faith: Account of Our Religion, Doctrine and Faith Given by Peter Rideman of the Brothers Whom Men Call Hutterians,* by Peter Rideman (Rifton, N.Y.: Plough Publishing House, 1970). Reprinted by permission.

CHAPTER 8

Excerpts from *Mother Caroline and the School Sisters of Notre Dame in North America,* vol. 1 (Saint Louis: Woodward and Tiernan Co., 1928).

CHAPTER 9

Excerpts from "Report of the Commission on Licensing and Ordaining Women" are from the *Journal of the Twenty-Ninth Delegated General Conference of the Methodist Episcopal Church Held at Springfield, Massachusetts.*

Excerpts from *Causes of Unrest among the Women of the Church,* by Katharine Bennett and Margaret E. Hodge (Philadelphia, 1927).

Excerpts from *The Service and Status of Women in the Churches,* by Kathleen Bliss (London: SCM Press, 1952), are reprinted by permission.

Excerpts from "Presbyterian Church U.S.A. Ordains First Woman Minister" are from *Presbyterian Life,* October 27, 1956, p. 18. Reprinted by permission of the Presbyterian Church U.S.A.

Excerpts from "Woman Looks at Herself" are from *The American Baptist Woman,* January 1971. Reprinted by permission.

Excerpts from *The Church and the Second Sex,* with the "Feminist Post-Christian Introduction" and "New Archaic After Words," by Mary Daly (1968, 1975; Boston: Beacon Press, 1985), are reprinted by permission of the author.

CHAPTER 10

Excerpts from "Declaration on the Question of the Admission of Women to the Ministerial Priesthood" are from *Women Priests: A Catholic Commentary on the Vatican Declaration,* edited by Leonard Swidler and Arlene Swidler. Copyright © 1977 by The Missionary Society of St. Paul the Apostle in the State of New York. Used by permission of Paulist Press.

Excerpts from "The Nun's Story" are from *Women and Religion: A Reader for the Clergy,* edited by Regina Coll, C.S.J. Copyright © 1982 by The Missionary Society of St. Paul the Apostle in the State of New York. Used by permission of Paulist Press.

Excerpts from "Expression of a Vision" are from *Women as Pastors,* edited by Lyle E. Schaller (Creative Leadership Series), copyright © 1982 by Abingdon Press. Excerpted by permission.

Excerpts from *Your Daughters Shall Prophesy: Feminist Alternatives in Theological Education,* by the Cornwall Collective (New York: Pilgrim Press, 1980), are reprinted by permission of the Pilgrim Press.

Excerpts from *An Inclusive Language Lectionary: Readings for Year B,* copyright © 1987 by the Division of Education and Ministry, National Council of the Churches of Christ in the U.S.A., are used by permission. All rights reserved.

Excerpts from *Human Liberation in a Feminist Perspective: A Theology,* by Letty M. Russell, copyright © 1974 by Letty M. Russell, are reprinted by permission of Westminster/John Knox Press.

Chapter 1

BIBLICAL IMAGES OF WOMEN

1 · JEPHTHAH'S DAUGHTER

The story of Jephthah's daughter is set in the days when the tribes of Israel depended upon judges raised up by God for their survival. The crisis in chapter 11 has been caused by an invasion of Gilead by the kingdom of Ammon. Jephthah, a social outcast, emerges as savior. Yet despite his anointing by the spirit of Yahweh, he feels he must bargain with God to guarantee victory. He promises to sacrifice "whoever" comes forth from his house to greet him on his return. His victory turns to tragedy when he is met by his one and only child, a daughter, who joins in an ancient ritual of celebration with timbrels and dances. Jephthah redeems his vow by inflicting upon this childless woman a violent and premature death. Although she has no heirs, she is remembered by all Israel.

Source: Judges 11:29-40.

²⁹Then the spirit of the LORD came upon Jephthah, and he passed through Gilead and Manasseh. He passed on to Mizpah of Gilead, and from Mizpah of Gilead he passed on to the Ammonites. ³⁰And Jephthah made a vow to the LORD, and said, "If you will give the Ammonites into my hand, ³¹then whoever comes out of the doors of my house to meet me, when I return victorious from the Ammonites, shall be the LORD's, to be offered up by me as a burnt offering." ³²So Jephthah crossed over to the Ammonites to fight against them; and the LORD gave them into his hand. ³³He inflicted a massive defeat on them from Aroer to the neighborhood of Minnith, twenty towns, and as far as Abel-keramim. So the Ammonites were subdued before the people of Israel.
³⁴Then Jephthah came to his home at Mizpah; and there was his daughter coming out to meet him with timbrels and with dancing. She was his only child; he had no son or daughter except her. ³⁵When he saw her, he tore his clothes, and said, "Alas, my daughter! You have brought me very low; you have become the cause of great trouble to me. For I have opened my mouth to the LORD, and I cannot take back my vow." ³⁶She said to him, "My father, if you have opened your mouth to the LORD, do to me

1

according to what has gone out of your mouth, now that the LORD has given you vengeance against your enemies, the Ammonites." [37]And she said to her father, "Let this thing be done for me: Grant me two months, so that I may go and wander on the mountains, and bewail my virginity, my companions and I." [38]"Go," he said and sent her away for two months. So she departed, she and her companions, and bewailed her virginity on the mountains. [39]At the end of two months, she returned to her father, who did with her according to the vow he had made. She had never slept with a man. So there arose an Israelite custom that [40]for four days every year the daughters of Israel would go out to lament the daughter of Jephthah the Gileadite.

2 ▪ THE MENSTRUAL TABOO

It was common in the religions of the ancient world to consider people under certain circumstances to be unclean or unholy. As such, it was unsafe for them to participate in or have contact with the ritual life of the community. These circumstances, as outlined in the legal codes of ancient Israel, included leprosy and other skin diseases, contact with a corpse, and bodily emissions of all types. In the fifteenth chapter of Leviticus, menstruation is detailed as an unclean condition, thus ensuring that women would be regularly excluded from ritual life.

Source: Leviticus 15:19-33.

[19]When a woman has a discharge of blood that is her regular discharge from her body, she shall be in her impurity for seven days, and whoever touches her shall be unclean until the evening. [20]Everything upon which she lies during her impurity shall be unclean; everything also upon which she sits shall be unclean. [21]Whoever touches her bed shall wash his clothes, and bathe in water, and be unclean until the evening. [22]Whoever touches anything upon which she sits shall wash his clothes, and bathe in water, and be unclean until the evening; [23]whether it is the bed or anything upon which she sits, when he touches it he shall be unclean until the evening. [24]If any man lies with her, and her impurity falls on him, he shall be unclean seven days; and every bed on which he lies shall be unclean.

[25]If a woman has a discharge of blood for many days, not at the time of her impurity, or if she has a discharge beyond the time of her impurity, all the days of the discharge she shall continue in uncleanness; as in the days of her impurity, she shall be unclean. [26]Every bed on which she lies during all the days of her discharge shall be treated as the bed of her impurity; and

everything on which she sits shall be unclean, as in the uncleanness of her impurity. ²⁷Whoever touches these things shall be unclean, and shall wash his clothes, and bathe in water, and be unclean until the evening. ²⁸If she is cleansed of her discharge, she shall count seven days, and after that she shall be clean. ²⁹On the eighth day she shall take two turtledoves or two pigeons and bring them to the priest to the entrance of the tent of meeting. ³⁰The priest shall offer one for a sin offering and the other for a burnt offering; and the priest shall make atonement on her behalf before the LORD for her unclean discharge.

³¹Thus you shall keep the people of Israel separate from their uncleanness, so that they do not die in their uncleanness by defiling my tabernacle that is in their midst.

³²This is the ritual for those who have a discharge: for him who has an emission of semen, becoming unclean thereby, ³³for her who is in the infirmity of her period, for anyone, male or female, who has a discharge, and for the man who lies with a woman who is unclean.

3 ▪ A CREATION STORY

The earlier of the two creation accounts in the Old Testament, Genesis 2–3 has been pointed to throughout history as divine sanction for the subordination of women. Such interpretations focus on the creation of woman after man and from his rib, on the use of the word helpmeet, *and on the role of woman in the fall. Other scholars, however, argue that a careful reading of the text affirms male-female equality. Woman is a helper who is not inferior and whose place in the creative process is parallel to her companion's. Her subjection after the fall is not a divine command but a prediction of what life would be like outside the gates of Eden.*

Source: Genesis 2:4—3:24.

⁴ᵇIn the day that the LORD God made the earth and the heavens, ⁵when no plant of the field was yet in the earth and no herb of the field had yet sprung up—for the LORD God had not caused it to rain upon the earth, and there was no one to till the ground; ⁶but a stream would rise from the earth, and water the whole face of the ground—⁷then the LORD God formed man from the dust of the ground, and breathed into his nostrils the breath of life; and the man became a living being. ⁸And the LORD God planted a garden in Eden, in the east; and there he put the man whom he had formed. ⁹Out of the ground the LORD God made to grow every tree

that is pleasant to the sight and good for food, the tree of life also in the midst of the garden, and the tree of the knowledge of good and evil. ¹⁰A river flows out of Eden to water the garden, and from there it divides and becomes four branches. ¹¹The name of the first is Pishon; it is the one that flows around the whole land of Havilah, where there is gold; ¹²and the gold of that land is good; bdellium and onyx stone are there. ¹³The name of the second river is Gihon; it is the one that flows around the whole land of Cush. ¹⁴The name of the third river is Tigris, which flows east of Assyria. And the fourth river is the Euphrates.

¹⁵The LORD God took the man and put him in the garden of Eden to till it and keep it. ¹⁶And the LORD God commanded the man, "You may freely eat of every tree of the garden; ¹⁷but of the tree of the knowledge of good and evil you shall not eat, for in the day that you eat of it you shall die."

¹⁸Then the LORD God said, "It is not good that the man should be alone; I will make him a helper as his partner." ¹⁹So out of the ground the LORD God formed every animal of the field and every bird of the air, and brought them to the man to see what he would call them; and whatever the man called every living creature, that was its name. ²⁰The man gave names to all cattle, and to the birds of the air, and to every animal of the field; but for the man there was not found a helper as his partner. ²¹So the LORD God caused a deep sleep to fall upon the man, and he slept; then he took one of his ribs and closed up its place with flesh. ²²And the rib that the LORD God had taken from the man he made into a woman and brought her to the man. ²³Then the man said,

> "This at last is bone of my bones
>   and flesh of my flesh;
> this one shall be called Woman,
>   for out of Man this one was taken."

²⁴Therefore a man leaves his father and his mother and clings to his wife, and they become one flesh. ²⁵And the man and his wife were both naked, and were not ashamed.

¹Now the serpent was more crafty than any other wild animal that the LORD God had made. He said to the woman, "Did God say, 'You shall not eat from any tree in the garden'?" ²The woman said to the serpent, "We may eat of the fruit of the trees in the garden; ³but God said, 'You shall not eat of the fruit of the tree that is in the middle of the garden, nor shall you touch it, or you shall die.'" ⁴But the serpent said to the woman, "You will not die; ⁵for God knows that when you eat of it your eyes will be opened, and you will be like God, knowing good and evil." ⁶So when the woman saw that the tree was good for food, and that it was a delight to the eyes, and that the tree was to be desired to make one wise, she took of its fruit and

ate; and she also gave some to her husband, who was with her, and he ate. [7]Then the eyes of both were opened, and they knew that they were naked; and they sewed fig leaves together and made loincloths for themselves.

[8]They heard the sound of the LORD God walking in the garden at the time of the evening breeze, and the man and his wife hid themselves from the presence of the LORD God among the trees of the garden. [9]But the LORD God called to the man, and said to him, "Where are you?" [10]He said, "I heard the sound of you in the garden, and I was afraid, because I was naked; and I hid myself." [11]He said, "Who told you that you were naked? Have you eaten from the tree of which I commanded you not to eat?" [12]The man said, "The woman whom you gave to be with me, she gave me fruit from the tree, and I ate." [13]Then the LORD God said to the woman, "What is this that you have done?" The woman said, "The serpent tricked me, and I ate." [14]The LORD God said to the serpent,

> "Because you have done this,
>   cursed are you among all animals
>   and among all wild creatures;
> upon your belly you shall go,
>   and dust you shall eat
>   all the days of your life.
> [15]I will put enmity between you and the woman,
>   and between your offspring and hers;
> he will strike your head,
>   and you will strike his heel."
> [16]To the woman he said,
> "I will greatly increase your pangs in childbearing;
>   in pain you shall bring forth children,
> yet your desire shall be for your husband,
>   and he shall rule over you."
> [17]And to the man he said,
> "Because you have listened to the voice of your wife,
>   and have eaten of the tree
> about which I commanded you,
>   'You shall not eat of it,'
> cursed is the ground because of you;
>   in toil you shall eat of it all the days of your life;
> [18]thorns and thistles it shall bring forth for you;
>   and you shall eat the plants of the field.
> [19]By the sweat of your face
>   you shall eat bread
> until you return to the ground,

for out of it you were taken;
you are dust,
   and to dust you shall return."

²⁰The man named his wife Eve, because she was the mother of all living. ²¹And the LORD God made garments of skins for the man and for his wife, and clothed them.

²²Then the LORD God said, "See, the man has become like one of us, knowing good and evil; and now, he might reach out his hand and take also from the tree of life, and eat, and live forever"—²³therefore the LORD God sent him forth from the garden of Eden, to till the ground from which he was taken. ²⁴He drove out the man; and at the east of the garden of Eden he placed the cherubim, and a sword flaming and turning to guard the way to the tree of life.

4 · EQUALITY IN LOVE

The Song of Solomon has been traditionally ascribed to Solomon, whose name appears in the text, but it is probably of much later origins. Many scholars believe the collection of poems was possibly influenced by Syrian wedding songs or the liturgical texts from ancient fertility rites. At face value, the poems express human passion in sensuous language and imagery. Many interpreters throughout history have understood the book as an allegory of the love between God and Israel or Christ and his bride, the church. Some feminist scholars see it as part of a biblical tradition that runs counter to patriarchal culture. They argue that the poems affirm a mutuality of the sexes and reject stereotyping. The female speaker, for example, earns her living and initiates lovemaking.

Source: Song of Solomon 1:1—3:5.

¹The Song of Songs, which is Solomon's.
²Let him kiss me with the kisses of his mouth!
 For your love is better than wine,
3   your anointing oils are fragrant,
  your name is perfume poured out;
     therefore the maidens love you.
⁴Draw me after you, let us make haste.
   The king has brought me into his chambers.
 We will exult and rejoice in you;
     we will extol your love more than wine;
     rightly do they love you.

⁵I am black and beautiful,
 O daughters of Jerusalem,
like the tents of Kedar,
 like the curtains of Solomon.
⁶Do not gaze at me because I am dark,
 because the sun has gazed on me.
My mother's sons were angry with me;
 they made me keeper of the vineyards,
 but my own vineyard I have not kept!
⁷Tell me, you whom my soul loves,
 where you pasture your flock,
 where you make it lie down at noon;
for why should I be like one who is veiled
 beside the flocks of your companions?

⁸If you do not know,
 O fairest among women,
follow the tracks of the flock,
 and pasture your kids
 beside the shepherds' tents.

⁹I compare you, my love,
 to a mare among Pharaoh's chariots.
¹⁰Your cheeks are comely with ornaments,
 your neck with strings of jewels.
¹¹We will make you ornaments of gold,
 studded with silver.

¹²While the king was on his couch,
 my nard gave forth its fragrance.
¹³My beloved is to me a bag of myrrh
 that lies between my breasts.
¹⁴My beloved is to me a cluster of henna blossoms
 in the vineyards of En-gedi.

¹⁵Ah, you are beautiful, my love;
 ah, you are beautiful;
 your eyes are doves.
¹⁶Ah, you are beautiful, my beloved,
 truly lovely.
Our couch is green;
¹⁷ the beams of our house are cedar,
 our rafters are pine.

¹I am a rose of Sharon,
    a lily of the valleys.

²As a lily among brambles,
    so is my love among maidens.

³As an apple tree among the trees of the wood,
    so is my beloved among young men.
With great delight I sat in his shadow,
    and his fruit was sweet to my taste.
⁴He brought me to the banqueting house,
    and his intention toward me was love.
⁵Sustain me with raisins,
    refresh me with apples;
    for I am faint with love.
⁶O that his left hand were under my head,
    and that his right hand embraced me!
⁷I adjure you, O daughters of Jerusalem,
    by the gazelles or the wild does:
do not stir up or awaken love
    until it is ready!

⁸The voice of my beloved!
    Look, he comes,
leaping upon the mountains,
    bounding over the hills.
⁹My beloved is like a gazelle
    or a young stag.
Look, there he stands
    behind our wall,
gazing in at the windows,
    looking through the lattice.
¹⁰My beloved speaks and says to me:
    "Arise, my love, my fair one,
    and come away;
¹¹for now the winter is past,
    the rain is over and gone.
¹²The flowers appear on the earth;
    the time of singing has come,
and the voice of the turtledove
    is heard in our land.
¹³The fig tree puts forth its figs,
    and the vines are in blossom;

they give forth fragrance.
   Arise, my love, my fair one,
      and come away.
14O my dove, in the clefts of the rock,
      in the covert of the cliff,
   let me see your face,
      let me hear your voice;
   for your voice is sweet,
      and your face is lovely.
15Catch us the foxes,
      the little foxes,
   that ruin the vineyards—
      for our vineyards are in blossom."

16My beloved is mine and I am his;
      he pastures his flock among the lilies.
17Until the day breathes
      and the shadows flee,
   turn, my beloved, be like a gazelle
      or a young stag on the cleft mountains.

1Upon my bed at night
      I sought him whom my soul loves;
   I sought him, but found him not;
      I called him, but he gave no answer.
2"I will rise now and go about the city,
      in the streets and in the squares;
   I will seek him whom my soul loves."
      I sought him, but found him not.

3The sentinels found me,
      as they went about in the city.
   "Have you seen him whom my soul loves?"
4Scarcely had I passed them,
      when I found him whom my soul loves.
   I held him, and would not let him go
      until I brought him into my mother's house,
         and into the chamber of her that conceived me.
5I adjure you, O daughters of Jerusalem,
      by the gazelles or the wild does:
   do not stir up or awaken love
      until it is ready!

5 · SOME RABBINIC TRADITIONS

Although some rabbis agreed that sons and daughters should be taught the Scriptures, the negative opinions of others concerning women and their role in the central activity of Jewish religious life cannot be ignored. In the first passage from the Mishnah, the second-century collection of laws that forms the superstructure of the Talmud, this ambivalence is evident. The second selection prescribes a domestic life for women.

Source: *The Mishnah; Translated from the Hebrew with Introduction and Brief Explanatory Notes.* Translated by Herbert Danby, 296, 252. Oxford: Oxford University Press, 1933.

Sotah 3.4

Hardly has she finished drinking before her face turns yellow and her eyes bulge and her veins swell, and they say, "Take her away! take her away! that the Temple Court be not made unclean!"[1] But if she had any merit this holds her punishment in suspense. Certain merits may hold punishment in suspense for one year, others for two years, and others for three years; hence Ben Azzai says: A man ought to give his daughter a knowledge of the Law so that if she must drink [the bitter water] she may know that the merit [that she had acquired] will hold her punishment in suspense. R. Eliezer says: If any man gives his daughter a knowledge of the Law it is as though he taught her lechery. R. Joshua says: A woman has more pleasure in one *kab* with lechery than in nine *kabs* with modesty.[2] He used to say: A foolish saint and a cunning knave and a woman that is a hypocrite and the wounds of the Pharisees, these wear out the world.

Ketuboth 5.5

These are works which the wife must perform for her husband: grinding flour and baking bread and washing clothes and cooking food and giving suck to her child and making ready his bed and working in wool. If she brought him in one bondwoman she need not grind or bake or wash; if two, she need not cook or give her child suck; if three, she need not make ready his bed or work in wool; if four, she may sit [all the day] in a chair. R. Eliezer says: Even if she brought him in a hundred bondwomen he should compel her to work in wool, for idleness leads to unchastity. Rabban Simeon b. Gamaliel says: Moreover if a man put his wife under a vow to do

1. The test of bitter water was a frightening and humiliating ordeal administered by religious authorities to determine whether a woman had committed adultery.—Ed.
2. A *kab* is a unit of liquid and dry measurement.—Ed.

no work he should put her away and give her *Ketubah*, for idleness leads to lowness of spirit.[3]

6 ▪ MARY AND MARTHA

Immediately following the parable of the Good Samaritan, Luke records the visit of Jesus to the house of his friends Mary and Martha. Here Jesus not only allows himself to be served by a woman, but he also rejects the idea that women should be restricted to domestic roles. Mary behaves like the male disciple of a male teacher or rabbi, and Jesus does not condemn her. She listens to his teaching while she "[sits] at the Lord's feet," a rabbinic phrase that means to study with a person. Mary is encouraged to feed her intellect and spirit.

Source: Luke 10:38-42.

[38]Now as they went on their way, he entered a certain village, where a woman named Martha welcomed him into her home. [39]She had a sister named Mary, who sat at the Lord's feet and listened to what he was saying. [40]But Martha was distracted by her many tasks; so she came to him and asked, "Lord, do you not care that my sister has left me to do all the work by myself? Tell her then to help me." [41]But the Lord answered her, "Martha, Martha, you are worried and distracted by many things; [42]there is need of only one thing. Mary has chosen the better part, which will not be taken away from her."

7 ▪ JESUS AND THE SAMARITAN WOMAN

The Gospel of John includes a story about Jesus and a Samaritan woman that reveals Jesus' willingness to violate conventional codes of male-female behavior. Tired from his journey, Jesus rests at Jacob's well outside the Samaritan village of Sychar while his disciples search for food. A Samaritan woman approaches to draw water and Jesus, despite the fact that he is a male and a Jew, talks to her. His disciples are clearly shocked, particularly because he is conversing in public with a woman. Jesus is also willing to take a drink from a woman considered by the Jews to be a menstruant from birth. He reveals his identity as Messiah to her and sends her back to her people where her "word" bears fruit like the "word" of the disciples in other parts of the Gospel.

---

3. The *Ketubah* is a sum of money previously agreed upon to be paid to a wife if her husband dies or divorces her.—Ed.

Source: John 4:1-42.

[1]Now when Jesus learned that the Pharisees had heard, "Jesus is making and baptizing more disciples than John" [2]—although it was not Jesus himself but his disciples who baptized—[3]he left Judea and started back to Galilee. [4]But he had to go through Samaria. [5]So he came to a Samaritan city called Sychar, near the plot of ground that Jacob had given to his son Joseph. [6]Jacob's well was there, and Jesus, tired out by his journey, was sitting by the well. It was about noon.

[7]A Samaritan woman came to draw water, and Jesus said to her, "Give me a drink." [8](His disciples had gone to the city to buy food.) [9]The Samaritan woman said to him, "How is it that you, a Jew, ask a drink of me, a woman of Samaria?" (Jews do not share things in common with Samaritans.) [10]Jesus answered her, "If you knew the gift of God, and who it is that is saying to you, 'Give me a drink,' you would have asked him, and he would have given you living water." [11]The woman said to him, "Sir, you have no bucket, and the well is deep. Where do you get that living water? [12]Are you greater than our ancestor Jacob, who gave us the well, and with his sons and his flocks drank from it?" [13]Jesus said to her, "Everyone who drinks of this water will be thirsty again, [14]but those who drink of the water that I will give them will never be thirsty. The water that I will give will become in them a spring of water gushing up to eternal life." [15]The woman said to him, "Sir, give me this water, so that I may never be thirsty or have to keep coming here to draw water."

[16]Jesus said to her, "Go, call your husband, and come back." [17]The woman answered him, "I have no husband." Jesus said to her, "You are right in saying, 'I have no husband'; [18]for you have had five husbands, and the one you have now is not your husband. What you have said is true!" [19]The woman said to him, "Sir, I see that you are a prophet. [20]Our ancestors worshiped on this mountain, but you say that the place where people must worship is in Jerusalem." [21]Jesus said to her, "Woman, believe me, the hour is coming when you will worship the Father neither on this mountain nor in Jerusalem. [22]You worship what you do not know; we worship what we know, for salvation is from the Jews. [23]But the hour is coming, and is now here, when the true worshipers will worship the Father in spirit and truth, for the Father seeks such as these to worship him. [24]God is spirit, and those who worship him must worship in spirit and truth." [25]The woman said to him, "I know that Messiah is coming" (who is called Christ). "When he comes, he will proclaim all things to us." [26]Jesus said to her, "I am he, the one who is speaking to you."

[27]Just then his disciples came. They were astonished that he was speaking with a woman, but no one said, "What do you want?" or, "Why are

you speaking with her?" [28]Then the woman left her water jar and went back to the city. She said to the people, [29]"Come and see a man who told me everything I have ever done! He cannot be the Messiah, can he?" [30]They left the city and were on their way to him.

[31]Meanwhile the disciples were urging him, "Rabbi, eat something." [32]But he said to them, "I have food to eat that you do not know about." [33]So the disciples said to one another, "Surely no one has brought him something to eat?" [34]Jesus said to them, "My food is to do the will of him who sent me and to complete his work. [35]Do you not say, 'Four months more, then comes the harvest'? But I tell you, look around you, and see how the fields are ripe for harvesting. [36]The reaper is already receiving wages and is gathering fruit for eternal life, so that sower and reaper may rejoice together. [37]For here the saying holds true, 'One sows and another reaps.' [38]I sent you to reap that for which you did not labor. Others have labored, and you have entered into their labor."

[39]Many Samaritans from that city believed in him because of the woman's testimony, "He told me everything I have ever done." [40]So when the Samaritans came to him, they asked him to stay with them; and he stayed there two days. [41]And many more believed because of his word. [42]They said to the woman, "It is no longer because of what you said that we believe, for we have heard for ourselves, and we know that this is truly the Savior of the world."

8 ▪ PAUL ON MARRIAGE

Scholars agree that this text, which is basically positive in its attitude toward women, is from the hand of the apostle Paul. Paul affirms the goodness of marriage and the legitimacy of sexuality within marriage. He repeats Jesus' prohibition on divorce for men and women but then qualifies it to permit dissolution of marriages between Christians and non-Christians, if faith were threatened. In the last section Paul offers his own opinion in favor of celibacy, arguing that marriage is unnecessary because the second coming is imminent and the chaste would be freer to devote themselves to prayer and good works. In this entire passage he is remarkably evenhanded in dealing with women and men. They each have rights and responsibilities and are subject to expectations and allowances.

Source: 1 Corinthians 7:1-40.

[1]Now concerning the matters about which you wrote: "It is well for a man not to touch a woman." [2]But because of cases of sexual immorality, each

man should have his own wife and each woman her own husband. ³The husband should give to his wife her conjugal rights, and likewise the wife to her husband. ⁴For the wife does not have authority over her own body, but the husband does; likewise the husband does not have authority over his own body, but the wife does. ⁵Do not deprive one another except perhaps by agreement for a set time, to devote yourselves to prayer, and then come together again, so that Satan may not tempt you because of your lack of self-control. ⁶This I say by way of concession, not of command. ⁷I wish that all were as I myself am. But each has a particular gift from God, one having one kind and another a different kind.

⁸To the unmarried and the widows I say that it is well for them to remain unmarried as I am. ⁹But if they are not practicing self-control, they should marry. For it is better to marry than to be aflame with passion.

¹⁰To the married I give this command—not I but the Lord—that the wife should not separate from her husband ¹¹(but if she does separate, let her remain unmarried or else be reconciled to her husband), and that the husband should not divorce his wife.

¹²To the rest I say—I and not the Lord—that if any believer has a wife who is an unbeliever, and she consents to live with him, he should not divorce her. ¹³And if any woman has a husband who is an unbeliever, and he consents to live with her, she should not divorce him. ¹⁴For the unbelieving husband is made holy through his wife, and the unbelieving wife is made holy through her husband. Otherwise, your children would be unclean, but as it is, they are holy. ¹⁵But if the unbelieving partner separates, let it be so; in such a case the brother or sister is not bound. It is to peace that God has called you. ¹⁶Wife, for all you know, you might save your husband. Husband, for all you know, you might save your wife.

¹⁷However that may be, let each of you lead the life that the Lord has assigned, to which God called you. This is my rule in all the churches. ¹⁸Was anyone at the time of his call already circumcised? Let him not seek to remove the marks of circumcision. Was anyone at the time of his call uncircumcised? Let him not seek circumcision. ¹⁹Circumcision is nothing, and uncircumcision is nothing; but obeying the commandments of God is everything. ²⁰Let each of you remain in the condition in which you were called.

²¹Were you a slave when called? Do not be concerned about it. Even if you can gain your freedom, make use of your present condition now more than ever. ²²For whoever was called in the Lord as a slave is a freed person belonging to the Lord, just as whoever was free when called is a slave of Christ. ²³You were bought with a price; do not become slaves of human masters. ²⁴In whatever condition you were called, brothers and sisters, there remain with God.

²⁵Now concerning virgins, I have no command of the Lord, but I give my opinion as one who by the Lord's mercy is trustworthy. ²⁶I think that, in view of the impending crisis, it is well for you to remain as you are. ²⁷Are you bound to a wife? Do not seek to be free. Are you free from a wife? Do not seek a wife. ²⁸But if you marry, you do not sin, and if a virgin marries, she does not sin. Yet those who marry will experience distress in this life, and I would spare you that. ²⁹I mean, brothers and sisters, the appointed time has grown short; from now on, let even those who have wives be as though they had none, ³⁰and those who mourn as though they were not mourning, and those who rejoice as though they were not rejoicing, and those who buy as though they had no possessions, ³¹and those who deal with the world as though they had no dealings with it. For the present form of this world is passing away.

³²I want you to be free from anxieties. The unmarried man is anxious about the affairs of the Lord, how to please the Lord; ³³but the married man is anxious about the affairs of the world, how to please his wife, ³⁴and his interests are divided. And the unmarried woman and the virgin are anxious about the affairs of the Lord, so that they may be holy in body and spirit; but the married woman is anxious about the affairs of the world, how to please her husband. ³⁵I say this for your own benefit, not to put any restraint upon you, but to promote good order and unhindered devotion to the Lord.

³⁶If anyone thinks that he is not behaving properly toward his fiancée, if his passions are strong, and so it has to be, let him marry as he wishes; it is no sin. Let them marry. ³⁷But if someone stands firm in his resolve, being under no necessity but having his own desire under control, and has determined in his own mind to keep her as his fiancée, he will do well. ³⁸So then, he who marries his fiancée does well; and he who refrains from marriage will do better.

³⁹A wife is bound as long as her husband lives. But if the husband dies, she is free to marry anyone she wishes, only in the Lord. ⁴⁰But in my judgment she is more blessed if she remains as she is. And I think that I too have the Spirit of God.

9 ▪ HEADCOVERING IN THE CHURCH

Probably concerned about the prevalence of homosexuality in Greco-Roman culture, Paul's primary objective in 1 Corinthians 11 is to maintain an orderly church that has clear distinctions between women and men. He is clearly ambivalent about the status of women here. He assumes it is proper for women to pray and prophesy out loud, but they must cover their heads, a traditional gesture of subjection. He searches the Scriptures and comes up with a rationale from the order of creation in Genesis 2 and "because of the angels," an argument not entirely clear. He hints, however, at male-female equality in verses 11 and 12.

Source: 1 Corinthians 11:2-16.

[2]I commend you because you remember me in everything and maintain the traditions just as I handed them on to you. [3]But I want you to understand that Christ is the head of every man, and the husband is the head of his wife, and God is the head of Christ. [4]Any man who prays or prophesies with something on his head disgraces his head, [5]but any woman who prays or prophesies with her head unveiled disgraces her head—it is one and the same thing as having her head shaved. [6]For if a woman will not veil herself, then she should cut off her hair; but if it is disgraceful for a woman to have her hair cut off or to be shaved, she should wear a veil. [7]For a man ought not to have his head veiled, since he is the image and reflection of God; but woman is the reflection of man. [8]Indeed, man was not made from woman, but woman from man. [9]Neither was man created for the sake of woman, but woman for the sake of man. [10]For this reason a woman ought to have a symbol of authority on her head, because of the angels. [11]Nevertheless, in the Lord woman is not independent of man or man independent of woman. [12]For just as woman came from man, so man comes through woman; but all things come from God. [13]Judge for yourselves: is it proper for a woman to pray to God with her head unveiled? [14]Does not nature itself teach you that if a man wears long hair, it is degrading to him, [15]but if a woman has long hair, it is her glory? For her hair is given to her for a covering. [16]But if anyone is disposed to be contentious—we have no such custom, nor do the churches of God.

Chapter 2

WOMEN AND
THE EARLY CHURCHES

10 • WOMEN KEEP SILENT

The First Letter to Timothy, probably written early in the second century, is believed by many biblical scholars to be the work not of Paul but of someone influenced by Paul's teaching. In addition to a lengthy discussion about widows, deacons, and bishops, the letter contains what can be seen as the most negative statement in the New Testament about women. Women are told that they are not to teach or exercise authority over men, but to keep silence. The author uses a contemporary Jewish interpretation of the fall—that it was caused by Eve—as the basis for these limitations.

Source: 1 Timothy 2:8-15.

[8]I desire, then, that in every place the men should pray, lifting up holy hands without anger or argument; [9]also that the women should dress themselves modestly and decently in suitable clothing, not with their hair braided, or with gold, pearls, or expensive clothes, [10]but with good works, as is proper for women who profess reverence for God. [11]Let a woman learn in silence with full submission. [12]I permit no woman to teach or to have authority over a man; she is to keep silent. [13]For Adam was formed first, then Eve; [14]and Adam was not deceived, but the woman was deceived and became a transgressor. [15]Yet she will be saved through childbearing, provided they continue in faith and love and holiness, with modesty.

11 • DEACONESSES IN THE EARLY CHURCH

The Didascalia Apostolorum, *a set of instructions ordering the ritual and moral life of the church as well as its polity, was probably composed in northern Syria in the beginning of the third century. It lays down, for example, a liturgy for public penance, rules for the election of a bishop, procedures for the ordination of priests, and moral instruction. Of interest here is its provision for the appointment of women as deaconesses. They are to be helpers to the bishop, appointed particularly for a ministry to women. The church is instructed to use them as visitors to Christian women in non-Christian homes and as assistants in the baptismal ritual, anointing the heads of women and receiving them from the water.*

Source: "On the Appointment of Deacons and Deaconesses." In *Didascalia Apostolorum: The Syriac Version Translated and Accompanied by the Verona Latin Fragments,* with an introduction and notes by R. Hugh Connolly, 146–48. Oxford: Clarendon Press, 1929.

Wherefore, O bishop, appoint thee workers of righteousness as helpers who may co-operate with thee unto salvation. Those that please thee out of all the people thou shalt choose and appoint as deacons: a man for the performance of the most things that are required, but a woman for the ministry of women. For there are houses whither thou canst not send a deacon to the women, on account of the heathen, but mayest send a deaconess. Also, because in many other matters the office of a woman deacon is required. In the first place, when women go down into the water, those who go down into the water ought . . . to be anointed by a deaconess with the oil of anointing; and where there is no woman at hand, and especially no deaconess, he who baptizes must of necessity anoint her who is being baptized. But where there is a woman, and especially a deaconess, it is not fitting that women should be seen by men: but with the imposition of hand do thou anoint the head only. As of old the priests and kings were anointed in Israel, do thou in like manner, with the imposition of hand, anoint the head of those who receive baptism, whether of men or of women; and afterwards—whether thou thyself baptize, or thou command the deacons or presbyters to baptize—let a woman deacon, as we have already said, anoint the women. But let a man pronounce over them the invocation of the divine Names in the water.

And when she who is being baptized has come up from the water, let the deaconess receive her, and teach and instruct her how the seal of baptism ought to be (kept) unbroken in purity and holiness. For this cause we say that the ministry of a woman deacon is especially needful and important. For our Lord and Savior also was ministered unto by women ministers, *Mary Magdalene, and Mary the daughter of James and mother of Jose, and the mother of the sons of Zebedee,* with other women beside. And thou also hast need of the ministry of a deaconess for many things; for a deaconess is required to go into the houses of the heathen where there are believing women, and to visit those who are sick, and to minister to them in that of which they have need, and to bathe those who have begun to recover from sickness.

12 ▪ CHRISTIAN WIDOWS

This selection comes from a collection of church law, the Apostolic Constitutions, *compiled in Syria around 380. In addition to incorporating the* Didascalia Apostolorum, *the legislation covers matters such as liturgical procedures, fasts and feasts, schism, heresy, and Christian burial. It also describes the duties of members of the Christian community. Women, when widowed, were entitled to the support of the church if they were sober, chaste, pious, and the wives of only one husband. They were not to discuss doctrine lest they misconstrue it. The church, in fact, was not to allow any woman to teach. Such teaching, the document argues, would be contrary to the example set by Jesus and the biblical injunction that women be subject to men. Widows, furthermore, were to remain within the confines of their homes to pray for the church.*

Source: "Concerning Christian Widows." In *The Work Claiming to Be the Constitutions of the Holy Apostles, Including the Canons*, translated by Irah Chase, 81–83. New York: D. Appleton, 1848.

That the widows are to be very careful of their deportment.
  Let every widow be meek, quiet, gentle, sincere, free from anger; not talkative, not clamorous, not hasty of speech, not given to evil-speaking, not captious, not double-tongued, not a busy-body. If she see or hear any thing that is not right, let her be as one that doth not see, and as one that doth not hear; and let the widow mind nothing but to pray for those that give, and for the whole church; and when she is asked any thing by any one, let her not easily answer, except questions concerning faith, and right-eousness, and hope in God; remitting to the rulers those that desire to be instructed in the doctrines of godliness. Let her answer only so as may tend to subvert the error of polytheism, and demonstrate the doctrine concerning the monarchy of God. But of the remaining doctrines, let her not answer any thing rashly, lest, by saying any thing unlearnedly, she should cause the Word to be blasphemed. For the Lord hath taught us, that the Word is like *a grain of mustard seed*, which is of a fiery nature; and, if any one useth it unskilfully, he will find it bitter. For in the mystical points we ought not to be rash, but cautious. For the Lord exhorteth us, saying, *Cast not your pearls before swine, lest they trample them with their feet, and turn again and rend you*. For unbelievers, when they hear the doctrine concerning Christ not explained as it ought to be, but defectively, and especially that concerning his incarnation or his passion, will rather reject it with scorn, and laugh

at it as false, than praise God for it. And so the aged women will be guilty of rashness, and of causing blasphemy, and will inherit a woe. For, saith he, *Woe to him by whom my name is blasphemed among the Gentiles.*

That women ought not to teach, because it is unseemly; and what women followed our Lord.

We do not permit our *women to teach in the church*, but only to pray, and to hear those that teach. For our Master and Lord, Jesus Christ himself, when he sent us, the twelve, to make disciples of the people and of the nations, did nowhere send out women to preach, although he did not want such; for there were with us the mother of our Lord, and his sisters; also Mary Magdalen; and Mary, the mother of James; and Martha and Mary, the sisters of Lazarus; Salome, and certain others. For, had it been necessary for women to teach, he himself would have first commanded these also to instruct the people with us. For if *the head of the wife be the man*, it is not reasonable that the rest of the body should govern the head.

Let the widow, therefore, own herself to be the *altar of God*, and let her sit in her house, and not enter into the houses of the faithful, under any pretense, to receive any thing; for the altar of God never runneth about, but is fixed in one place. Let, therefore, the virgin and the widow be such as do not run about, or gad to the houses of those who are alien from the faith. For such as these are gadders and impudent; they do not make their feet to rest in one place, because they are not widows, but purses ready to receive, triflers, evil speakers, counsellors of strife, without shame, impudent; who, being such, are not worthy of him that called them. For they do not come to the common resting place of the congregation on the Lord's day, as those that are watchful. But they either slumber, or trifle, or allure men, or beg, or ensnare others, bringing them to the evil one; not suffering them to be watchful in the Lord; but taking care that they go out as vain as they came in, because they do not hear the Word of the Lord either taught or read. For of such as these the prophet Isaiah saith, *Hearing ye shall hear, and shall not understand; and seeing ye shall see, and not perceive; for the heart of this people is waxen gross.*

13 ▪ GNOSTIC IMAGES OF THE DIVINE

The Thunder, Perfect Mind *is a short discourse from the extensive collection of fourth-century gnostic writings discovered near the Egyptian city of Nag Hammadi in 1946. The collection, containing many literary types and many forms of Gnosticism, has enabled scholars to study the tradition from gnostic sources and not simply the accounts of Christian opponents. In* The Thunder *a female revealer speaks from the world of the divine. The absolute transcendence and unfathomable character of the revealer is demonstrated by her use of antithetical or paradoxical descriptors.*

Source: "The Thunder, Perfect Mind" 6.2. In *The Nag Hammadi Library in English*, translated by members of the Coptic Gnostic Library Project of the Institute for Antiquity and Christianity, James M. Robinson, Director, 271–72. San Francisco: Harper & Row, 1977.

I was sent forth from [the] power,
    and I have come to those who reflect upon me,
    and I have been found among those who seek after me.
Look upon me, you (pl.) who reflect upon me,
    and you hearers, hear me.
    You who are waiting for me, take me to yourselves.
And do not banish me from your sight.
    And do not make your voice hate me, nor your hearing.
    Do not be ignorant of me anywhere or any time. Be on your
        guard!
    Do not be ignorant of me.
For I am the first and the last.
I am the honored one and the scorned one.
I am the whore and the holy one.
I am the wife and the virgin.
I am <the mother> and the daughter.
I am the members of my mother.
I am the barren one
    and many are her sons.
I am she whose wedding is great,
    and I have not taken a husband.
I am the midwife and she who does not bear.
I am the solace of my labor pains.
I am the bride and the bridegroom,
    and it is my husband who begot me.
I am the mother of my father
    and the sister of my husband,
    and he is my offspring.
I am the slave of him who prepared me.
I am the ruler of my offspring.
    But he is the one who [begot me] before the time on a birthday.
    And he is my offspring [in] (due) time, and my power is from
        him.

I am the staff of his power in his youth,
  [and] he is the rod of my old age.
  And whatever he wills happens to me.
I am the silence that is incomprehensible
  and the idea whose remembrance is frequent.
I am the voice whose sound is manifold
  and the word whose appearance is multiple.
I am the utterance of my name.
Why, you who hate me, do you love me,
  and you hate those who love me?
You who deny me, confess me,
  and you who confess me, deny me.
You who tell the truth about me, lie about me,
  and you who have lied about me, tell the truth about me.
You who know me, be ignorant of me,
  and those who have not known me, let them know me.

14 ▪ WOMEN IN GNOSTIC RITUAL

After studying in Rome and serving as a presbyter, Irenaeus (c. 130–200) was appointed bishop of Lyons in 178. His chief work, Against Heresies, *is a detailed attack on Gnosticism and some aspects of Montanism in the name of orthodoxy as it had developed by the end of the second century. Here he scorns women who follow Marcus not only because of his tricks but also because he promises them unity with the divine. They are participants in gnostic ritual, being given the cup and told to pray and prophesy. Grace, whose presence they desire, is a female essence.*

Source: Irenaeus. *Against Heresies* 1.13.1–4. Translated by Mary R. Lefkowitz. In *Women's Life in Greece and Rome*, compiled by Mary R. Lefkowitz and Maureen B. Fant, 275–76. Baltimore: Johns Hopkins University Press, 1982.

There is another one of those Gnostics who prides himself on having improved on his teacher. His name is Marcus. He is skilled in the art of false magic, and has used it to deceive many men and not a few women and to convert them to his cult, on the grounds that he is the most knowledgeable and has the greatest access to hidden and indescribable places. One could call him the One before the Antichrist (if such a person existed)....He pretends to say grace over a cup with wine in it; while he strings out his prayer at great length, he makes the wine turn red and purple, so that they will believe that the true Grace of the Company of the Most High is letting her blood drop into his cup during his prayer, and that those present should strongly desire to taste of that cup so that into them too Grace would drop, because she is summoned by that magician. Again, he gives women cups full of wine and orders them to say grace in his presence. When this is done he offers another cup much larger than the one over which the deceived woman has said grace; he then pours from the smaller cup (over which the woman said grace) into the much larger one which he has brought forward; at the same time he says as follows: "May grace who is before all things, who cannot be known or imagined, fill your inner person and multiply in you her understanding, sowing her mustard seed in good soil." By saying this sort of thing he makes the poor woman insane, while he appears to be working wonders, since the bigger cup is filled up by the smaller cup, so that it spills over. By performing other tricks like that he has destroyed many people, and steals them for his cult. . . .

He spends his time mainly with women, and particularly with those who come from good families and who have fine clothes and are very rich. He frequently deceives them with flattery, and seduces them by saying: "I want you to share in my grace, since the Father of All always sees your angel before his face. The place of your greatness is in *us;* it is right that we come together into one being. Take grace first from me and through me. Prepare yourself as a bride to receive your bridegroom so that you may be what I am, and I be what you are. Set in your bridal chamber the seed of light. Receive from me your bridegroom, take him, and be taken in him. Behold grace descends on you. Open your mouth and prophesy." But when the woman answers "I have never prophesied and I have nothing to prophesy," he offers new prayers, to the bewilderment of the woman who is being deluded: "Open your mouth and speak whatever comes to you, and you will prophesy." And she in her delusion, excited by what has already been said, her courage stimulated by the notion that she can prophesy, with her heart pounding harder than it should, takes the chance, and speaks in her delirium, and all sorts of things come out, foolishly and brazenly. . . . From that time on she thinks she is a Prophetess and gives thanks to Marcus because he shared his grace with her. She offers to pay him, not only by giving him her possessions (by which means he has amassed a huge amount of wealth) but also by intercourse with her body, and in addition she seeks to be united with him in everything so that she may enter with him into the One. . . . This same Marcus uses love potions and aphrodisiacs so that he can inflict violence on the bodies of some women—not of all. Those who return to the Church of God very often confess that not only have their bodies been corrupted by him but that they were passionately in love with him.

15 • THE MARTYRDOM OF PERPETUA

One of Christianity's oldest and most descriptive accounts of martyrdom is in large part written by a woman. The author, Vibia Perpetua, daughter of a wealthy Carthaginian family, was arrested along with five friends in 202 or 203 at the direction of Septimus Severus. The account of her imprisonment and visions was supplemented and verified by fellow martyr Satarus and later given an introduction and conclusion. In these sections from Perpetua's story, she makes clear her willingness to defy the norms of family, society, and state although she does so with regret. They also illustrate the androgynous character of the story, presenting Perpetua as both daughter and combatant, nurturer and rebel.

Source: "The Martyrdom of Saints Perpetua and Felicitas." In *The Acts of the Christian Martyrs*, introduction, texts, and translations by Herbert Musurillo, 109–19. Oxford: Clarendon Press, 1972.

While we were still under arrest (she said) my father out of love for me was trying to persuade me and shake my resolution. "Father," said I, "do you see this vase here, for example, or waterpot or whatever?"

"Yes, I do," said he.

And I told him: "Could it be called by any other name than what it is?"

And he said: "No."

"Well, so too I cannot be called anything other than what I am, a Christian."

At this my father was so angered by the word "Christian" that he moved towards me as though he would pluck my eyes out. But he left it at that and departed, vanquished along with his diabolical arguments.

For a few days afterwards I gave thanks to the Lord that I was separated from my father, and I was comforted by his absence. During these few days I was baptized, and I was inspired by the Spirit not to ask for any other favor after the water but simply the perseverance of the flesh. A few days later we were lodged in the prison; and I was terrified, as I had never before been in such a dark hole. What a difficult time it was! With the crowd the heat was stifling; then there was the extortion of the soldiers; and to crown all, I was tortured with worry for my baby there.

Then Tertius and Pomponius, those blessed deacons who tried to take care of us, bribed the soldiers to allow us to go to a better part of the prison to refresh ourselves for a few hours. Everyone then left that dungeon and shifted for himself. I nursed my baby, who was faint from hunger. In my anxiety I spoke to my mother about the child, I tried to comfort my brother, and I gave the child in their charge. I was in pain because I saw them suffering out of pity for me. These were the trials I had to endure for many days. Then I got permission for my baby to stay with me in prison. At once I recovered my health, relieved as I was of my worry and anxiety over the child. My prison had suddenly become a palace, so that I wanted to be there rather than anywhere else....

A few days later there was a rumor that we were going to be given a hearing. My father also arrived from the city, worn with worry, and he came to see me with the idea of persuading me.

"Daughter," he said, "have pity on my grey head—have pity on me your father, if I deserve to be called your father, if I have favored you above all your brothers, if I have raised you to reach this prime of your life. Do not abandon me to be the reproach of men. Think of your brothers, think of your mother and your aunt, think of your child, who will not be able to live once you are gone. Give up your pride! You will destroy all of us! None of us will ever be able to speak freely again if anything happens to you."

This was the way my father spoke out of love for me, kissing my hands and throwing himself down before me. With tears in his eyes he no longer addressed me as his daughter but as a woman. I was sorry for my father's sake, because he alone of all my kin would be unhappy to see me suffer.

I tried to comfort him saying: "It will all happen in the prisoner's dock as God wills; for you may be sure that we are not left to ourselves but are all in his power."

And he left me in great sorrow.

One day while we were eating breakfast we were suddenly hurried off for a hearing. We arrived at the forum, and straight away the story went about the neighborhood near the forum and a huge crowd gathered. We walked up to the prisoner's dock. All the others when questioned admitted their guilt. Then, when it came my turn, my father appeared with my son, dragged me from the step, and said: "Perform the sacrifice—have pity on your baby!"

Hilarianus the governor, who had received his judicial powers as the successor of the late proconsul Minucius Timinianus, said to me: "Have pity on your father's grey head; have pity on your infant son. Offer the sacrifice for the welfare of the emperors."

"I will not," I retorted.

"Are you a Christian?" said Hilarianus.

And I said: "Yes, I am."

When my father persisted in trying to dissuade me, Hilarianus ordered him to be thrown to the ground and beaten with a rod. I felt sorry for father, just as if I myself had been beaten. I felt sorry for his pathetic old age.

Then Hilarianus passed sentence on all of us: we were condemned to the beasts, and we returned to prison in high spirits. But my baby had got used to being nursed at the breast and to staying with me in prison. So I sent the deacon Pomponius straight away to my father to ask for the baby. But father refused to give him over. But as God willed, the baby had no further desire for the breast, nor did I suffer any inflammation; and so I was relieved of any anxiety for my child and of any discomfort in my breasts. . . .

The day before we were to fight with the beasts I saw the following vision. Pomponius the deacon came to the prison gates and began to knock violently. I went out and opened the gate for him. He was dressed in an unbelted white tunic, wearing elaborate sandals. And he said to me: "Perpetua, come; we are waiting for you."

Then he took my hand and we began to walk through rough and broken country. At last we came to the amphitheater out of breath, and he led me into the center of the arena.

Then he told me: "Do not be afraid. I am here, struggling with you." Then he left.

I looked at the enormous crowd who watched in astonishment. I was surprised that no beasts were let loose on me; for I knew that I was condemned to die by the beasts. Then out came an Egyptian against me, of vicious appearance, together with his seconds, to fight with me. There also came up to me some handsome young men to be my seconds and assistants.

My clothes were stripped off, and suddenly I was a man. My seconds began to rub me down with oil (as they are wont to do before a contest). Then I saw the Egyptian on the other side rolling in the dust. Next there came forth a man of marvellous stature, such that he rose above the top of the amphitheater. He was clad in a beltless purple tunic with two stripes (one on either side) running down the middle of his chest. He wore sandals that were wondrously made of gold and silver, and he carried a wand like an athletic trainer and a green branch on which there were golden apples.

And he asked for silence and said: "If this Egyptian defeats her he will slay her with the sword. But if she defeats him, she will receive this branch." Then he withdrew.

We drew close to one another and began to let our fists fly. My opponent tried to get hold of my feet, but I kept striking him in the face with the heels of my feet. Then I was raised up into the air and I began to pummel him without as it were touching the ground. Then when I noticed there was a lull, I put my two hands together linking the fingers of one hand with those of the other and thus I got hold of his head. He fell flat on his face and I stepped on his head.

The crowd began to shout and my assistants started to sing psalms. Then I walked up to the trainer and took the branch. He kissed me and said to me: "Peace be with you, my daughter!" I began to walk in triumph towards the Gate of Life. Then I awoke. I realized that it was not with wild animals that I would fight but with the Devil, but I knew that I would win the victory. So much for what I did up until the eve of the contest. About what happened at the contest itself, let him write of it who will.

16 · ADORNING WOMEN

One of the thirty-eight surviving treatises written by Tertullian (c. 160–220), a presbyter in Carthage, deals with appropriate apparel for women. Probably written in 202, the text reflects Tertullian's hatred of North African, non-Christian culture and his growing interest in the puritanical and uncompromising life-style of Montanism. It has been both applauded and denounced as an indictment of women, although the writer does urge modesty on men and never questions women's equal access to grace. Tertullian's purpose is to persuade Christian women to abandon elaborate dress, ornaments, and cosmetics. He reasons that the sex that brought sin into the world should wear humble garb and renounce the skills of adornment that were taught by the angels of darkness. He also reminds women that such attire tempts men and betrays impure impulses within their own souls.

Source: Tertullian. "On the Apparel of Women." Translated by S. Thelwall. In *Ante-Nicene Fathers: Translations of the Writings of the Fathers down to A.D. 325*, edited by Alexander Roberts and James Donaldson. Volume 4:14–15, 18–21, 25. Buffalo: The Christian Literature Publishing Co., 1885.

If there dwelt upon earth a faith as great as is the reward of faith which is expected in the heavens, no one of you at all, best beloved sisters, from the time that she had first "known the Lord," and learned (the truth) concerning her own (that is, woman's) condition, would have desired too gladsome (not to say too ostentatious) a style of dress; so as not rather to go about in humble garb, and rather to affect meanness of appearance, walking about as Eve mourning and repentant, in order that by every garb of penitence she might the more fully expiate that which she derives from Eve,—the ignominy, I mean, of the first sin, and the odium (attaching to her as the cause) of human perdition. "In pains and in anxieties dost thou bear (children), woman; and toward thine husband (is) thy inclination, and he lords it over thee." And do you not know that you are (each) an Eve? The sentence of God on this sex of yours lives in this age: the guilt must of necessity live too. *You* are the devil's gateway: *you* are the unsealer of that (forbidden) tree: *you* are the first deserter of the divine law: *you* are she who persuaded him whom the devil was not valiant enough to attack. *You* destroyed so easily God's image, man. On account of *your* desert—that is, death—even the Son of God had to die. And do you think about adorning yourself over and above your tunics of skins? Come, now; if from the beginning of the world the Milesians sheared sheep, and the Serians spun trees, and the Tyrians dyed, and the Phrygians embroidered with the needle, and the Babylonians with the loom, and pearls gleamed, and onyx-stones flashed; if gold itself also had already issued, with the cupidity (which accompanies it), from the ground; if the mirror, too, already had license to lie so largely, Eve, expelled from paradise, (Eve) already dead, would also have coveted *these* things, I imagine! No more, then, ought she *now* to crave, or be acquainted with (if she desires to live again), what, when she *was* living, she had neither had nor known. Accordingly these things are all the baggage of woman in her condemned and dead state, instituted as if to swell the pomp of her funeral. . . .

For they, withal, who instituted them are assigned, under condemnation, to the penalty of death,—those angels, to wit, who rushed from heaven on the daughters of men; so that this ignominy also attaches to woman. For when to an age much more ignorant (than ours) they had disclosed certain well-concealed material substances, and several not well-revealed scientific arts—if it is true that they had laid bare the operations of metallurgy, and had divulged the natural properties of herbs, and had promulgated the powers of enchantments, and had traced out every curious art, even to the interpretation of the stars—they conferred properly and as it were peculiarly upon women that instrumental mean of womanly ostentation, the radiances of jewels wherewith necklaces are variegated, and the circlets of gold wherewith the arms are compressed, and the medicaments of orchil with which wools are colored, and that black powder itself wherewith the eyelids and eyelashes are made prominent. What is the quality of these things may be declared meantime, even at this point, from the quality and condition of their teachers: in that sinners could never have either shown or supplied anything conducive to integrity, unlawful lovers anything conducive to chastity, renegade spirits anything conducive to the fear of God. If (these things) are to be called *teachings*, ill masters must of necessity have taught ill; if as *wages of lust*, there is nothing base of which the wages are honorable. But why was it of so much importance to show these things as well as to confer them? Was it that women, without material causes of splendor, and without ingenious contrivances of grace, could not please *men*, who, while still unadorned, and uncouth, and—so to say— crude and rude, had moved (the mind of) *angels*? or was it that the lovers would appear sordid and—through gratuitous use—contumelious, if they had conferred no (compensating) gift on the women who had been enticed into connubial connection with them? But these questions admit of no calculation. Women who possessed angels (as husbands) could desire nothing more; they had, forsooth, made a grand match! Assuredly they who, of course, did sometimes think whence they had fallen, and, after the heated impulses of their lusts, looked up toward heaven, thus requited that very excellence of women, natural beauty, as (having proved) a cause of evil, in order that their good fortune might profit them nothing; but that, being turned from simplicity and sincerity, they, together with (the angels) themselves, might become offensive to God. Sure they were that all ostentation, and ambition, and love of pleasing by carnal means, was *dis*pleasing to God. And these are the angels whom we are destined to judge: these are the angels whom in baptism we renounce: these, of course, are the reasons why they have deserved to be judged by man. What business, then, have their *things* with their *judges?* What commerce have they who are to condemn with them who are to be condemned? The same, I take it, as Christ has with Belial. With what consistency do we mount that (future) judgment-seat to pronounce sentence against those whose gifts we (now) seek after? For you too, (women as you are,) have the self-same angelic nature promised as your reward, the self-same sex as men: the self-same advancement to the dignity of judging, does (the Lord) promise you. Unless, then, we begin even here to *pre*-judge, by pre-condemning their *things*, which we are hereafter to condemn in *themselves*, *they* will rather judge and condemn *us.* . . .

Handmaids of the living God, my fellow-servants and sisters, the right which I enjoy with you—I, the most meanest in that right of fellow-servantship and brotherhood—emboldens me to address to you a discourse, not, of course, of affection, but paving the way for affection in the cause of your salvation. That salvation—and not (the salvation) of women only, but likewise of men—consists in the exhibition principally of modesty. For since, by the introduction into an appropriation (in) us of the Holy Spirit, we are all "the temple of God," Modesty is the sacristan and priestess of that temple, who is to suffer nothing unclean or profane to be introduced (into it), for fear that the God who inhabits it should be offended, and quite forsake the polluted abode. But on the present occasion we (are to speak) not about modesty, for the enjoining and exacting of which the divine precepts which press (upon us) on every side are sufficient; but about the matters which pertain to it, that is, the manner in which it behoves you to walk. For most women (which very thing I trust God may permit me, with a view, of course, to my own personal censure, to censure in all), either from simple ignorance or else from dissimulation, have the hardihood so to walk as if modesty consisted only in the (bare) integrity of the flesh, and in turning away from (actual) fornication; and there were no need for anything extrinsic to boot—in the matter (I mean) of the arrangement of dress and ornament, the studied graces of form and brilliance:—wearing in their gait the self-same appearance as the women of the nations, from whom the sense of *true* modesty is absent, because in those who know not God, the Guardian and Master of truth, there is *nothing* true. For if any modesty can be believed (to exist) in Gentiles, it is plain that it must be imperfect and undisciplined to such a degree that, although it be actively tenacious of itself in the *mind* up to a certain point, it yet allows itself to relax into licentious extravagances of attire; just in accordance with Gentile perversity, in craving after that of which it carefully shuns the effect. How many a one, in short, is there who does not earnestly desire even to look pleasing to strangers? who does not on that very account take care to have herself painted out, and denies that she has (ever) been an object of (carnal) appetite? And yet, granting that even this is a practice familiar to Gentile modesty—(namely,) not actually to *commit* the sin, but still to be *willing* to do so; or even not to be *willing*, yet still not *quite* to refuse—what wonder? for all things which are not God's are perverse. Let those women therefore look to it, who, by not holding fast the *whole* good, easily mingle with evil even what they do hold fast. Necessary it is that *you* turn aside from them, as in all other things, so also in your gait; since you ought to be "perfect, as (is) your Father who is in the heavens...."

You must know that in the eye of perfect, that is, Christian, modesty, (carnal) desire of one's self (on the part of others) is not only not to be desired, but even execrated, by you: first, because the study of making personal grace (which we know to be naturally the inviter of lust) a mean of pleasing does not spring from a sound conscience: why therefore excite toward yourself that evil (passion)? why invite (that) to which you profess yourself a stranger? secondly, because we ought not to open a way to temptations, which, by their instancy, sometimes achieve (a wickedness) which God expels from them who are His; (or,) at all events, put the spirit into a thorough tumult by (presenting) a stumbling-block (to it). We ought indeed to walk so holily, and with so entire substantiality of faith, as to be confident and secure in regard of our own conscience, *desiring* that that (gift) may abide in us to the end, yet not *presuming* (that it will). For he who presumes feels less apprehension; he who feels less apprehension takes less precaution; he who takes less precaution runs more risk. Fear is the foundation of salvation; presumption is an impediment to fear. More useful, then, is it to apprehend that we may possibly fail, than to presume that we cannot; for apprehending will lead us to fear, fearing to caution, and caution to salvation. On the other hand, if we presume, there will be neither fear nor caution to save us. He who acts securely, and not at the same time warily, possesses no safe and firm security; whereas he who is wary will be truly able to be secure. For His own servants, may the Lord by His mercy take care that to *them* it may be lawful even to *presume* on His goodness! But why are we a (source of) danger to our neighbor? why do we import concupiscence into our neighbor? which concupiscence, if God, in "amplifying the law," do not dissociate in (the way of) penalty from the actual commission of fornication, I know not whether He allows impunity to him who has been the cause of perdition to some other. For that other, as soon as he has felt concupiscence after your beauty, and has mentally already committed (the deed) which his concupiscence pointed to, perishes; and you have been made the sword which destroys him: so that, albeit you be free from the (actual) crime, you are not free from the odium (attaching to it); as, when a robbery has been committed on some man's estate, the (actual) crime indeed will not be laid to the owner's charge, while yet the domain is branded with ignominy, (and) the owner himself aspersed with the infamy. Are we to paint ourselves out that our neighbors may perish? Where, then, is (the command), "Thou shalt love thy neighbor as thyself"? "Care not merely about your own (things), but (about your) neighbor's"? No enunciation of the Holy Spirit ought to be (confined) to the subject immediately in hand merely, and not applied and carried out with a view to *every* occasion to which its application is useful. Since, therefore, both our own interest and that of others is implicated in the studious pursuit of most perilous (outward) comeliness, it is time for you to know that not merely must the pageantry of fictitious and elaborate beauty be rejected by you; but that of even natural grace must be obliterated by concealment and negligence, as equally dangerous to the glances of (the beholder's) eyes. For, albeit comeliness is not to be *censured*, as being a bodily happiness, as being an additional outlay of the divine plastic art, as being a kind of goodly garment of the soul; yet it is to be *feared*, just on account of the injuriousness and violence of suitors: which (injuriousness and violence) even the father of the faith, Abraham, greatly feared in regard of his own wife's grace; and Isaac, by falsely representing Rebecca as his sister, purchased safety by insult! . . .

These suggestions are not made to you, of course, to be developed into an entire crudity and wildness of appearance; nor are we seeking to persuade you of the good of squalor and slovenliness; but of the limit and norm and just measure of cultivation of the person. There must be no overstepping of that line to which simple and sufficient refinements limit their desires—that line which is pleasing to God. For they who rub their skin with medicaments, stain their cheeks with rouge, make their eyes prominent with antimony, sin against HIM. To them, I suppose, the plastic skill of God is displeasing! In their own persons, I suppose, they convict, they censure, the Artificer of all things! For censure they do when they amend, when they add to, (His work;) taking these their additions, of course, from the adversary artificer. That adversary artificer is the devil. For who would show the way to change the *body*, but he who by wickedness transfigured man's *spirit?* He it is, undoubtedly, who adapted ingenious devices of this kind; that in your persons it may be apparent that you, in a certain sense, do violence to God. Whatever is *born* is the work of God. Whatever, then, is *plastered on* (that), is the devil's work. To superinduce on a divine work Satan's ingenuities, how criminal is it! Our servants borrow nothing from our personal enemies: soldiers eagerly desire nothing from the foes of their own general; for, to demand for (your own) use anything from the adversary of Him in whose hand you are, is a transgression. Shall a Christian be assisted in anything by that evil one? (If he do,) I know not whether this name (of "Christian") will continue (to belong) to him; for he will be *his* in whose lore he eagerly desires to be instructed. But how alien from *your* schoolings and professions are (these things)! How unworthy the Christian name, to wear a fictitious face, (you,) on whom simplicity in every form is enjoined!—to lie in your appearance, (you,) to whom (lying) with the tongue is not lawful!—to seek after what is another's, (you,) to whom is delivered (the precept of) abstinence from what is another's!—to practise adultery in your mien, (you,) who make modesty your study! Think, blessed (sisters), how will you keep God's precepts if you shall not keep in your own persons His lineaments? ...

Perhaps some (woman) will say: "To me it is not necessary to be approved by men; for I do not require the testimony of men: God is the inspector of the heart." (That) we all know; provided, however, we remember what the same (God) has said through the apostle: "Let your probity appear before men." For what purpose, except that malice may have no access at all to you, or that you may be an example and testimony to the evil? Else, what is (that): "Let your works shine"? Why, moreover, does the Lord call us the light of the world; why has He compared us to a city built upon a mountain; if we do not shine in (the midst of) darkness, and stand eminent amid them who are sunk down? If you hide your lamp beneath a bushel, you must necessarily be left quite in darkness, and be run against by many. The things which make us luminaries of the world are these—our good works. What is *good*, moreover, provided it be true and full, loves not darkness: it joys in being seen, and exults over the very pointings which are made at it. To Christian modesty it is not enough to *be* so, but to *seem* so too. For so great ought its plenitude to be, that it may flow out from the mind to the garb, and burst out from the conscience to the outward appearance; so that even from the outside it may gaze, as it were, upon its own furniture,—(a furniture) such as to be suited to retain faith as its inmate perpetually. For such delicacies as tend by their softness and effeminacy to unman the manliness of faith are to be discarded. Otherwise, I know not whether the wrist that has been wont to be surrounded with the palmleaf-like bracelet will endure till it grow into the numb hardness of its own chain. I know not whether the leg that has rejoiced in the anklet will suffer itself to be squeezed into the gyve! I fear the neck, beset with pearl and emerald nooses, will give no room to the broadsword! Wherefore, blessed (sisters), let us meditate on hardships, and we shall not feel them; let us abandon luxuries, and we shall not regret them. Let us stand ready to endure every violence, having nothing which we may fear to leave behind. It is these things which are the bonds which retard our hope. Let us cast away earthly ornaments if we desire heavenly. Love not gold; in which (one substance) are branded all the sins of the people of Israel. You ought to *hate* what ruined your fathers; what was adored by them who were forsaking God. Even *then* (we find) gold is food for the fire. But Christians always, and now more than ever, pass their times not in gold but in iron: the stoles of martyr-dom are (now) preparing: the angels who are to carry us are (now) being awaited! Do you go forth (to meet them) already arrayed in the cosmet-ics and ornaments of prophets and apostles; drawing your whiteness from simplicity, your ruddy hue from modesty; painting your eyes with bash-fulness, and your mouth with silence; implanting in your ears the words of God; fitting on your necks the yoke of Christ. Submit your head to your husbands, and you will be enough adorned. Busy your hands with spinning; keep your feet at home; and you will "please" better than (by ar-raying yourselves) in gold. Clothe yourselves with the silk of uprightness, the fine linen of holiness, the purple of modesty. Thus painted, you will have God as your Lover!

17 ▪ A MODEL OF CHRISTIAN ASCETICISM

A Roman of considerable wealth and social status, Paula was converted to Christianity and, in keeping with fourth-century asceticism, shunned the riches and attention of the world. She eventually left her family to journey to Nitria and the holy land and to settle in Bethlehem, where she established separate monasteries for men and women. Jerome (c. 342–419), one of the church's foremost biblical scholars, spent much of his life ruling the male community. In 404 he wrote a long letter to Paula's daughter Eustochium in order to console her on her mother's death. He heaps praise upon Paula for her humility, chastity, and complete trust in God, being somewhat anxious that his readers will find his evaluation of Paula hardly "credible" because of her sex. Despite his own formidable scholarship, he acknowledges Paula's "docile" mind and lucid Hebrew.

Source: Jerome. "To Eustochium, Memorials of Her Mother Paula." In *A Select Library of Nicene and Post-Nicene Fathers of the Christian Church*, translated by W. H.

Fremantle and edited by Philip Schaff and Henry Wace. Second series. Volume 16:195–97, 202–3, 206, 209–10. New York: The Christian Literature Co., 1893.

If all the members of my body were to be converted into tongues, and if each of my limbs were to be gifted with a human voice, I could still do no justice to the virtues of the holy and venerable Paula. Noble in family, she was nobler still in holiness; rich formerly in this world's goods, she is now more distinguished by the poverty that she has embraced for Christ. Of the stock of the Gracchi and descended from the Scipios, the heir and representative of that Paulus whose name she bore, the true and legitimate daughter of that Martia Papyria who was mother to Africanus, she yet preferred Bethlehem to Rome, and left her palace glittering with gold to dwell in a mud cabin. We do not grieve that we have lost this perfect woman; rather we thank God that we have had her, nay that we have her still. For "all live unto" God, and they who return unto the Lord are still to be reckoned members of his family. We have lost her, it is true, but the heavenly mansions have gained her; for as long as she was in the body she was absent from the Lord and would constantly complain with tears:— "Woe is me that I sojourn in Mesech, that I dwell in the tents of Kedar; my soul hath been this long time a pilgrim." It was no wonder that she sobbed out that even she was in darkness (for this is the meaning of the word Kedar) seeing that, according to the apostle, "the world lieth in the evil one"; and that, "as its darkness is, so is its light"; and that "the light shineth in darkness and the darkness comprehended it not." She would frequently exclaim: "I am a stranger with thee and a sojourner as all my fathers were," and again, I desire "to depart and to be with Christ." As often too as she was troubled with bodily weakness (brought on by incredible abstinence and by redoubled fastings), she would be heard to say: "I keep under my body and bring it into subjection; lest that by any means, when I have preached to others, I myself should be a castaway"; and "It is good neither to eat flesh nor to drink wine"; and "I humbled my soul with fasting"; and "thou wilt make all" my "bed in" my "sickness"; and "Thy hand was heavy upon me: my moisture is turned into the drought of summer." And when the pain which she bore with such wonderful patience darted through her, as if she saw the heavens opened she would say: "Oh that I had wings like a dove! for then would I fly away and be at rest."

I call Jesus and his saints, yes and the particular angel who was the guardian and the companion of this admirable woman to bear witness that these are no words of adulation and flattery but sworn testimony every one of them borne to her character. They are, indeed, inadequate to the virtues of one whose praises are sung by the whole world, who is admired by bishops, regretted by bands of virgins, and wept for by crowds of monks and poor....

In what terms shall I speak of her distinguished, and noble, and formerly wealthy house; all the riches of which she spent upon the poor? How can I describe the great consideration she shewed to all and her far reaching kindness even to those whom she had never seen? What poor man, as he lay dying, was not wrapped in blankets given by her? What bedridden person was not supported with money from her purse? She would seek out such with the greatest diligence throughout the city, and would think it a misfortune were any hungry or sick person to be supported by another's food. So lavish was her charity that she robbed her children; and, when her relatives remonstrated with her for doing so, she declared that she was leaving to them a better inheritance in the mercy of Christ.

Nor was she long able to endure the visits and crowded receptions, which her high position in the world and her exalted family entailed upon her. She received the homage paid to her sadly, and made all the speed she could to shun and to escape those who wished to pay her compliments. It so happened that at that time the bishops of the East and West had been summoned to Rome by letter from the emperors to deal with certain dissensions between the churches, and in this way she saw two most admirable men and Christian prelates, Paulinus bishop of Antioch and Epiphanius, bishop of Salamis or, as it is now called, Constantia, in Cyprus. Epiphanius, indeed, she received as her guest; and, although Paulinus was staying in another person's house, in the warmth of her heart she treated him as if he too were lodged with her. Inflamed by their virtues she thought more and more each moment of forsaking her home. Disregarding her house, her children, her servants, her property, and in a word everything connected with the world, she was eager—alone and unaccompanied (if ever it could be said that she was so)—to go to the desert made famous by its Pauls and by its Antonies. And at last when the winter was over and the sea was open, and when the bishops were returning to their churches, she also sailed with them in her prayers and desires. Not to prolong the story, she went down to Portus accompanied by her brother, her kinsfolk and above all her own children eager by their demonstrations of affection to overcome their loving mother. At last the sails were set and the strokes of the rowers carried the vessel into the deep. On the shore the little Toxotius stretched forth his hands in entreaty, while Rufina, now grown up, with silent sobs besought her mother to wait till she should be married. But still Paula's eyes were dry as she turned them heavenwards; and she overcame her love for her children by her love for God. She knew herself no more as a mother, that she might approve herself a handmaid of Christ. Yet her heart was rent within her, and she wrestled with her grief, as though she were being forcibly separated from parts of herself....

I will now pass on to Egypt, pausing for a while on the way at Socoh, and at Samson's well which he clave in the hollow place that was in the jaw. Here I will lave my parched lips and refresh myself before visiting Moresheth; in old days famed for the tomb of the prophet Micah, and now for its church. Then skirting the country of the Horites and Gittites, Mareshah, Edom, and Lachish, and traversing the lonely wastes of the desert where the tracks of the traveller are lost in the yielding sand, I will come to the river of Egypt called Sihor, that is "the muddy river," and go through the five cities of Egypt which speak the language of Canaan, and through the land of Goshen and the plains of Zoan on which God wrought his marvellous works. And I will visit the city of No, which has since become Alexandria; and Nitria, the town of the Lord, where day by day the filth of multitudes is washed away with the pure nitre of virtue. No sooner did Paula come in sight of it than there came to meet her the reverend and estimable bishop, the confessor Isidore, accompanied by countless multitudes of monks, many of whom were of priestly or of Levitical rank. On seeing these Paula rejoiced to behold the Lord's glory manifested in them; but protested that she had no claim to be received with such honor. Need I speak of the Macarii, Arsenius, Serapion, or other pillars of Christ! Was there any cell that she did not enter? Or any man at whose feet she did not throw herself? In each of His saints she believed that she saw Christ Himself; and whatever she bestowed upon them she rejoiced to feel that she had bestowed it upon the Lord. Her enthusiasm was wonderful and her endurance scarcely credible in a woman. Forgetful of her sex and of her weakness she even desired to make her abode, together with the girls who accompanied her, among these thousands of monks. And, as they were all willing to welcome her, she might perhaps have sought and obtained permission to do so; had she not been drawn away by a still greater passion for the holy places. Coming by sea from Pelusium to Maioma on account of the great heat, she returned so rapidly that you would have thought her a bird. Not long afterwards, making up her mind to dwell permanently in holy Bethlehem, she took up her abode for three years in a miserable hostelry; till she could build the requisite cells and monastic buildings, to say nothing of a guest house for passing travellers where they might find the welcome which Mary and Joseph had missed. At this point I conclude my narrative of the journeys that she made accompanied by Eustochium and many other virgins.

I am now free to describe at greater length the virtue which was her peculiar charm; and in setting forth this I call God to witness that I am no flatterer. I add nothing. I exaggerate nothing. On the contrary I tone down much that I may not appear to relate incredibilities. My carping critics must not insinuate that I am drawing on my imagination or decking Paula, like Æsop's crow, with the fine feathers of other birds. Humility is the first of Christian graces, and hers was so pronounced that one who had never seen her, and who on account of her celebrity had desired to see her, would have believed that he saw not her but the lowest of her maids. When she was surrounded by companies of virgins she was always the least remarkable in dress, in speech, in gesture, and in gait. From the time that her husband died until she fell asleep herself she never sat at meat with a man, even though she might know him to stand upon the pinnacle of the episcopate. She never entered a bath except when dangerously ill. Even in the severest fever she rested not on an ordinary bed but on the hard ground covered only with a mat of goat's hair; if that can be called rest which made day and night alike a time of almost unbroken prayer. Well did she fulfil the words of the psalter: "All the night make I my bed to swim; I water my couch with my tears"! Her tears welled forth as it were from fountains, and she lamented her slightest faults as if they were sins of the deepest dye. Constantly did I warn her to spare her eyes and to keep them for the reading of the gospel; but she only said: "I must disfigure that face which contrary to God's commandment I have painted with rouge, white lead, and antimony. I must mortify that body which has been given up to many pleasures. I must make up for my long laughter by constant weeping. I must exchange my soft linen and costly silks for rough goat's hair. I who have pleased my husband and the world in the past, desire now to please Christ." Were I among her great and signal virtues to select her chastity as a subject of praise, my words would seem superfluous; for, even when she was still in the world, she set an example to all the matrons of Rome, and bore herself so admirably that the most slanderous never ventured to couple scandal with her name. No mind could be more considerate than hers, or none kinder towards the lowly. She did not court the powerful; at the same time, if the proud and the vainglorious sought her, she did not turn from them with disdain. If she saw a poor man, she supported him: and if she saw a rich one, she urged him to do good. Her liberality alone knew no bounds. Indeed, so anxious was she to turn no needy person away that she borrowed money at interest and often contracted new loans to pay off old ones. I was wrong, I admit; but when I saw her so profuse in giving, I reproved her alleging the apostle's words: "I mean not that other men be eased and ye burthened; but by an equality that now at this time your abundance may be a supply for their want, that their abundance also may be a supply for your want." I quoted from the gospel the Savior's words: "he that hath two coats, let him impart one of them to him that hath none"; and I warned her that she might not always have means to do as she would wish. Other arguments I adduced to the same purpose; but with admirable modesty and brevity she overruled them all. "God is my witness," she said, "that what I do I do for His sake. My prayer is that I may die a beggar not leaving a penny to my daughter and indebted to strangers for my winding sheet." She then concluded with these words: "I, if I beg, shall find many to give to me; but if this beggar does not obtain help from me who by borrowing can give it to him, he will die; and if he dies, of whom will his soul be required?" I wished her to be more careful in managing her concerns, but she with a faith more glowing than mine clave to the Savior with her whole heart and poor in spirit followed the Lord in His poverty, giving back to Him what she had received and becoming poor for His sake. She obtained her wish at last and died leaving her daughter overwhelmed with a mass of debt. This Eustochium still owes and indeed cannot hope to pay off by her own exertions; only the mercy of Christ can free her from it. . . .

I shall now describe the order of her monastery and the method by which she turned the continence of saintly souls to her own profit. She sowed carnal things that she might reap spiritual things; she gave earthly things that she might receive heavenly things; she forwent things temporal that she might in their stead obtain things eternal. Besides establishing a monastery for men, the charge of which she left to men, she divided into three companies and monasteries the numerous virgins whom she had gathered out of different provinces, some of whom are of noble birth while others belonged to the middle or lower classes. But, although they worked and had their meals separately from each other, these three companies met together for psalm-singing and prayer. After the chanting of the Alleluia—the signal by which they were summoned to the Collect—no one was permitted to remain behind. But either first or among the first Paula used to await the arrival of the rest, urging them to diligence rather by her own modest example than by motives of fear. At dawn, at the third, sixth, and ninth hours, at evening, and at midnight they recited the psalter each in turn. No sister was allowed to be ignorant of the psalms, and all had every day to learn a certain portion of the holy scriptures. On the Lord's day only they proceeded to the church beside which they lived, each company following its own mother-superior. Returning home in the same order, they then devoted themselves to their allotted tasks, and made garments either for themselves or else for others. If a virgin was of noble birth, she was not allowed to have an attendant belonging to her own household lest her maid having her mind full of the doings of old days and of the license of childhood might by constant converse open old wounds and renew former errors. All the sisters were clothed alike. Linen was not used except for drying the hands. So strictly did Paula separate them from men that she would not allow even eunuchs to approach them; lest she should give occasion to slanderous tongues (always ready to cavil at the religious) to console themselves for their own misdoing. When a sister was backward in coming to the recitation of the psalms or shewed herself remiss in her work, Paula used to approach her in different ways. Was she quick-tempered? Paula coaxed her. Was she phlegmatic? Paula chid her, copying the example of the apostle who said: "What will ye? Shall I come to you with a rod or in love and in the spirit of meekness?" Apart from food and raiment she allowed no one to have anything she could call her own, for Paul had said, "Having food and raiment let us be therewith content." She was afraid lest the custom of having more should breed covetousness in them; an appetite which no wealth can satisfy, for the more it has the more it requires, and neither opulence nor indigence is able to diminish it. When the sisters quarrelled one with another she reconciled them with soothing words. If the younger ones were troubled with fleshly desires, she broke their force by imposing redoubled fasts; for she wished her virgins to be ill in body rather than to suffer in soul. If she chanced to notice any sister too attentive to her dress, she reproved her for her error with knitted brows and severe looks, saying[:] "a clean body and a clean dress mean an unclean soul. A virgin's lips should never utter an improper or an impure word, for such indicate a lascivious mind and by the outward man the faults of the inward are made manifest." When she saw a sister verbose and talkative or forward and taking pleasure in quarrels, and when she found after frequent admonitions that the offender shewed no signs of improvement; she placed her among the lowest of the sisters and outside their society, ordering her to pray at the door of the refectory instead of with the rest, and commanding her to take her food by herself, in the hope that where rebuke had failed shame might bring about a reformation. The sin of theft she loathed as if it were sacrilege; and that which among men of the world is counted little or nothing she declared to be in a monastery a crime of the deepest dye. How shall I describe her kindness and attention towards the sick or the wonderful care and devotion with which she nursed them? Yet, although when others were sick she freely gave them every indulgence, and even allowed them to eat meat; when she fell ill herself, she made no concessions to her own weakness, and seemed unfairly to change in her own case to harshness the kindness which she was always ready to shew to others. . . .

To revert then to that description of her character which I began a little time ago; no mind was ever more docile than was hers. She was slow to speak and swift to hear, remembering the precept, "Keep silence and hearken, O Israel." The holy scriptures she knew by heart, and said of the history contained in them that it was the foundation of the truth; but, though she loved even this, she still preferred to seek for the underlying spiritual meaning and made this the keystone of the spiritual building raised within her soul. She asked leave that she and her daughter might read over the old and new testaments under my guidance. Out of modesty I at first refused compliance, but as she persisted in her demand and frequently urged me to consent to it, I at last did so and taught her what I had learned not from myself—for self-confidence is the worst of teachers—but from the church's most famous writers. Wherever I stuck fast and honestly confessed myself at fault she would by no means rest content but would force me by fresh questions to point out to her which of many different solutions seemed to me the most probable. I will mention here another fact which to those who are envious may well seem incredible. While I myself beginning as a young man have with much toil and effort partially acquired the Hebrew tongue and study it now unceasingly lest if I leave it, it also may leave me; Paula, on making up her mind that she too would learn it, succeeded so well that she could chant the psalms in Hebrew and could speak the language without a trace of the pronunciation peculiar to Latin. The same accomplishment can be seen to this day in her daughter Eustochium, who always kept close to her mother's side, obeyed all her commands, never slept apart from her, never walked abroad or took a meal without her, never had a penny that she could call her own, rejoiced when her mother gave to the poor her little patrimony, and fully believed that in filial affection she had the best heritage and the truest riches.

18 · EGERIA IN THE HOLY LAND

This text is part of an account of a pilgrimage to various sacred sites in and around the holy land, to which is added a description of the liturgy used in Jerusalem. It was probably written by Egeria, a wealthy woman of high social status, sometime between 404 and 417 and addressed to a group of learned and devout women serving the church where she lived. She does not simply list the places she visits but enhances her account with details such as the quality of King Agbar's portrait and the customs linked with the feast day of Saint Helpidius. She reveals that she is well-read in Scripture and worthy of the hospitality of great bishops and monks.

Source: "The Pilgrimage of Egeria." In *A Lost Tradition: Women Writers of the Early Church*, edited by Patricia Wilson-Kastner et al., 102–3, 105–7. Lanham, Md.: University Press of America, 1981.

And so again making my way through several rest-stations, I came to the city whose name we find in Scripture, Batanis, which is a city even today.

The church, with a holy bishop who is both a monk and confessor, has several martyria. The city contains multitudes of people, for an army with its tribune is based here.

Setting out from there, we arrived in the name of Christ our God at Edessa. When we had arrived there, we immediately went to the church and martyrium of Saint Thomas. Thus having prayed according to our custom, and having done all these things we habitually do in holy places, we also read there some things about Saint Thomas. The church there is large and very beautiful and newly built, and truly worthy to be a house of God. Because there were so many things there which I wanted to see, I had to stay there three days. So I saw many martyria and also holy monks, some living by the martyria and others having their dwellings far from the city in secluded places.

Then the holy bishop of the city, a truly religious monk and confessor, having hospitably received me, told me: "Because I see, daughter, that you have taken such a great work upon yourself, because of your piety coming even from the ends of the earth to these places, we will show you whatever you want, whatever it would please Christians to see." First giving thanks to God, I then asked him to be so kind as to do as he had offered. He first led me to the palace of King Agbar, and showed me there a large portrait of him, quite like him, they say, and as lustrous as if it were made of pearls. Looking at Agbar face to face, he seems to be truly a wise and honorable man. Then the holy bishop said to me: "Here is King Agbar, who before he saw the Lord believed in him as truly the Son of God." Next to that portrait was one also made of marble, said to be his son Magnus, whose countenance was also gracious. . . .

Having passed three days there, I had to go all the way to Carrae, as they now call it [Charra = Haran]. But in Scripture it is called Charra where Saint Abraham lived, as it is written in Genesis that the Lord said to Abraham, "Go from your land and from the house of your father and go into Haran," and so forth [Gen. 12:1]. When I reached there, that is, Charra, I went immediately to the church which is within the city itself. I soon saw the bishop of the place, a truly holy man of God, himself a monk and confessor, who kindly offered to show us all the places we wished. Then he led us immediately to the church outside the city which is on the site where Saint Abraham's house was, a church made from its stones and on its foundations, as the holy bishop told us. When we had come into that church he prayed and read a passage from the book of Genesis, sang a psalm, and the bishop having said another prayer and blessed us, we went outside. He then kindly agreed to lead us to the well from which Saint Rebecca carried water. The holy bishop told us: "Here is the well from which Saint Rebecca gave water to the camels of the servant of Abraham, Eleazar" [Gen. 24:15-20]. He consented to show us everything.

The church, which, as I said, ladies, venerable sisters, is outside the city, where once was the house of Abraham, now has there a martyrium to a certain holy monk called Helpidius. It was our good fortune to arrive there the day before the martyr's day of Saint Helpidius, nine days before the kalends of May [April 23]. On this day from everywhere within the borders of Mesopotamia all the monks come to Haran, even the great monks who dwell in solitude and are called aescetics, both for that feast which is very highly celebrated here, and for the memory of Saint Abraham, whose house was where the church now is in which is laid the body of the holy martyr. It was more than we had hoped to see these truly holy men of God, the Mesopotamian monks, whose reputation and life are heard of afar. I never thought that I would be able to see them, not because it would be impossible for God to grant this to me, because he has deigned to grant everything, but because I had heard that they did not come down from their dwellings except on the Pasch and on this day, and because these are the sort who do marvelous works. And I did not even know on what day was the martyr's feast, as I said. Thus, God willing, the day arrived for which I had not dared hope when we had come. We stayed there two days, for the martyr's feast and for seeing all the holy men who graciously agreed to receive me and speak with me, even though I did not deserve it. Immediately after the martyr's feast they are not to be seen there, because soon after nightfall they seek the desert and each of them goes to the cell where he lives. In this city, apart from a few clerics and holy monks, I found not a single Christian, for all are pagans. Just as we reverence the place where Saint Abraham first dwelt, honoring his memory, so also the pagans greatly reverence a place about a mile outside the city, where are tombs of Nahor and Bethuel [Gen. 29:24].

Because the bishop of the city is very learned in Scripture, I asked him, "I beg you, my Lord, tell me something I would like to know about." He replied, "Ask what you will, daughter, and I will tell you if I know." "I know through Scripture that Saint Abraham with his father Terah and Sarah his wife and Lot his brother's son came into this place, but I have not read that either Nahor or Bethuel traveled here [Gen. 11:31]. I know that only the servant of Abraham afterwards came to Charra to seek Rebecca, daughter of Bethuel son of Nahor, for Isaac, the son of his master Abraham." "Truly, daughter, it is written as you have said in Genesis, that Saint Abraham came here with his family; the Canonical Scriptures do not say at what time Nahor with his family and Bethuel arrived here [Gen. 11:31]. But clearly at sometime afterward they must have come here, for their tombs are about a mile from the city. For Scripture testifies truly that the servant of Saint Abraham came here to receive Saint Rebecca, and again that Saint Jacob came here that he might take the daughters of Laban the Syrian" [Gen. 24:28].

Then I asked him where the well was from which Saint Jacob gave water to the sheep which were herded by Rachel the daughter of Laban the Syrian [Gen. 11:28]. The bishop told me: "Within about six miles of here is a place next to a village which then was the land of Laban the Syrian; when you wish to go there we will go with you and show it to you, for there are many holy monks and aescetics, as well as a holy church in that place." I also asked the holy bishop where was the place where first Terah and his family lived among the Chaldeeans. Then the holy bishop responded: "The place of which you speak is from here ten days journey into Persia. From here Nisibis is five days, and from there to Ur, the city of the Chaldeeans, is five more days. But now there is no access for Romans there, because the Persians hold the whole territory. Particularly this part which is on the Roman borders of Persia and Chaldee is called Syria Orientalis." He kindly told me many other things, as had also many other holy bishops and monks, always about the Scriptures and the deeds of holy men, of monks, that is; if they were dead, of the marvels they had done, if they are still in the body, of what is done daily by those called aescetics [2 Cor. 12:3]. For I do not wish your affection to think that the monks have any other stories than those of the divine Scriptures and the deeds of the great monks.

Chapter 3

VIRGIN AND WITCH: WOMEN IN MEDIEVAL CHRISTIANITY

19 • SPIRITUAL MARRIAGE CONDEMNED

John Chrysostom's (c. 347–407) two treatises on the cohabitation of Christian men and women devoted to celibacy represent the most extensive treatment of this subject in Christian literature. As a priest in Antioch and as bishop of Constantinople, Chrysostom used pen and pulpit to call for moral reformation. This document is taken from his treatise urging monks in spiritual marriages to abandon the practice. He appeals to his readers not only through wit and sarcasm but also by using the popular device of dialogue, in this case between the monks and an interrogator representing conventional asceticism. Rather than accuse the men of engaging in sexual intercourse, he focuses on the fact that the piety that motivated their spiritual marriage was misplaced because it caused offense to others. Chrysostom also points out the practical disadvantages of such an arrangement. Women had many more household needs than men; they required separate, furnished bedrooms; and they would inevitably involve their companions in the maintenance of their personal "paraphernalia."

Source: John Chrysostom. "Instruction and Refutation Directed against Those Men Cohabiting with Virgins." In *Jerome, Chrysostom and Friends: Essays and Translations*, by Elizabeth A. Clark, 186–92. Studies in Women and Religion, volume 2. New York: Edwin Mellen Press, 1979.

Although you claim that you do everything for the sake of God, you behave in a manner characteristic of his foes, for to do that which blasphemes and slanders his name is characteristic of the enemies of God. And I will add something further. Let us grant that the person saying these things was speaking the truth, is innocent of all lust, and undertakes this patronage from no other motivation than piety alone. But even then we will not find him exempt from punishment. For if he did not lack other opportunities through which he could prove his piety and could do so without scandalizing souls, then he ought not to spend his time on the kind of projects in which the disadvantage is greater than the benefit. For tell me, how is there an equivalence between managing the worldly affairs of one or two virgins and the scandal caused to the souls of a limitless multitude? Yet it is not in this that the condemnation is grievous. Rather, when you find a thousand ways which do not entail condemnation, are free from scandal, and yield a greater gain, why do you so rashly and pointlessly become entangled in practical concerns, undermining your profit, and building a house in an unstable and dishonorable fashion when you could do it with considerable security and glory?

Do you not know that the life of a Christian ought to shine brightly on all sides and that he who sullies his own honor will not be of use anywhere later on, will not be able to reap any reward even if he should perform heroic acts of virtue? "For if the salt loses its savor," Jesus says, "with what strength shall it salt the rest?" God wills for us to be salt and light and leaven, so that others can have a share in our utility. For if men living irreproachably can scarcely convert the careless, are we not in all ways responsible for their ruin if we provide them with even an opportunity for their behavior? Just as he who lives a corrupted life is never to be saved, neither can he who wraps himself up in an evil reputation escape punishment.

If, however, it is incumbent upon me to utter something quite shocking, I will contribute the following: even if someone sins greatly but does so without being observed and causes no scandal, he will be given a lighter penalty than the one who sins to a lesser degree but does so openly, giving offense to many people....

Therefore let us do everything so that no cause for scandal may arise. Even if we believe that people are making unjust accusations, let us put an end to their complaints; let us imitate the saints who had such abundant zeal for God's glory and for their own glory, theirs for the sake of his. Let us not imagine that it suffices for our defense if we say, after having knocked everything down and trampled it under foot, "We have purchased a cloak and shoes for a virgin and have conveniently made every arrangement for her bodily needs."

"And who will manage our household?" our opponent continues. "Who will keep an eye on our possessions? Who will direct the operation when we are spending time elsewhere, if we don't have a woman at home?..."

For what, tell me, do they say these household matters are for which they deem it necessary to utilize the virgin's managerial skills? Do you have a crowd of recently purchased foreign maids who need to be trained in woolworking and in other duties? Do you have a storeroom for your tremendous treasures and expensive garments? Is it necessary for a guard to sit at home all the time, for the virgin's eyes to serve as a fortress against the wickedness of the servants? Or do you continually prepare feasts and banquets and require the house to be decorated? Do you have cooks and waiters who receive the benefit of the virgin's advance planning? Or are there a variety of frequent expenses, and is it necessary for someone always to be in charge, carefully guarding things, so that items do not disappear at random from the house?

"For none of these reasons," he replies. "Rather I need a woman so that she can oversee my chest of drawers, my cloak, and my other poor needs, such as setting the table, making the bed, lighting the fire, washing my feet, and providing for every other comfort. Surely on account of these rather trivial and dreary forms of relaxation we will not fear such condemnation and be subject to such censure, will we?"

Yet how much better, how much more easily a brother will serve in these matters, for a man is by nature stronger than a woman, more like us in his needs, and not so extravagant. For the woman, since she is more delicate, requires a softer bed, finer clothes, and perhaps a maid to wait on her; she does not provide us with as much service as we must give her. But a brother is aloof from all these problems. If he has needs, they will be the same as ours. It is no small advantage for housemates not to differ in their requirements but to have identical ones—the very thing which is not the case with the virgin.

In the first place, if she needs to bathe or if she becomes physically ill, surely a brother should not attend her in these circumstances, even if he might opt for such dreadful self-disgrace, nor will she be able to make do on her own. But if it is brothers who are living together, they will render each other this service. Furthermore, when sleep calls, if there is a virgin in the house you need two beds, two carpets and sets of covers, and if you are thinking clearly, also two bedrooms. But if the two are brothers, then the need is reduced, since they are more alike; indeed, one house, one pillow, one bed, and the same covers suffice for both of them. In short, if anyone should make a list of all these requirements, he will find it very easy to supply them if two men are living together, but very difficult if it is a woman and a man who are housemates—and I pass over the disgrace occasioned by the household.

For what shall we think when we enter a monk's house and see women's shoes hanging up, and girdles, headbands, baskets, a distaff, various items of weaving equipment, and all the other things women have, too numerous to be counted? And if you review the situation of a virgin who is well-provided for, the laughter increases. First of all, the monk twists and turns in the midst of so many serving girls, a veritable herd of them, as if he were the dancer in the orchestra of a theater accompanied by the singing of the women's chorus. Could anything be more disgraceful, more dishonorable?

Then he is bursting with irritation at the domestics all day long because of incidents pertaining to the woman; either he has to keep quiet, disregard everything which concerns her and take the blame, or speak out in rebuke and disgrace himself.

Just see what happens. He who has been forbidden even to approach worldly affairs not only immerses himself in them, but also in those which concern women. Indeed, these men will not refuse to devote themselves to matters concerning women's paraphernalia; instead, they will constantly be stopping in at the silversmith's to inquire if the mistress's mirror is ready yet, if he has finished the urn, if he has delivered the perfume flask. For things are in such a state of corruption that the majority of these virgins has greater need of such items than women in secular life do.

20 ▪ MELANIA THE YOUNGER AS ASCETIC TEACHER

Born into a wealthy Roman family at the end of the fourth century, Melania the Younger married Valerius Pinian when she was fourteen. After burying two infants, she persuaded her husband to join her in a celibate life. She eventually converted their home into a hostel for religious pilgrims and sold her vast properties, distributing proceeds to the poor. With Pinian she fled the Gothic invasion of northern Italy, settling first in Sicily, then North Africa, and eventually Jerusalem. There Melania founded a monastery for women on the Mount of Olives and one for men several years later. An account of her life was written, probably in Greek, in 452 or 453 by her close associate, the priest Gerontius. This section involves her visit to Constantinople in 436 on which she converts her uncle, an exprefect of Rome, and "talks theology from dawn to dusk" in an effort to thwart the spread of Nestorianism. She also teaches Emperor Theodosius and embarks, with his wife, on an arduous journey to Palestine.

Source: *The Life of Melania the Younger.* Introduction, translation, and commentary by Elizabeth A. Clark, 66–69. Studies in Women and Religion, volume 14. New York: Edwin Mellen Press, 1985.

Just then the Devil threw the souls of simple people into great trouble through the polluted doctrine of Nestorius. Therefore many of the wives of senators and some of the men illustrious in learning came to our holy mother in order to investigate the orthodox faith with her. And she, who had the Holy Spirit indwelling, did not cease talking theology from dawn to dusk. She turned many who had been deceived to the orthodox faith and sustained others who doubted; quite simply, she benefited all those who chanced to come to her divinely inspired teaching. Thus the Devil, the enemy of truth, was very jealous both on account of those who came to her for edification and on account of her uncle's salvation. He changed into a young black man, came to her, and said the following: "For how long do you destroy my hopes through your words? Know, then, that if I am strong enough to harden the hearts of Lausus and the emperors . . . I [can] inflict on your body such tortures that you will fear even for your life, so that you may be kept silent by necessity." After she had made him disappear by calling on our Lord Jesus Christ, she sent for my most humble self to tell me the threats of the Black One. And she had not yet finished speaking to me when she began to feel a pain in her hip. Suddenly her suffering was so strong that she remained mute for three hours. After we had made an offering on her behalf, she scarcely recovered herself. She spent six days in that unspeakable suffering, feeling far greater pain at that hour when she had seen the Black One. And when on the seventh day it seemed as if she would be released from this temporal life, someone came to announce that her uncle was in danger of dying, and he was still a catechumen.

Melania's grief at this announcement was greater than her suffering and her pains. She kept repeating to us, "Take me to him before I die." But we feared even to touch her because her foot was like dry wood. She lay there saying, "Carry me to my uncle, for if you don't, I am in more danger from that affliction." So according to her command we brought a litter and with much labor we hoisted her on it. I arrived before them at the palace and inquired how the ex-prefect was. And some of the famous people answered me, "Yesterday he asked for the saint and upon learning that she was seriously ill, he called lady Eleutheria, the nurse of Eudoxia the most pious empress, and through God he was enlightened." When I heard these things, I was cheered in the Lord and speedily sent off a horseman so that it might be announced to the blessed woman. When she heard that her uncle had been baptized, she was able to move her foot without pain because of her great joy. The Devil, disgraced, withdrew at that hour and with him all the pains totally left the blessed woman, so that she who had not been able to raise herself up, walked up all the stairs and through the side door of the palace, and entered the dwelling of the friend of Christ, the empress Eudoxia. Everyone was amazed and glorified the Lord because of the defeat of the Enemy of our salvation.

Melania herself sat all night at her uncle's bedside comforting him by saying things such as these: "You are truly blessed, my lord, because you have been sufficiently glorified in this life, and in the future one you are going towards the Lord, justified in having received the holy bath of incorruption." She had him participate three times in the holy mysteries and at dawn—it being the feast of Holy Epiphany—she joyfully sent him on in peace to the Lord. And while everybody was giving thanks to the One who did great wonders, the blessed woman said, praising his unutterable love for humans, "How great is his concern for even one soul, that in his goodness he arranged for Volusian to come from Rome and moved us to come from Jerusalem, so that a soul who had lived an entire lifetime in ignorance should be saved!"

Melania remained at Constantinople until she had done her time of forty days. She greatly benefited all who were there, most particularly the Christ-loving imperial women. She also edified the most pious emperor Theodosius. And since his wife had a desire to worship at the Holy Places, Melania begged him to let her go. We departed from there at the end of the month of February.

At that time the winter was so fierce that the Galatian and Cappadocian bishops asserted that they had never seen such a winter. And although we were completely covered with snow all day, we made our journey without faltering. We saw neither the ground nor the mountains, nothing except the hostels in which we stayed at night. Melania, who was like adamant, did not let up on her fasting at all. She said, "We ought now to fast more and to give thanks to God, the ruler of everything, because of the great wonders he has accomplished with me." Persevering in her unceasing prayer, she prevented both herself and us from suffering anything disagreeable in that most terrible cold. She showed that the prayer of a just person is a very strong weapon through which even the very elements are moved and overcome.

While all the holy men tried to delay us en route, she was not persuaded by any of them to do so, but had one wish, to celebrate Christ's Passion in Jerusalem. This God granted to her, according to the trustworthy promise he spoke through his most holy prophet, "He will do the desire of those who fear him and will hear their prayer."

21 · REJECTING PATRIARCHAL MARRIAGE

The text of The Life of Christina of Markyate, *a celebrated English ascetic, is probably a fourteenth-century abridgment of the story originally written two centuries earlier by an unknown Benedictine monk from St. Albans. Born into a wealthy, noble family of Huntingdon at the end of the eleventh century, Christina vowed to live as a virgin of Christ. Much of her story is an account of her clever and desperate efforts to defy a conspiracy of family members and church authorities to force her to consummate her marriage to Burthred. After spending a year imprisoned in her home, Christina escapes and settles into a hermit life with Roger in his cell at Markyate. She gathers virgin women around*

*her and together they form the nucleus of a female monastery at Markyate,
of which Christina becomes prioress. Parts of the text given below describe her
parents' unsuccessful use of flattery, force, and church law to intimidate her into
submission. She is accused of bringing dishonor upon the family by her obstinacy
and disobedience. Christina, however, has a firm sense of where her loyalty rests,
and she summons the courage to argue with her superiors accordingly.*

Source: *The Life of Christina of Markyate: A Twelfth Century Recluse.* Edited and
translated by C. H. Talbot, 49–63. Oxford: Clarendon Press, 1959.

See finally how she acted, how she behaved herself at what is called the
Gild merchant, which is one of the merchants' greatest and best-known
festivals. One day, when a great throng of nobles were gathered together
there, Autti and Beatrix held the place of honor, as being the most important amongst them. It was their pleasure that Christina, their eldest
and most worthy daughter, should act as cup-bearer to such an honorable gathering. Wherefore they commanded her to get up and lay aside
the mantle which she was wearing, so that, with her garments fastened
to her sides with bands and her sleeves rolled up her arms, she should
courteously offer drinks to the nobility. They hoped that the compliments
paid to her by the onlookers and the accumulation of little sips of wine
would break her resolution and prepare her body for the deed of corruption. Carrying out their wishes, she prepared a suitable defense against
both attacks. Against the favors of human flattery she fixed in her memory the thought of the Mother of God, and for this purpose she was not
a little helped by the hall where the gathering took place, for because of
its size it had several entrances. One of these before which Christina had
frequently to pass looked out on the monastery of the blessed Mother of
God. . . . Against the urge to drunkenness, she opposed her burning thirst.
What wonder is there that she felt dry, since though she had been pour-
ing out wine all day for others to drink their fill, she had tasted nothing?
But in the evening, when it was late and she was fainting with the heat
and thirst, she drank a little water and thus satisfied both desires at the
same time.

But as her parents had been outwitted in this, they tried something else.
And at night they let her husband secretly into her bedroom in order that,
if he found the maiden asleep, he might suddenly take her by surprise and
overcome her. But even through that providence to which she had commended herself, she was found dressed and awake, and she welcomed the
young man as if he had been her brother. And sitting on her bed with him,
she strongly encouraged him to live a chaste life, putting forward the saints
as examples. She recounted to him in detail the story of St. Cecilia and

her husband Valerian, telling him how, at their death they were accounted worthy to receive crowns of unsullied chastity from the hands of an angel. Not only this: but both they and many others after them had followed the path of martyrdom and thus, being crowned twice by the Lord, were honored both in heaven and on earth. "Let us, therefore," she exhorted him, "follow their example, so that we may become their companions in eternal glory. Because if we suffer with them, we shall also reign with them. Do not take it amiss that I have declined your embraces. In order that your friends may not reproach you with being rejected by me, I will go home with you: and let us live together there for some time, ostensibly as husband and wife, but in reality living chastely in the sight of the Lord. But first let us join hands in a compact that neither meanwhile will touch the other unchastely, neither will look upon the other except with a pure and angelic gaze, making a promise that in three or four years' time we will receive the religious habit and offer ourselves . . . to some monastery which providence shall appoint." When the greater part of the night had passed with talk such as this, the young man eventually left the maiden. When those who had got him into the room heard what had happened, they joined together in calling him a spineless and useless fellow. And with many reproaches they goaded him on again, and thrust him into her bedroom another night, having warned him not to be misled by her deceitful tricks and naïve words nor to lose his manliness. Either by force or entreaty he was to gain his end. And if neither of these sufficed, he was to know that they were at hand to help him: all he had to mind was to act the man.

When Christina sensed this, she hastily sprang out of bed and clinging with both hands to a nail which was fixed in the wall, she hung trembling between the wall and the hangings. Burthred meanwhile approached the bed and, not finding what he expected, he immediately gave a sign to those waiting outside the door. They crowded into the room forthwith and with lights in their hands ran from place to place looking for her, the more intent on their quest as they knew she was in the room when he entered it and could not have escaped without their seeing her. What, I ask you, were her feelings at that moment? How she kept trembling as they noisily sought after her. Was she not faint with fear? She saw herself already dragged out in their midst, all surrounding her, looking upon her, threatening her, given up to the sport of her destroyer. At last one of them touched and held her foot as she hung there, but since the curtain in between deadened his sense of touch, he let it go, not knowing what it was. Then the maiden of Christ, taking courage, prayed to God, saying: "Let them be turned backward, that desire my hurt": and straightway they departed in confusion, and from that moment she was safe. . . .

Her father brought her back there[1] another time, and placing her before Fredebert, the reverend prior, and the rest of the canons of the house, addressed them with these doleful words: "I know, my fathers, I know, and I admit to my daughter, that I and her mother have forced her against her will into this marriage and that against her better judgement she has received this sacrament. Yet, no matter how she was led into it, if she resists our authority and rejects it, we shall be the laughing-stock of our neighbors, a mockery and derision to those who are round about. Wherefore, I beseech you, plead with her to have pity on us: let her marry in the Lord and take away our reproach. Why must she depart from tradition? Why should she bring this dishonor on her father? Her life of poverty will bring the whole of the nobility into disrepute. Let her do now what we wish and she can have all that we possess." When Autti had said this, Fredebertus asked him to leave the assembly and with his canons about him began to address the maiden with these words: "We are surprised, Theodora, at your obstinacy, or rather we should say, your madness. We know that you have been betrothed according to ecclesiastical custom. We know that the sacrament of marriage, which has been sanctioned by divine law, cannot be dissolved, because what God has joined together, no man should put asunder. For this a man will leave his father and mother and cleave to his wife. And they shall be two in one flesh. And the Apostle says: let the husband render unto the wife due benevolence and likewise also the wife unto the husband. The woman has no power over her own body, but the husband: and likewise also the husband has not power over his own body, but the wife. Unto the married I command, yet not I, but the Lord, let not the wife depart from her husband and let not the husband put away his wife. And we know the commandment given to children: obey your parents and show them respect. These two commandments, about obedience to parents and faithfulness in marriage, are great, much commended in the Old and New Testaments. Yet the bond of marriage is so much more important than the authority of parents that if they commanded you to break off the marriage you should not listen to them. Now, however, that they order you to do something which we know on divine authority to be more important than obedience itself, and you do not listen to them, you are doubly at fault. Nor should you think that only virgins are saved: for whilst many virgins perish, many mothers of families are saved, as we well know. And since this is so, nothing remains but that you accept our advice and teaching and submit yourself to the lawful embraces of the man to whom you have been legally joined in marriage."

To these exhortations Christina replied: "I am ignorant of the scriptures

---

1. The Augustinian priory of St. Mary's, Huntingdon.—Ed.

which you have quoted, father prior. But from their sense I will give my answers thereto. My father and mother, as you have heard, bear me witness that against my will this sacrament, as you call it, was forced on me. I have never been a wife and have never thought of becoming one. Know that from my infancy I have chosen chastity and have vowed to Christ that I would remain a virgin: this I did before witnesses, but even if they were not present God would be witness to my conscience continuously. This I showed by my actions as far as I was allowed. And if my parents have ordered me to enter into a marriage which I never wanted and to break the vow to Christ which they know I made in my childhood, I leave you, who are supposed to excel other men in the knowledge of the scriptures, to judge how wicked a thing this is. If I do all in my power to fulfil the vow I made to Christ, I shall not be disobedient to my parents. What I do, I do on the invitation of Him whose voice, as you say, is heard in the Gospel: Every one who leaves house or brothers or sisters or father or mother or wife or children or possessions for My name's sake shall receive a hundredfold and possess eternal life. Nor do I think that virgins only will be saved. But I say as you do, and it is true, that if many virgins perish, so rather do married women. And if many mothers of families are saved, which you likewise say, and it is true, certainly virgins are saved more easily."

22 · HUNTING FOR WITCHES

The Malleus Maleficarum *was published in 1486 by the German inquisitors Heinrich Kraemer and Jacob Sprenger. It was only one of several treatises on witchcraft produced at the height of the witch hunt, but it had particular significance in several respects. It was prefaced by a bull from Pope Innocent VIII ordering the extirpation of witchcraft, and thus carried great authority. The* Malleus *was also important in that it systematized and transmitted the cumulative popular picture of witchcraft, a picture that included grotesque rituals, sacrilegious orgies, and devil worship. But perhaps the most novel feature of this treatise was its vicious attack on women. In the style of scholastic disputation, the authors raise the question of why more women than men are witches, and then answer it by pointing out that women are feebler in mind and body, carnal, prone to jealousy, and quicker to waver in their faith.*

Source: Heinrich Kraemer and Jacob Sprenger. *Malleus Maleficarum.* Translated by Montague Summers, 44–47. New York: Dover, 1971.

But because in these times this perfidy is more often found in women than in men, as we learn by actual experience, if anyone is curious as to the reason, we may add to what has already been said the following: that since they are feebler both in mind and body, it is not surprising that they should come more under the spell of witchcraft.

For as regards intellect, or the understanding of spiritual things, they seem to be of a different nature from men; a fact which is vouched for by the logic of the authorities, backed by various examples from the Scriptures. Terence says: Women are intellectually like children. And Lactantius (*Institutiones* 3): No woman understood philosophy except Temeste. And Proverbs 6, as it were describing a woman, says: As a jewel of gold in a swine's snout, so is a fair woman which is without discretion.

But the natural reason is that she is more carnal than a man, as is clear from her many carnal abominations. And it should be noted that there was a defect in the formation of the first woman, since she was formed from a bent rib, that is, a rib of the breast, which is bent as it were in a contrary direction to a man. And since through this defect she is an imperfect animal, she always deceives. For Cato says: When a woman weeps she weaves snares. And again: When a woman weeps, she labors to deceive a man. And this is shown by Samson's wife, who coaxed him to tell her the riddle he had propounded to the Philistines, and told them the answer, and so deceived him. And it is clear in the case of the first woman that she had little faith; for when the serpent asked why they did not eat of every tree in Paradise, she answered: Of every tree, etc.—Lest perchance we die. Thereby she showed that she doubted, and had little faith in the word of God. And all this is indicated by the etymology of the word; for *Femina* comes from *Fe* and *Minus*, since she is ever weaker to hold and preserve the faith. And this as regards faith is of her very nature; although both by grace and nature faith never failed in the Blessed Virgin, even at the time of Christ's Passion, when it failed in all men.

Therefore a wicked woman is by her nature quicker to waver in her faith, and consequently quicker to abjure the faith, which is the root of witchcraft.

And as to her other mental quality, that is, her natural will; when she hates someone whom she formerly loved, then she seethes with anger and impatience in her whole soul, just as the tides of the sea are always heaving and boiling. Many authorities allude to this cause. Ecclesiasticus 25: There is no wrath above the wrath of a woman. And Seneca (*Tragedies* 8): No might of the flames or of the swollen winds, no deadly weapon, is so much to be feared as the lust and hatred of a woman who has been divorced from the marriage bed.

This is shown too in the woman who falsely accused Joseph, and caused him to be imprisoned because he would not consent to the crime of adultery with her (Genesis 30). And truly the most powerful cause which contributes to the increase of witches is the woeful rivalry between married folk and unmarried women and men. This is so even among holy women, so what must it be among the others? For you see in Genesis 21 how impatient and envious Sarah was of Hagar when she conceived: how jealous Rachel was of Leah because she had no children (Genesis 30): and Hannah, who was barren, of the fruitful Peninnah (1 Kings 1): and how Miriam (Numbers 12) murmured and spoke ill of Moses, and was therefore stricken with leprosy: and how Martha was jealous of Mary Magdalen, because she was busy and Mary was sitting down (Luke 10). To this point is Ecclesiasticus 37: Neither consult with a woman touching her of whom she is jealous. Meaning that it is useless to consult with her, since there is always jealousy, that is, envy, in a wicked woman. And if women behave thus to each other, how much more will they do so to men.

Valerius Maximus tells how, when Phoroneus, the king of the Greeks, was dying, he said to his brother Leontius that there would have been nothing lacking to him of complete happiness if a wife had always been lacking to him. And when Leontius asked how a wife could stand in the way of happiness, he answered that all married men well knew. And when the philosopher Socrates was asked if one should marry a wife, he answered: If you do not, you are lonely, your family dies out, and a stranger inherits; if you do, you suffer perpetual anxiety, querulous complaints, reproaches concerning the marriage portion, the heavy displeasure of your relations, the garrulousness of a mother-in-law, cuckoldom, and no certain arrival of an heir. This he said as one who knew. For S. Jerome in his *Contra Iouinianum* says: This Socrates had two wives, whom he endured with much patience, but could not be rid of their contumelies and clamorous vituperations. So one day when they were complaining against him, he went out of the house to escape their plaguing, and sat down before the house; and the women then threw filthy water over him. But the philosopher was not disturbed by this, saying, "I knew that the rain would come after the thunder."

There is also a story of a man whose wife was drowned in a river, who, when he was searching for the body to take it out of the water, walked up the stream. And when he was asked why, since heavy bodies do not rise but fall, he was searching against the current of the river, he answered: "When that woman was alive she always, both in word and deed, went contrary to my commands; therefore I am searching in the contrary direction in case even now she is dead she may preserve her contrary disposition."

And indeed, just as through the first defect in their intelligence they are more prone to abjure the faith; so through their second defect of inordinate affections and passions they search for, brood over, and inflict various vengeances, either by witchcraft, or by some other means. Wherefore it is no wonder that so great a number of witches exist in this sex.

Women also have weak memories; and it is a natural vice in them not to be disciplined, but to follow their own impulses without any sense of what is due; this is her whole study, and all that she keeps in her memory. So Theophrastus says: If you hand over the whole management of the house to her, but reserve some minute detail to your own judgement, she will think that you are displaying a great want of faith in her, and will stir up strife; and unless you quickly take counsel, she will prepare poison for you, and consult seers and soothsayers; and will become a witch.....

It is this which is lamented in Ecclesiastes 7, and which the Church even now laments on account of the great multitude of witches. And I have found a woman more bitter than death, who is the hunter's snare, and her heart is a net, and her hands are bands. He that pleaseth God shall escape from her; but he that is a sinner shall be caught by her. More bitter than death, that is, than the devil: Apocalypse 6:8, His name was Death. For though the devil tempted Eve to sin, yet Eve seduced Adam. And as the sin of Eve would not have brought death to our soul and body unless the sin had afterwards passed on to Adam, to which he was tempted by Eve, not by the devil, therefore she is more bitter than death.

More bitter than death, again, because that is natural and destroys only the body; but the sin which arose from woman destroys the soul by depriving it of grace, and delivers the body up to the punishment for sin.

More bitter than death, again, because bodily death is an open and terrible enemy, but woman is a wheedling and secret enemy.

And that she is more perilous than a snare does not speak of the snare of hunters, but of devils. For men are caught not only through their carnal desires, when they see and hear women: for S. Bernard says: Their face is a burning wind, and their voice the hissing of serpents: but they also cast wicked spells on countless men and animals. And when it is said that her heart is a net, it speaks of the inscrutable malice which reigns in their hearts. And her hands are as bands for binding; for when they place their hands on a creature to bewitch it, then with the help of the devil they perform their design.

To conclude. All witchcraft comes from carnal lust, which is in women insatiable. See Proverbs 30: There are three things that are never satisfied, yea, a fourth thing which says not, It is enough; that is, the mouth of the womb. Wherefore for the sake of fulfilling their lusts they consort even with devils. More such reasons could be brought forward, but to the understanding it is sufficiently clear that it is no matter for wonder that there are more women than men found infected with the heresy of witchcraft. And in consequence of this, it is better called the heresy of witches than of wizards, since the name is taken from the more powerful party. And blessed be the Highest Who has so far preserved the male sex from so great a crime:

for since He was willing to be born and to suffer for us, therefore He has granted to men this privilege.

23 · VIRTUOUS WOMEN

The author of this selection, Christine de Pizan (c. 1363–1431), received a solid education in the French court of Charles V. Left a widow with three young children when she was twenty-five, Christine turned to writing to earn a living. She acquired a reputation as an outstanding writer on diverse subjects but was particularly noted for her ardent campaign to disprove the myths about women held by her contemporaries. In The Book of the City of Ladies, *published in 1405, the author talks to three allegorical figures, Justice, Reason, and Rectitude, whose comments demonstrate the indispensable contributions women have made to human civilization and cleverly refute those who denigrated the female sex. Christine draws upon classical sources in her attempt to present history from a woman's point of view, but she is firmly grounded in the Christian tradition. Her title, in fact, alludes directly to Augustine's* City of God. *Here she reminds us of the virtuous Susanna and the countless deeds of goodness performed by Christian women. She also reminds readers that Mary, as the queen of heaven and first among her sex, makes it imperative that women be treated with reverence and not reproach.*

Source: Christine de Pizan. *The Book of the City of Ladies.* Translated by Earl Jeffrey Richards, 155–56, 217–18, and 251–54. New York: Persea Books, 1982.

"From what I see, my lady, all good and virtuous things are found in women. Where does the opinion that there are so few chaste women come from? Were this so, then all their other virtues would be nothing, since chastity is the supreme virtue in women. But from what I have heard you say, the complete opposite of what those men claim seems to be the case."

She replied, "From what I have already actually told you and from what you know about this, the contrary is quite obvious to you, and I could tell you more about this and then some. How many valiant and chaste ladies does Holy Scripture mention who chose death rather than transgress against the chastity and purity of their bodies and thoughts, just like the beautiful and good Susanna, wife of Joachim, a rich man of great authority among the Jews? Once when this valiant lady Susanna was alone relaxing in her garden, two old men, false priests, entered the garden, approached her, and demanded that she sin with them. She refused them totally, whereupon, seeing their request denied, they threatened to denounce her to the authorities and to claim that they had discovered her with a young man.

Hearing their threats and knowing that women in such a case were customarily stoned, she said, 'I am completely overwhelmed with anguish, for
if I do not do what these men require of me, I risk the death of my body,
and if I do it, I will sin before my Creator. However, it is far better for
me, in my innocence, to die than to incur the wrath of my God because
of sin.' So Susanna cried out, and the servants came out of the house, and,
to put the matter briefly, with their disloyal testimony, these false priests
managed to have Susanna condemned to death. Yet God, who always provides for those dear to Him, opened the mouth of the prophet Daniel, who
was a little child in his mother's arms and who, as Susanna was being led to
her execution, with a great procession of people in tears following her, cried
out that the innocent Susanna had been condemned because of a very grave
mistake. So she was led back, and the false priests were thoroughly inter-
rogated and found guilty by their own confessions. The innocent Susanna
was freed and these men executed. . . . "

Lady Justice then turned to me in her sublime manner and said, "Christine, to tell the truth, it seems to me that you have worked extraordinarily
well at building the City of Ladies, according to your capacities and with
the aid of my sisters which you have put to excellent use. Now it is time
for me to undertake the rest, just as I promised you. That is, to bring
and to lodge here the most excellent Queen, blessed among women, with
her noble company, so that she may rule and govern the City, inhabited
by the multitude of noble ladies from her court and household, for I
see the palaces and tall mansions ready and furnished, the streets paved
to receive her most excellent and honorable company and assembly. Let
princesses, ladies, and all women now come forward to receive her with
the greatest honor and reverence, for she is not only their Queen but
also has ministry and dominion over all created powers after the only
Son whom she conceived of the Holy Spirit and carried and who is the
Son of God the Father. And it is right that the assembly of all women
beg this most lofty and excellent sovereign princess to reside here below in her humility with them in their City and congregation without
disdain or spite because of their insignificance compared to her high-
ness. Yet, there is no need to fear that her humility, which surpasses all
others, and her more than angelic goodness will allow her to refuse to
inhabit and reside in the City of Ladies, and above all, in the palace already prepared for her by my sister Rectitude, which is constructed solely
of glory and praise. Let all women now accompany me, and let us say
to her:

"'We greet you, Queen of Heaven, with the greeting which the Angel
brought you, when he said, *Hail Mary*, which pleased you more than all
other greetings. May all the devout sex of women humbly beseech you

that it please you well to reside among them with grace and mercy, as their defender, protector, and guard against all assaults of enemies and of the world, that they may drink from the fountain of virtues which flows from you and be so satisfied that every sin and vice be abominable to them. Now come to us, Heavenly Queen, Temple of God, Cell and Cloister of the Holy Spirit, Vessel of the Trinity, Joy of the Angels, Star and Guide to those who have gone astray, Hope of the True Creation. My Lady, what man is so brazen to dare think or say that the feminine sex is vile in beholding your dignity? For if all other women were bad, the light of your goodness so surpasses and transcends them that any remaining evil would vanish. Since God chose His spouse from among women, most excellent Lady, because of your honor, not only should men refrain from reproaching women but should also hold them in great reverence.'"

The Virgin replied as follows: "O Justice, greatly beloved by my Son, I will live and abide most happily among my sisters and friends, for Reason, Rectitude, and you, as well as Nature, urge me to do so. They serve, praise, and honor me unceasingly, for I am and will always be the head of the feminine sex. This arrangement was present in the mind of God the Father from the start, revealed and ordained previously in the council of the Trinity."

Here Justice answered, while all the women knelt with their heads bowed, "My Lady, may honor and praise be given to you forever. Save us, our Lady, and pray for us to your Son who refuses you nothing. . . .

"What more do you want me to tell you, my fair friend, Christine? I could recall other similar examples to you without stop. But because I see that you are surprised—for you said earlier, that every classical author attacked women—I tell you that, in spite of what you may have found in the writings of pagan authors on the subject of criticizing women, you will find little said against them in the holy legends of Jesus Christ and His Apostles; instead, even in the histories of all the saints, just as you can see yourself, you will find through God's grace many cases of extraordinary firmness and strength in women. Oh, the beautiful service, the outstanding charity which they have performed with great care and solicitude, unflinchingly, for the servants of God! Should not such hospitality and favors be considered? And even if some foolish men deem them frivolous, no one can deny that such works in accordance with our Faith are the ladders leading to Heaven. So it is written regarding Drusiana, an honest widow who received Saint John the Evangelist in her home and waited on him and served him meals. It happened when this same Saint John returned from exile that the city dwellers held a large feast for him just as Drusiana was being led to burial, for she had died from grief over his long absence. And the neighbors said, 'John, here is Drusiana, your good hostess, who died from sorrow at your absence. She will never wait on you again.' Whereupon Saint John addressed her, 'Drusiana, get up and go home and prepare my meal for me.' And she came back to life.

"Likewise, a valiant and noble lady from the city of Limoges, named Susanna, was the first to give lodging to Saint Martial, who had been sent there by Saint Peter in order to convert the country. And this lady did many good things for him.

"Similarly, the good lady Maximilla removed Saint Andrew from the cross and buried him and in so doing risked death.

"The holy virgin Ephigenia in like manner followed Saint Matthew the Evangelist with great devotion and waited upon him. And after his death she had a church built in his honor.

"Similarly, another good lady was so taken with holy love for Saint Paul that she followed him everywhere and served him diligently.

"Likewise, during the time of the Apostles, a noble queen named Helen (not the mother of Constantine but the queen of Adiabene, in Assyria) went to Jerusalem, where there was a terrible shortage of foodstuffs because of the famine there. And when she learned that the saints of our Lord, who were in the city to preach to the people and to convert them, were dying of hunger, she had enough food purchased to provide them food as long as the famine lasted.

"Similarly, when Saint Paul was led to be beheaded at Nero's command, a good lady named Plautilla, who had customarily waited on him, walked ahead of him, weeping profoundly. And Saint Paul asked her for the scarf which she had on her head. And she gave it to him, whereupon the evil men who were there taunted her, saying that it was a fine thing for her to forfeit such a beautiful scarf. Saint Paul himself tied it around his eyes, and when he was dead, the angels gave it back to the woman, and it was completely smeared with blood, for which she cherished it dearly. And Saint Paul appeared to her and told her that because she had served him on Earth, he would serve her in Heaven by praying for her. I will tell you many more similar cases.

"Basilissa was a noble lady by virtue of her chastity. She was married to Saint Julian, and both of them took a vow of virginity on their wedding night. No one could conceive of the holy way of life of this virgin, nor the multitude of women and maidens who were saved and drawn to a holy life through her sacred preaching. And, in short, she was so deserving of grace because of her great chastity that our Lord spoke to her as she was dying.

"I do not know what more I could tell you, Christine, my friend. I could tell of countless ladies of different social backgrounds, maidens, married women, and widows, in whom God manifested His virtues with amazing force and constancy. But let this suffice for you, for it seems to me that I have acquitted myself well of my office in completing the high roofs of your City and in populating it for you with outstanding ladies, just as I promised. These last examples will serve as the doorways and gates into our City. And even though I have not named all the holy ladies who have lived, who are living, and who will live—for I could name only a handful!—they can all be included in this City of Ladies. Of it may be said, *'Gloriosa dicta sunt de te, civitas Dei.'* So I turn it over to you, finished perfectly and well enclosed, just as I promised. Farewell and may the peace of the Lord be always with you."

24 ▪ MARGERY KEMPE

The spiritual biography of Margery Kempe is one of the rare vernacular works by women from the fifteenth century. Born in Kings Lynn in 1373, Kempe married a prominent citizen and bore fourteen children before she and her husband agreed to live celibately. This selection from The Book of Margery Kempe *reveals much about her activities, relationships, and spirituality. She makes a number of pilgrimages to local and foreign holy places, in this case Canterbury. Here, as elsewhere, her emotional outbursts and her pointed condemnation of the monks and priests lead the churchmen to accuse her of heresy. She is rescued not by her husband, who has abandoned her, but by two strangers who appear in answer to her prayers. They in turn ask her to pray for them. Following these incidents, Kempe experiences a period of close communion with God.*

Source: Margery Kempe. *The Book of Margery Kempe, Fourteen Hundred & Thirty-six.* A modern version by W. Butler-Bowden, 20–22. New York: Devin-Adair Co., 1944.

On a time, as this creature was at Canterbury in the church amongst the monks, she was greatly despised and reproved because she wept so fast, both by the monks and priests, and by secular men, nearly all day both forenoon and afternoon also, so much indeed that her husband went away from her as if he had not known her, and left her alone amongst them, choose how she might. Further comfort had she none of him that day.

So an old monk, who had been Treasurer with the Queen whilst he was in secular clothing, a rich man, and greatly dreaded by many people, took her by the hand, saying unto her:—

"What canst thou say of God?"

"Sir," she said, "I will both speak of Him, and hear of Him," repeating to the monk a story of Scripture.

The monk said:—"I would thou wert enclosed in a house of stone, so that, there, no man should speak with thee."

"Ah! Sir," she said, "ye should maintain God's servants. Ye are the first that hold against them. Our Lord amend you."

Then a young monk said to her:—"Either thou hast the Holy Ghost, or else thou hast the devil within thee, for what thou speakest to us here is Holy Writ, and that hast thou not of thyself."

Then said this creature:—"I pray you, sir, give me leave to tell you a tale."

Then the people said to the monk:—"Let her say what she will."

Then she said:—"There was once a man who had sinned greatly against God, and when he was shriven, his confessor enjoined him as part of his penance, that he should for one year hire men to chide him and reprove him for his sins, and he should give them silver for their labor. And one day he came amongst many great men, such as are now here, God save you all, and stood among them as I do now amongst you, despising him as ye do me, the man laughing and smiling and having good game at their words. The greatest master of them said to the man:—

'Why laughest thou, wretch? Thou are greatly despised!'

'Ah! Sir, I have great cause to laugh, for I have many days put silver out of my purse and hired men to chide me for remission of my sin, and this day I may keep my silver in my purse. I thank you all.

'Right so I say to you, worshipful sirs. Whilst I was at home in my own country, day by day with great weeping and mourning, I sorrowed because I had no shame, scorn or contempt, as I was worthy. I thank you all, sirs, highly for what, forenoon and afternoon, I have had in good measure this day, blessed be God for it.'"

Then she went out of the monastery, they following and crying upon her:—

"Thou shalt be burnt, false Lollard. Here is a cartful of thorns ready for thee, and a tun to burn thee with."

And the creature stood outside the gates of Canterbury, for it was in the evening, many people wondering at her.

Then said the people:—"Take and burn her!"

She stood still, trembling and quaking full sore in her flesh, without earthly comfort, and knew not where her husband had gone.

Then prayed she in her heart to Our Lord in this manner:—

"Here came I, Lord, for Thy love. Blessed Lord, help me and have mercy on me."

And anon, after she had made her prayer in her heart to Our Lord, there came two fair young men, who said to her:—

"Damsel, art thou neither heretic nor Lollard?"

And she said:—"No, sirs, I am neither heretic nor Lollard."

They asked her, where was her inn. She said she knew not what street;

nevertheless it would be at a Dewchman's house. Then these two young men brought her home to her hostel, and made her great cheer, asking her to pray for them, and there she found her husband.

And many people in N . . . had said evil of her whilst she was out, and slandered her over many things she was said to have done whilst she was in the country.

Then, after this, she was in great rest of soul a long while, and had high contemplation day by day, and much holy speech and dalliance with Our Lord Jesus Christ, both forenoon and afternoon with many sweet tears of high devotion, so plenteously and continually, that it was a marvel that her eyes endured, or that her heart should last, without being consumed with the ardor of love, which was kindled with the holy dalliance of Our Lord, when He said to her many times:—

"Dear daughter, love thou Me with all thy heart, for I love thee with all My heart and the might of My Godhead, for thou wert a chosen soul without beginning in My sight and a pillar of Holy Church. My merciful eyes are ever upon thee. It would be impossible for thee to suffer the scorn and contempt that thou shalt have, were not My grace supporting thee."

25 ▪ JESUS AS MOTHER

Julian of Norwich (b. c. 1342) spent much of her life in an anchorage attached to the Church of St. Julian and St. Edward in the Norwich area. She was sought out as a sympathetic, shrewd, and learned spiritual adviser by many, including Margery Kempe. She was probably still living at home in May 1373 when she experienced a series of mystical "showings" or revelations during a serious illness. After giving her the church's last rites, a priest left Julian with a crucifix that he urged her to meditate upon. The result was fifteen revelations in five hours and an additional one the next day. Twenty years later, she committed her experiences and her reflections upon them to writing in The Sixteen Revelations of Divine Love. *As this document illustrates, her visions of the Trinity and the passion of Christ give rise to extensive meditations particularly on the love of God. Here this love is understood in terms of mother-love.*

Source: Julian of Norwich. *Revelations of Divine Love.* Translated with an introduction by M. L. Del Mastro, 191–93. New York: Doubleday, 1977.

But now it is necessary for me to say a little more about this "spreading forth," as I understood it in our Lord's meaning—how we are brought again, by the motherhood of mercy and grace, into our natural place, for which we were created by the motherhood of natural love. This natural love never leaves us.

Our natural mother, our gracious mother, because he willed to become our mother entirely in everything, took the ground for his work most humbly and most mildly in the maiden's womb. That he showed in the first showing, where he brought that meek maiden before the eye of my understanding in the simple stature she had when she conceived. That is to say, our high God, the sovereign wisdom of all, arrayed himself in this low place and made himself entirely ready in our poor flesh in order to do the service and the office of motherhood himself in all things.

A mother's service is nearest, readiest and surest. It is nearest because it is most natural. It is readiest because it is most loving. And it is surest because it is most true. This office no one but him alone might or could ever have performed to the full.

We realize that all our mothers bear us for pain and for dying, and what is that? But our true mother, Jesus—All love—alone bears us for joy and for endless living, blessed may he be! Thus he sustains us within himself in love and hard labor, until the fulness of time. Then he willed to suffer the sharpest thorns and the most grievous pains there ever were or ever will be, and to die at the last.

When he had done this and so borne us to bliss, all this still could not satisfy his marvelous love. That he showed in these noble, surpassing words of love: "If I could suffer more, I would suffer more." He could not die any more, but he would not stop working.

Therefore it was necessary for him to feed us, for the most precious love of motherhood had made him a debtor to us. A mother can give her child her milk to suck, but our precious mother, Jesus, can feed us with himself. He does so most courteously and most tenderly, with the Blessed Sacrament, which is the precious food of true life. With all the sweet sacraments he sustains us most mercifully and graciously. That is what he meant in these blessed words, where he said, "I am that which holy Church preaches and teaches you," that is to say, "All the health and the life of the sacraments, all the virtue and the grace of my word, all the goodness that is ordained for you in holy Church, that I am."

The mother can hold her child tenderly to her breast, but our tender mother, Jesus, can lead us in friendly fashion into his blessed breast by means of his sweet open side and there show us something of the godhead and the joys of heaven with a spiritual assurance of endless bliss. This he showed in the ninth revelation, giving the same understanding in the sweet word where he said, "See how I loved you!" Look into his blessed side, rejoicing.

This fair, lovely word "mother" is so sweet and so natural in itself that it cannot truly be said of anyone but him, or to anyone but him, who is the true mother of life and of everything.

To motherhood as properties belong natural love, wisdom and knowledge—and this is God. For though it is true that our bodily bringing forth is very little, low and simple compared to our spiritual bringing forth, yet it is he who does the mothering in the creatures by whom it is done.

The natural loving mother, who recognizes and knows the need of her child, takes care of it most tenderly, as the nature and condition of motherhood will do. And continually, as the child grows in age and size, she changes what she does but not her love. When the child has grown older, she allows it to be punished, breaking down vices to enable the child to receive virtues and grace.

This work, with all that is fair and good, our Lord does in those by whom it is done. Thus he is our mother in nature, by the working of grace in the lower part for love of the higher. And he wills that we know it, for he wills to have all our love fastened to him.

In this I saw that all the debts that we owe, by God's command, to fatherhood and motherhood by reason of God's fatherhood and motherhood, are repaid in the true loving of God. This blessed love Christ works in us. And this was showed in everything, especially in the noble, plenteous words, where he says, "I am what you love."

26 · PERSUADING A POPE

Catherine Benincasa (d. 1380), the daughter of a Sienese dyer, joined the Third Order of St. Dominic when she was sixteen. She was renowned for her saintly life and gifted with the power of persuasion. Both of these qualities are evident in this letter, which is one of a series written to Pope Gregory XI (1370–1378). Gregory XI was residing in Avignon, France, as his predecessors had done since 1305. This "Babylonian Captivity" of the church by the French government had, in the eyes of many, including Catherine, made the holy see partisan, avaricious, and virtually impotent. Here Catherine urges Gregory to purge the church of its self-serving priests and rulers and to return to Rome despite the turbulence and violence of Italian city-state politics. The holy see was finally reestablished there in 1377. Gregory's death a year later, however, began another long period of scandal and turmoil in the church.

Source: Catherine of Siena. "To Gregory XI." In *Saint Catherine of Siena as Seen in Her Letters*, translated, edited, and introduced by Vida D. Scudder, 130–33. London: J. M. Dent, 1911.

Most holy and dear and sweet father in Christ sweet Jesus: I your unworthy daughter Catherine, servant and slave of the servants of Jesus Christ, write to you in His precious Blood. With desire have I desired to see in you the fulness of divine grace, in such wise that you may be the means, through divine grace, of pacifying all the universal world. Therefore, I beg you, sweet my father, to use the instrument of your power and virtue, with zeal, and hungry desire for the peace and honor of God and the salvation of souls. And should you say to me, father—"The world is so ravaged! How shall I attain peace?" I tell you, on behalf of Christ crucified, it befits you to achieve three chief things through your power. Do you uproot in the garden of Holy Church the malodorous flowers, full of impurity and avarice, swollen with pride: that is, the bad priests and rulers who poison and rot that garden. Ah me, you our Governor, do you use your power to pluck out those flowers! Throw them away, that they may have no rule! Insist that they study to rule themselves in holy and good life. Plant in this garden fragrant flowers, priests and rulers who are true servants of Jesus Christ, and care for nothing but the honor of God and the salvation of souls, and are fathers of the poor. Alas, what confusion is this, to see those who ought to be a mirror of voluntary poverty, meek as lambs, distributing the possessions of Holy Church to the poor: and they appear in such luxury and state and pomp and worldly vanity, more than if they had turned them to the world a thousand times! Nay, many seculars put them to shame who live a good and holy life. But it seems that Highest and Eternal Goodness is having that done by force which is not done by love; it seems that He is permitting dignities and luxuries to be taken away from His Bride, as if He would show that Holy Church should return to her first condition, poor, humble, and meek as she was in that holy time when men took note of nothing but the honor of God and the salvation of souls, caring for spiritual things and not for temporal. For ever since she has aimed more at temporal than at spiritual, things have gone from bad to worse. See therefore that God, in judgment, has allowed much persecution and tribulation to befall her. But comfort you, father, and fear not for anything that could happen, which God does to make her state perfect once more, in order that lambs may feed in that garden, and not wolves who devour the honor that should belong to God, which they steal and give to themselves. Comfort you in Christ sweet Jesus; for I hope that His aid will be near you, plenitude of divine grace, aid and support divine in the way that I said before. Out of war you will attain greatest peace; out of persecution, greatest unity; not by human power, but by holy virtue, you will discomfit those visible demons, wicked men, and those invisible demons who never sleep around us.

But reflect, sweet father, that you could not do this easily unless you accomplished the other two things which precede the completion of the other: that is, your return to Rome and uplifting of the standard of the most holy Cross. Let not your holy desire fail on account of any scandal or rebellion of cities which you might see or hear; nay, let the flame of holy desire be more kindled to wish to do swiftly. Do not delay, then, your coming. Do not believe the devil, who perceives his own loss, and so exerts himself to rob you of your possessions in order that you may lose your love and charity and your coming be hindered. I tell you, father in Christ Jesus, come swiftly like a gentle lamb. Respond to the Holy Spirit who calls you. I tell you, Come, come, come, and do not wait for time, since time does not wait for you. Then you will do like the Lamb Slain whose place you hold, who without weapons in His hand slew our foes, coming in gentleness, using only the weapons of the strength of love, aiming only at care of spiritual things, and restoring grace to man who had lost it through sin.

Alas, sweet my father, with this sweet hand I pray you, and tell you to come to discomfit our enemies. On behalf of Christ crucified I tell it you: refuse to believe the counsels of the devil, who would hinder your holy and good resolution. Be manly in my sight, and not timorous. Answer God, who calls you to hold and possess the seat of the glorious Shepherd St. Peter, whose vicar you have been. And raise the standard of the holy Cross; for as we were freed by the Cross—so Paul says—thus raising this standard, which seems to me the refreshment of Christians, we shall be freed—we from our wars and divisions and many sins, the infidel people from their infidelity. In this way you will come and attain the reformation, giving good priests to Holy Church. Fill her heart with the ardent love that she has lost; for she has been so drained of blood by the iniquitous men who have devoured her that she is wholly wan. But comfort you, and come, father, and no longer make to wait the servants of God, who afflict themselves in desire. And I, poor, miserable woman, can wait no more; living, I seem to die in my pain, seeing God thus reviled. Do not, then, hold off from peace because of the circumstance which has occurred at Bologna, but come; for I tell you that the fierce wolves will put their heads in your bosom like gentle lambs, and will ask mercy from you, father.

I say no more. I beg you, father, to hear and hark that which Fra Raimondo will say to you, and the other sons with him, who come in the Name of Christ crucified and of me; for they are true servants of God and sons of Holy Church. Pardon, father, my ignorance, and may the love and grief which make me speak excuse me to your benignity. Give me your benediction. Remain in the holy and sweet grace of God. Sweet Jesus, Jesus Love.

Chapter 4

WOMEN IN AN ERA
OF REFORMATION

27 ▪ LUTHER ON MARRIAGE

Martin Luther (1483–1546) had already written and preached on marriage several times when he returned to Wittenberg from the Wartburg in March 1522. His more in-depth treatment in "The Estate of Marriage" probably appeared by the end of that year. Although the exact circumstances behind the work are not clear, Luther may have been responding to practical questions about marriage that had arisen during his absence from Wittenberg and that he encountered on a short tour of surrounding towns. In the treatise he discusses legitimate marriages, grounds for divorce, and the character of Christian marriage. Marriage is an estate ordained by and most pleasing to God. The duties and sorrows it might bring—even death in childbirth—are made "sweet and tolerable" because they are God's will. People are created to reproduce and to fill the earth with children who have been taught by both parents to love God. If they do not respond to these natural impulses, they will become sick in soul and body.

Source: Martin Luther. "The Estate of Marriage." Translated by Walter I. Brandt. In *Luther's Works*, volume 45, edited by Walter I. Brandt, 38–46. Philadelphia: Fortress Press, 1962.

The world says of marriage, "Brief is the joy, lasting the bitterness." Let them say what they please; what God wills and creates is bound to be a laughingstock to them. The kind of joy and pleasure they have outside of wedlock they will be most acutely aware of, I suspect, in their consciences. To recognize the estate of marriage is something quite different from merely being married. He who is married but does not recognize the estate of marriage cannot continue in wedlock without bitterness, drudgery, and anguish; he will inevitably complain and blaspheme like the pagans and blind, irrational men. But he who recognizes the estate of marriage will find therein delight, love, and joy without end; as Solomon says, "He who finds a wife finds a good thing," etc. [Prov. 18:22].

Now the ones who recognize the estate of marriage are those who firmly believe that God himself instituted it, brought husband and wife together, and ordained that they should beget children and care for them. For this they have God's word, Genesis 1[:28], and they can be certain that he does not lie. They can therefore also be certain that the estate of marriage and everything that goes with it in the way of conduct, works, and suffering is pleasing to God. Now tell me, how can the heart have greater good, joy, and delight than in God, when one is certain that his estate, conduct, and work is pleasing to God?

That is what it means to find a wife. Many *have* wives, but few *find* wives. Why? They are blind; they fail to see that their life and conduct with their wives is the work of God and pleasing in his sight. Could they but find that, then no wife would be so hateful, so ill-tempered, so ill-mannered, so poor, so sick that they would fail to find in her their heart's delight and would always be reproaching God for his work, creation, and will. And because they see that it is the good pleasure of their beloved Lord, they would be able to have peace in grief, joy in the midst of bitterness, happiness in the midst of tribulations, as the martyrs have in suffering.

We err in that we judge the work of God according to our own feelings, and regard not his will but our own desire. This is why we are unable to recognize his works and persist in making evil that which is good, and regarding as bitter that which is pleasant. Nothing is so bad, not even death itself, but what it becomes sweet and tolerable if only I know and am certain that it is pleasing to God. Then there follows immediately that of which Solomon speaks, "He obtains favor from the Lord" [Prov. 18:22].

Now observe that when that clever harlot, our natural reason (which the pagans followed in trying to be most clever), takes a look at married life, she turns up her nose and says, "Alas, must I rock the baby, wash its diapers, make its bed, smell its stench, stay up nights with it, take care of it when it cries, heal its rashes and sores, and on top of that care for my wife, provide for her, labor at my trade, take care of this and take care of that, do this and do that, endure this and endure that, and whatever else of bitterness and drudgery married life involves? What, should I make such a prisoner of myself? O you poor, wretched fellow, have you taken a wife? Fie, fie upon such wretchedness and bitterness! It is better to remain free and lead a peaceful, carefree life; I will become a priest or a nun and compel my children to do likewise."

What then does Christian faith say to this? It opens its eyes, looks upon all these insignificant, distasteful, and despised duties in the Spirit, and is aware that they are all adorned with divine approval as with the costliest gold and jewels. It says, "O God, because I am certain that thou hast created me as a man and hast from my body begotten this child, I also know for a

certainty that it meets with thy perfect pleasure. I confess to thee that I am
not worthy to rock the little babe or wash its diapers, or to be entrusted
with the care of the child and its mother. How is it that I, without any
merit, have come to this distinction of being certain that I am serving thy
creature and thy most precious will? O how gladly will I do so, though
the duties should be even more insignificant and despised. Neither frost
nor heat, neither drudgery nor labor, will distress or dissuade me, for I am
certain that it is thus pleasing in thy sight."

A wife too should regard her duties in the same light, as she suckles the
child, rocks and bathes it, and cares for it in other ways; and as she busies
herself with other duties and renders help and obedience to her husband.
These are truly golden and noble works. This is also how to comfort and
encourage a woman in the pangs of childbirth, not by repeating St. Margaret legends and other silly old wives' tales but by speaking thus, "Dear
Grete, remember that you are a woman, and that this work of God in you
is pleasing to him. Trust joyfully in his will, and let him have his way with
you. Work with all your might to bring forth the child. Should it mean
your death, then depart happily, for you will die in a noble deed and in
subservience to God. If you were not a woman you should now wish to
be one for the sake of this very work alone, that you might thus gloriously
suffer and even die in the performance of God's work and will. For here
you have the word of God, who so created you and implanted within you
this extremity." Tell me, is not this indeed (as Solomon says [Prov. 18:22])
"to obtain favor from the Lord," even in the midst of such extremity?

Now you tell me, when a father goes ahead and washes diapers or performs some other mean task for his child, and someone ridicules him as
an effeminate fool—though that father is acting in the spirit just described
and in Christian faith—my dear fellow you tell me, which of the two is
most keenly ridiculing the other? God, with all his angels and creatures, is
smiling—not because that father is washing diapers, but because he is doing so in Christian faith. Those who sneer at him and see only the task but
not the faith are ridiculing God with all his creatures, as the biggest fool on
earth. Indeed, they are only ridiculing themselves; with all their cleverness
they are nothing but devil's fools.

St. Cyprian, that great and admirable man and holy martyr, wrote that
one should kiss the newborn infant, even before it is baptized, in honor of
the hands of God here engaged in a brand new deed. What do you suppose
he would have said about a baptized infant? There was a true Christian, who
correctly recognized and regarded God's work and creature. Therefore, I
say that all nuns and monks who lack faith, and who trust in their own
chastity and in their order, are not worthy of rocking a baptized child or
preparing its pap, even if it were the child of a harlot. This is because their

order and manner of life has no word of God as its warrant. They cannot boast that what they do is pleasing in God's sight, as can the woman in childbirth, even if her child is born out of wedlock. . . .

It is certainly a fact that he who refuses to marry must fall into immorality. How could it be otherwise, since God has created man and woman to produce seed and to multiply? Why should one not forestall immorality by means of marriage? For if special grace does not exempt a person, his nature must and will compel him to produce seed and to multiply. If this does not occur within marriage, how else can it occur except in fornication or secret sins? But, they say, suppose I am neither married nor immoral, and force myself to remain continent? Do you not hear that restraint is impossible without the special grace? For God's word does not admit of restraint; neither does it lie when it says, "Be fruitful and multiply" [Gen. 1:28]. You can neither escape nor restrain yourself from being fruitful and multiplying; it is God's ordinance and takes its course.

Physicians are not amiss when they say: If this natural function is forcibly restrained it necessarily strikes into the flesh and blood and becomes a poison, whence the body becomes unhealthy, enervated, sweaty, and foul-smelling. That which should have issued in fruitfulness and propagation has to be absorbed within the body itself. Unless there is terrific hunger or immense labor or the supreme grace, the body cannot take it; it necessarily becomes unhealthy and sickly. Hence, we see how weak and sickly barren women are. Those who are fruitful, however, are healthier, cleanlier, and happier. And even if they bear themselves weary—or ultimately bear themselves out—that does not hurt. Let them bear themselves out. This is the purpose for which they exist. It is better to have a brief life with good health than a long life in ill health.

But the greatest good in married life, that which makes all suffering and labor worth while, is that God grants offspring and commands that they be brought up to worship and serve him. In all the world this is the noblest and most precious work, because to God there can be nothing dearer than the salvation of souls. Now since we are all duty bound to suffer death, if need be, that we might bring a single soul to God, you can see how rich the estate of marriage is in good works. God has entrusted to its bosom souls begotten of its own body, on whom it can lavish all manner of Christian works. Most certainly father and mother are apostles, bishops, and priests to their children, for it is they who make them acquainted with the gospel. In short, there is no greater or nobler authority on earth than that of parents over their children, for this authority is both spiritual and temporal. Whoever teaches the gospel to another is truly his apostle and bishop. Mitre and staff and great estates indeed produce idols, but teaching the gospel produces apostles and bishops. See therefore how good and great is God's work and ordinance!

28 · CALVIN ON THE CREATION OF WOMAN

John Calvin's (1509–1564) commentaries on the books of the Old Testament were written after 1555 when his influence over the city of Geneva was at its height. Calvin, a lawyer and scholar, had been prevailed upon to give the Reformation direction in this city-state. His commentary on Genesis is clearly shaped by his understanding of Paul and his desire to affirm the goodness of marriage. Woman in paradise, therefore, was created as a fit companion for man and as one who also bears the divine image. She was, however, in a state of gentle subjection as his helper. After the fall—for which, according to Calvin, they shared responsibility—she was cast into bondage and punished with a harsher form of subordination.

Source: John Calvin. *Commentaries on the First Book of Moses Called Genesis.* Translated by John King. Volume 1:128–30 and 171–72. Edinburgh: Calvin Translation Society, 1947.

It is not good that the man should be alone. Moses now explains the design of God in creating the woman; namely, that there should be human beings on the earth who might cultivate mutual society between themselves. Yet a doubt may arise whether this design ought to be extended to progeny, for the words simply mean that since it was not expedient for man to be alone, a wife must be created, who might be his helper. I, however, take the meaning to be this, that God begins, indeed, at the first step of human society, yet designs to include others, each in its proper place. The commencement, therefore, involves a general principle, that man was formed to be a social animal. Now, the human race could not exist without the woman; and, therefore, in the conjunction of human beings, that sacred bond is especially conspicuous, by which the husband and the wife are combined in one body, and one soul; as nature itself taught Plato, and others of the sounder class of philosophers, to speak. But although God pronounced, concerning Adam, that it would not be profitable for him to be alone, yet I do not restrict the declaration to his person alone, but rather regard it as a common law of man's vocation, so that every one ought to receive it as said to himself, that solitude is not good, excepting only him whom God exempts as by a special privilege. Many think that celibacy conduces to their advantage, and, therefore, abstain from marriage, lest they should be miserable. Not only have heathen writers defined that to be a happy life which is passed without a wife, but the first book of Jerome, against Jovinian, is stuffed with petulant reproaches, by which he attempts to render hallowed wedlock both hateful and infamous. To these wicked suggestions of Satan let the faithful learn to oppose this declaration of God, by which he ordains the conjugal life for man, not to his destruction, but to his salvation.

I will make him an help. It may be inquired, why this is not said in the plural number, *Let us make,* as before in the creation of man. Some suppose that a distinction between the two sexes is in this manner marked, and that it is thus shown how much the man excels the woman. But I am better satisfied with an interpretation which, though not altogether contrary, is yet different; namely, since in the person of the man the human race had been created, the common dignity of our whole nature was without distinction, honored with one eulogy, when it was said, "Let us make man"; nor was it necessary to be repeated in creating the woman, who was nothing else than an accession to the man. Certainly, it cannot be denied, that the woman also, though in the second degree, was created in the image of God; whence it follows, that what was said in the creation of the man belongs to the female sex. Now, since God assigns the woman as a help to the man, he not only prescribes to wives the rule of their vocation, to instruct them in their duty, but he also pronounces that marriage will really prove to men the best support of life. We may therefore conclude, that the order of nature implies that the woman should be the helper of the man. The vulgar proverb, indeed, is, that she is a necessary evil; but the voice of God is rather to be heard, which declares that woman is given as a companion and an associate to the man, to assist him to live well. I confess, indeed, that in this corrupt state of mankind, the blessing of God, which is here described, is neither perceived nor flourishes; but the cause of the evil must be considered, namely, that the order of nature, which God had appointed, has been inverted by us. For if the integrity of man had remained to this day such as it was from the beginning, that divine institution would be clearly discerned, and the sweetest harmony would reign in marriage; because the husband would look up with reverence to God; the woman in this would be a faithful assistant to him; and both, with one consent, would cultivate a holy, as well as friendly and peaceful intercourse. Now, it has happened by our fault, and by the corruption of nature, that this happiness of marriage has, in a great measure, perished, or, at least, is mixed and infected with many inconveniences. Hence arise strifes, troubles, sorrows, dissensions, and a boundless sea of evils; and hence it follows, that men are often disturbed by their wives, and suffer through them many discouragements. Still, marriage was not capable of being so far vitiated by the depravity of men, that the blessing which God has once sanctioned by his word should be utterly abolished and extinguished. Therefore, amidst many inconveniences of marriage, which are the fruits of degenerate nature, some residue of divine good remains; as in the fire apparently smothered, some sparks still glitter. On this main point hangs another, that women, being instructed in their duty of helping their husbands, should study to keep this divinely appointed order. It is also the part of men to consider what they owe in return to the other half of their kind, for the obligation of both sexes is mutual, and on this condition is the woman assigned as a help to the man, that he may fill the place of her head and leader. One thing more is to be noted, that, when the woman is here called the help of the man, no allusion is made to that necessity to which we are reduced since the fall of Adam; for the woman was ordained to be the man's helper, even although he had stood in his integrity. But now, since the depravity of appetite also requires a remedy, we have from God a double benefit: but the latter is accidental....

Unto the woman he said. In order that the majesty of the judge may shine the more brightly, God uses no long disputation; whence also we may perceive of what avail are all our tergiversations with him. In bringing the serpent forward, Eve thought she had herself escaped. God, disregarding her cavils, condemns her. Let the sinner, therefore, when he comes to the bar of God, cease to contend, lest he should more severely provoke against himself the anger of him whom he has already too highly offended. We must now consider the kind of punishment imposed upon the woman. When he says, "I will multiply thy pains," he comprises all the trouble women sustain during pregnancy.... It is credible that the woman would have brought forth without pain, or at least without such great suffering, if she had stood in her original condition; but her revolt from God subjected her to inconveniences of this kind. The expression, "pains and conception," is to be taken by the figure *hypallage*, for the pains which they endure in consequence of conception. The second punishment which he exacts is *subjection*. For this form of speech, "Thy desire shall be unto thy husband," is of the same force as if he had said that she should not be free and at her own command, but subject to the authority of her husband and dependent upon his will; or as if he had said, "Thou shalt desire nothing but what thy husband wishes." As it is declared afterwards, "Unto thee shall be his desire" (4:7). Thus the woman, who had perversely exceeded her proper bounds, is forced back to her own position. She had, indeed, previously been subject to her husband, but that was a liberal and gentle subjection; now, however, she is cast into servitude.

29 ▪ LUTHER ON FEMALE PREACHING

In 1520, in his Babylonian Captivity of the Church, *Luther publicly announced his opposition to withholding the cup from the laity, the doctrine of transubstantiation, and the understanding of the mass as sacrifice. His supporters in Wittenberg, amid some confusion, began to act on these ideas while Luther was in the Wartburg. He wrote his treatise calling for the abrogation of the mass to aid and comfort the innovators. It was published in January 1522. While much of the work examines the mass in detail in order to refute any sacrificial connotations, the first section discusses the priestly office as one of preaching, to which all Christians are called. Luther, therefore, must argue that women have the right to preach, but only if no men are willing to do so. Men are "by nature" more fit for this task because they have better memories and voices.*

Source: Martin Luther. "The Misuse of the Mass." In *Luther's Works*, volume 36, edited by Abdel Ross Wentz, 151–52. Philadelphia: Muhlenberg Press, 1959.

Now, however, the papists quote to us the saying of Paul (1 Cor. 14[:34]): "The women should keep silence in the church; it is not becoming for a woman to preach. A woman is not permitted to preach, but she should be subordinate and obedient." They argue from this that preaching cannot be common to all Christians because women are excluded. My answer to this is that one also does not permit the dumb to preach, or those who are otherwise handicapped or incompetent. Although everyone has the right to preach, one should not use any person for this task, nor should anyone undertake it, unless he is better fitted than the others. To him the rest should yield and give place, so that the proper respect, discipline, and order may be maintained. Thus Paul charges Timothy to entrust the preaching of the Word of God to those who are fitted for it and who will be able to teach and instruct others [2 Tim. 2:2]. The person who wishes to preach needs to have a good voice, good eloquence, a good memory, and other natural gifts; whoever does not have these should properly keep still and let somebody else speak. Thus Paul forbids women to preach in the congregation where men are present who are skilled in speaking, so that respect and discipline may be maintained; because it is much more fitting and proper for a man to speak, a man is also more skilled at it.

Paul did not forbid this out of his own devices, but appealed to the law, which says that women are to be subject [Gen. 3:16]. From the law Paul was certain that the Spirit was not contradicting Himself by now elevating the women above the men after He had formerly subjected them to the men; but rather, being mindful of His former institution, He was arousing the men to preach, as long as there is no lack of men. How could Paul otherwise have singlehandedly resisted the Holy Spirit, who promised in Joel [2:28]: "And your daughters shall prophesy"[?] Moreover, we read in Acts 4 [21:8-9]: "Philip had four unmarried daughters, who all prophesied." "And Miriam the sister of Moses was also a prophetess" [Exod. 15:20]. And Huldah the prophetess gave advice to pious King Josiah [2 Kings 22:14-20], and Deborah did the same to Duke Barak [Judg. 4:4-7]; and finally, the song of the Virgin Mary [Luke 1:46-55] is praised throughout the world. Paul himself in 1 Corinthians 11[:5] instructs the women to pray and prophesy with covered heads. Therefore order, discipline, and respect demand that women keep silent when men speak; but if no man were to preach, then it would be necessary for the women to preach.

30 • CALVIN ON THE SILENCE OF WOMEN

The final edition of John Calvin's Institutes of the Christian Religion, *an exposition of his fundamental beliefs, was published in 1559. Intended both as a tool for teaching and a defense of Calvin's doctrine, the* Institutes *subsequently did much to shape Reformed theology. In the last section on the means of grace and the church, Calvin deals with the question of how to promote peace and order in the churches without binding Christian consciences to laws that are not perpetual divine commands. Two legitimate kinds of church laws can be made—laws for order that bind Christians together and laws for decorum that promote a fitting way to do things. Head coverings for women are a matter of decorum while the silence of women in churches is a matter of order. When such laws cease to build up or edify the church as a culture changes, they can be altered.*

Source: John Calvin. *Institutes of the Christian Religion,* 4.10.28–31. Edited by John T. MacNeill. Translated by Ford Lewis Battles. Volume 2:1206–9. Philadelphia: Westminster Press, 1960.

But it is worth-while to define still more clearly what is included under that decorum which Paul commends, and also under order [1 Cor. 14:40].

The purpose of decorum is in part that, when rites are used which promote reverence toward sacred things, we be aroused to piety by such aids; in part, also, that modesty and gravity, which ought to be seen in all honorable acts, may greatly shine there. The first point in order is that those in charge know the rule and law of good governing, but that the people who are governed become accustomed to obedience to God and to right discipline. The second point is, when we have the church set up in good order, we provide for its peace and quietness....

As a consequence, we shall not say that decorum exists where there is nothing but vain pleasure. We see such an example in the theatrical props that the papists use in their sacred rites, where nothing appears but the mask of useless elegance and fruitless extravagance. But decorum for us will be something so fitted to the reverence of the sacred mysteries that it may be a suitable exercise for devotion, or at least will serve as an appropriate adornment of the act. And this should not be fruitless but should indicate to believers with how great modesty, piety, and reverence they ought to treat sacred things. Now, ceremonies, to be exercises of piety, ought to lead us straight to Christ.

Similarly, we shall not establish an order in those trifling pomps which have nothing but fleeting splendor, but in that arrangement which takes away all confusion, barbarity, obstinacy, turbulence, and dissension.

There are examples of the first sort in Paul: that profane drinking bouts should not be mingled with the Sacred Supper of the Lord [1 Cor. 11:21-22], and that women should not go out in public with uncovered heads [1 Cor. 11:5]. And we have many others in daily use, such as: that we pray with knees bent and head bare; that we administer the Lord's sacraments not negligently, but with some dignity; that in burying the dead we use some decency; and other practices that belong to the same class.

Of the other kind are the hours set for public prayers, sermons, and sacraments. At sermons there are quiet and silence, appointed places, the singing together of hymns, fixed days for the celebration of the Lord's Supper, the fact that Paul forbids women to teach in the church [1 Cor. 14:34], and the like. Especially are there those things which maintain discipline, such as catechizing, church censures, excommunication, fasting, and whatever can be referred to the same list.

Thus all ecclesiastical constitutions which we accept as holy and salutary should be reckoned under two heads: the first type pertains to rites and ceremonies; the second, to discipline and peace. . . .

But there is danger here lest, on the one hand, false bishops seize from this the pretext to excuse their impious and tyrannous laws, and on the other, lest some be overscrupulous and, warned of the above evils, leave no place whatever for holy laws. Consequently, it behooves me to declare that I approve only those human constitutions which are founded upon God's authority, drawn from Scripture, and, therefore, wholly divine.

Let us take, for example, kneeling when solemn prayers are being said. The question is whether it is a human tradition, which any man may lawfully repudiate or neglect. I say that it is human, as it is also divine. It is of God insofar as it is a part of that decorum whose care and observance the apostle has commended to us [1 Cor. 14:40]. But it is of men insofar as it specifically designates what had in general been suggested rather than explicitly stated.

By this one example we may judge what opinion we should have of this whole class. I mean that the Lord has in his sacred oracles faithfully embraced and clearly expressed both the whole sum of true righteousness, and all aspects of the worship of his majesty, and whatever was necessary to salvation; therefore, in these the Master alone is to be heard. But because he did not will in outward discipline and ceremonies to prescribe in detail what we ought to do (because he foresaw that this depended upon the state of the times, and he did not deem one form suitable for all ages), here we must take refuge in those general rules which he has given, that whatever the necessity of the church will require for order and decorum should be tested against these. Lastly, because he has taught nothing specifically, and because these things are not necessary to salvation, and for the upbuilding of the church ought to be variously accommodated to the customs of each nation and age, it will be fitting (as the advantage of the church will require) to change and abrogate traditional practices and to establish new ones. Indeed, I admit that we ought not to charge into innovation rashly, suddenly, for insufficient cause. But love will best judge what may hurt or edify; and if we let love be our guide, all will be safe. . . .

Now it is the duty of Christian people to keep the ordinances that have been established according to this rule with a free conscience, indeed, without superstition, yet with a pious and ready inclination to obey; not to despise them, not to pass over them in careless negligence. So far ought we to be from openly violating them through pride and obstinacy!

What sort of freedom of conscience could there be in such excessive attentiveness and caution? Indeed, it will be very clear when we consider that these are no fixed and permanent sanctions by which we are bound, but outward rudiments for human weakness. Although not all of us need them, we all use them, for we are mutually bound, one to another, to nourish mutual love. This may be recognized in the examples set forth above. What? Does religion consist in a woman's shawl, so that it is unlawful for her to go out with a bare head? Is that decree of Paul's concerning silence so holy that it cannot be broken without great offense? Is there in bending the knee or in burying a corpse any holy rite that cannot be neglected without offense? Not at all. For if a woman needs such haste to help a neighbor that she cannot stop to cover her head, she does not offend if she runs to her with head uncovered. And there is a place where it is no less proper for her to speak than elsewhere to remain silent. Also, nothing prohibits a man who cannot bend his knees because of disease from standing to pray. Finally, it is better to bury a dead man in due time than, where a shroud is lacking, or where there are no pallbearers to carry him, to wait until the unburied corpse decays. Nevertheless, the established custom of the region, or humanity itself and the rule of modesty, dictate what is to be done or avoided in these matters. In them a man commits no crime if out of imprudence or forgetfulness he departs from them; but if out of contempt, this willfulness is to be disapproved. Similarly, the days themselves, the hours, the structure of the places of worship, what psalms are to be sung on what day, are matters of no importance. But it is convenient to have definite days and stated hours, and a place suitable to receive all, if there is any concern for the preservation of peace. For confusion in such details would become the seed of great contentions if every man were allowed, as he pleased, to change matters affecting public order! For it will never happen that the same thing will please all if matters are regarded as indifferent and left to individual choice. But if anyone loudly complains and wishes here to be wiser than he ought, let him see with what reason he can defend his overscrupulousness before the Lord. This saying of Paul's ought to satisfy us: that it is not our custom to contend, or that of the churches of God [1 Cor. 11:16].

31 ▪ CATHOLIC WOMEN IN GENEVA

Jeanne de Jussie, a nun in the order of St. Claire, provides evidence that women played an active part in both bringing about and opposing the Reformation. Her chronicle of events in Geneva between 1526 and 1535 includes descriptions of many visits made by Protestants to her convent. On one occasion, the elderly abbess, aided by her vicar, firmly resists the efforts of the city officials to compel the nuns to leave their cloister to attend a debate planned to teach Protestant doctrine. Later, a group of city officials and Protestant ministers enter the convent to persuade the sisters to leave while women outside engage the nuns in debate. Especially vocal is the sister of one of the nuns who would later convert to Calvinism. The nuns of St. Claire eventually found the atmosphere in Geneva so hostile that they reestablished their convent at Annecy, France.

Source: Jeanne de Jussie. *The Rise of Calvinism or the Beginning of the Heresy of Geneva, by the Reverend Sister Jeanne de Jussie, Sometime Nun at Sainte Claire de Genève, and after Her Departure Abbess at the Convent of Anyssi.* Edited by Ad.-C. Grivel, with an appended notice by Albert Rilliet. Translated by Allan C. Lane, 124–30, 142–45. Geneva: Imprimerie de Jules-Guillaume Fick, 1865–1866.

As, then, the stated deadline approached, the Syndics in person ordered the Father Confessor of the Sisters of Sainte Claire to appear without fail at the Convent of St. Francis for the debate.

Then on the Friday of the Octave of Corpus Christi at five in the afternoon, when the sisters were gathered in the refectory to have their light meal, the Syndics came to the door along with several other great heretics, telling the mother doorkeeper that they were coming to announce to the Ladies that they had to be present at the debate the following Sunday. The mother doorkeeper sent this pitiful news to the sisters at once, and asked that the mother abbess and her vicar should come speak to the men and give an answer. They went there together. Those women who remained in the refectory to keep community were soaked in the abundance of the wine of anguish, and sang compline in tears lamentably. The mother abbess and vicar greeted the Syndics humbly, and these men told them that all the nuns were bound by the command of the Messieurs to appear without fail at the debate. The women answered humbly, "Sirs, you have to excuse us, for we cannot obey this order. All our lives we have been obedient to your lordships and to your commands in what was legitimate for us. But this order we must not obey, for we have taken a vow of holy perpetual enclosure, and we wish to observe it."

The Syndics answered, "We have nothing to do with your ceremonies; you must obey the commands of Messieurs. In any case, solid citizens have been called together for this debate in order to become acquainted with and to demonstrate the truth of the Gospel, because we must come to a unity of faith." "How is that?" said the mother abbess and the vicar. "It is not the profession of women to take part in debates, for such things are not prescribed for women. You don't think that they should take part in debate, seeing that it is even forbidden to uneducated men to get at all involved in explaining holy Scripture. A woman has never been called to debate, nor to give testimony, and in this we do not wish to be the first. It would not do you honor to want to force us to be there."

So the Syndics answered them, "All these reasons are useless to us: you will come there with your father confessors, whether you wish to or not." The mother vicar told them, "Sirs, we beg you in the name of God, turn away from the desire to force us to do such a thing and don't prevent us in any way from going to the service of worship. We certainly don't believe that you are the Syndics, given your simple questions. For we believe the Syndics to be so wise and considered that they would not deign to think of wishing to give us any trouble or displeasure. But these are wicked boys who have no other pastime than to molest the servants of God."

The Syndics said to the lady vicar, "Don't try to trifle with us! Open your doors! We will come in, and then you will see who we are and what authority we have. You have in there five or six young ladies who have lived in the city and when they see us they will tell you just who we are, for we are solid citizens, Governors and Councillors of the city." "In good time," said the mother Vicar, "but for right now you can't come in here, nor can you speak to the ones you want, for they are worshipping at compline, and we wish to go there, too, bidding you a good evening."

The Syndics answered the lady vicar: "They are not all of your mind, for there are some of them that you are holding by force in there, by your traditions and bribes, and who would soon turn to the truth of the Gospel, if it were preached to them. And in order that no one should claim ignorance, the Messieurs have ordered this debate in the presence of everyone and wish that all of you should come there together." "Sirs," said the sisters, "save your grace, for we have all come inspired by the grace of the Holy Spirit and not by constraint in order to do penance and to pray for the world, and not for the sake of laziness. We are not at all hypocrites, as you say, but pure virgins."

So one of the Syndics answered, "You have really fallen from truth, for God has not at all commanded so many rules, which human beings have contrived; and in order to deceive the world and under the title of religion they are servants of the great Devil. You want us to believe that you are chaste, a thing which is not possible by nature: but you are totally corrupt women."

"What," said the mother vicar, "you who call yourselves Evangelists, do you find in the gospel that you ought to speak ill of someone else? The devil can well take away from what is good, but he has no part in us." The Syndic said, "You name the devil and you make yourselves seem so holy." "It is following your example," she said, "for you name him at your pleasure, and I do it as a reproach." The Syndic said, "Madam Vicar, be quiet and let the others speak who are not at all of your opinion." The mother vicar said, "I am willing. My sisters," she said, "tell the Messieurs our intention." And then the three doorkeepers, the bursar and two cooks, the nurse and several of the old mothers who were there to hear the conclusion all cried out together in full voice, "We speak as she does and wish to live and die in our holy vocation." And then the men were all astonished to hear such cries, telling each other, "Listen, Sirs, what a terrible racket these women inside are making, and what an outcry there is." The mother vicar answered, "Sirs, this is nothing. You will hear much more if you take us to your Synagogue, for when we will all be together, we will make such a noise that we will remain unvanquished." "Now," said the Syndics, "you are in high dudgeon, but you will come there." The mother vicar answered, "We will not." "We will take you there ourselves," they said, "and so you will never go back to your own land, for each of us will take one of you to his house, and we will take her every day to the preaching services, for she must change her wicked life and live according to God. We have lived wickedly in the past. I have been," said the Syndic, "a thief, a bandit and a Sybarite, not knowing the truth of the Gospel until now." The mother vicar answered, "All those works are wicked and against the divine commandment. You do well to amend your life, for you have lived badly. But neither my companions nor I, thanks be to the Lord, have ever committed a murder or any such works so as to need to take up a new life, and so we don't wish to change at all, but to continue in the service of God." And she spoke to them so forcefully along with the mother abbess, and the doorkeeper, that they were all amazed. "Lady Vicar," said the Syndic, "you are very arrogant, but if you make us angry, we will make you sorry." "Sirs," she said, "you can do nothing but punish my body, which is what I most desire for the love of my God. For on behalf of the holy faith, neither my company nor I wish at all to be dissemblers; our Lord wants us to confess him before human beings and if I say something which displeases you, I want to accept the punishment for it all by myself. So that you may know better who I am, and that others may not have unhappiness on my account, my name is sister Pernette of Montleul, or of Chasteau-fort."

When these evil men saw that they were wasting their time, they left, ending the conversation by saying furiously all together, "We enjoin you all a second time, on behalf of the Messieurs, not to fail to be present with your father confessors next Sunday, early, at the convent of St. Francis at the debate we have mentioned, and we do not intend that someone will have to come to get you," and so they left.

When they had gone away, the reverend mother abbess, the vicar, and the doorkeepers went up to the church with the others and then lifted the cloth from the grille to adore the holy Sacrament which was lying on the altar, as is the very praiseworthy custom. Then, lying prostrate on the ground, all together in a loud voice representing themselves as poor sinners and asking God for mercy—it was enough to break a pious heart, seeking from this good Jesus and the blessed Holy Spirit grace to be able to escape these dangers and perils. . . .

The sister of our poor apostate, hoping to make her leave, was there waiting, and in order to make her come and be perverted, had risen from her childbed, for she had given birth only eight days before. Her heretical husband had carried the child in his arms, and had held it in baptism without any other godparent. When that poor woman saw, I say, that her sister was not coming out at all, she proceeded to go up to the grille with some other women of the city, pretending to want to speak to the sisters in all friendship, to find out what had been done to them by these preachers. Then she asked to speak to her sister. The mother abbess, along with several discreet nuns, spoke to them devoutly, and then a false, serpentine tongue, preaching with sweet words, believing she could do more than the above-mentioned preachers, begins to speak of the Gospel, saying "Poor Ladies, you are very obstinate and blind! Don't you know that God has said that his yoke is easy and light, has said 'Come to me all you who labor and are weary and I will unburden you,' and has not said that one should lock oneself up and torture oneself with harsh penances as you are doing[?]" Then she said words about the holy sacrament which I would shrink from writing, as her "holy" words were quite contrary to salvation. The mother abbess, who knew the Holy Scriptures well, replied to her sharply, as did this poor apostate, but still she showed great friendship and intimacy to her sister, who was making the sisters very suspicious. Some of them went to beg the mother vicar to go there and put an end to their discussion. And she went at once to take the mother abbess by the arms, saying, "My Mother, seeing that these good ladies have changed from one law to another, and have chosen a course opposite to salvation, and to ourselves, you ought not to hear them out." And then she said to the mentioned Lady, "If you wish to converse here about our Lord and in honest words, as in the past, we will speak with you willingly, but we don't want to hear anything at all about these innovations in the law, because it is forbidden to us." Then without further ado she shut the door and left them frustrated. So they were very angry, and shouted there for more than half an hour, saying "Ha, false hypocrites, you despise the Word of God, and want to obey your hypocrites, and ministers of the Devil." And then this poor woman began to say, "You see how they treat my poor sister and keep her subject so that the poor young girl didn't dare declare her heart, however willingly she would listen to us."

And since that day they haven't ceased even a single day from sending someone from their sect to trouble and spy on the poor nuns, and often they would say scurrilous and detestable words. But the mother doorkeeper was sober and discreet and would not speak to them for long at all before she closed her little door. If she was forced to respond, she would have the mother abbess come, and the mother vicar and the sisters would start to pray and our Lord would always let them respond to great effect and they left the visitors conquered and confused. The truth is, they would often threaten the mother vicar with criminal imprisonment, and we sometimes feared that they would in fact do it—but some hesitated, saying, "She is too highly born and could be the cause of some high feeling against the city. Moreover the Duke of Savoy supports them, and so they only pray for him. Besides, we would be reproachable to lay hands on a foolish woman."

Several solid citizens used to come to warn us of the threats that they were making to come and take the young sisters in order to marry them, and especially the poor perverted woman, and to warn us that daily her sister begged the Messieurs and the Council to act. Therefore, some Catholic women from the city, and even some of their relatives, would come to weep, exhorting the nuns to be constant and to have good patience and perseverance, for indeed it had been resolved to oust us from the convent and to separate us from each other shortly.

32 · MARRIAGE AND ADULTERY AMONG THE HUTTERITES

Peter Rideman (1506–1556) spent his life as a Servant of the Word in the Church of the Brothers, or Hutterites. In 1540, while visiting Hesse to build up the Anabaptist communities there, he was captured and imprisoned. While confined, he wrote his Account of Our Religion, *which includes sections on marriage and adultery. Rideman contends that three grades of marriage exist, the highest of which is the marriage between God and the spirit. Implied in this discussion is the Anabaptist claim that a person's obligations to Christ take precedence over obligations to a spouse. Nevertheless, Rideman believes that the marriage of one body with another is a useful analogy to the spiritual union. As such, it is spoken of as a covenant or agreement between a woman who pledges obedience and a man who promises compassion. Like other Anabaptists, Rideman also believes that the marriage bond can be broken by adultery, but not just by adultery in a physical sense. One who ignores the moral imperatives of earthly marriage or who forsakes Christ is guilty of the same sin.*

Source: Peter Rideman. "Concerning Marriage" and "Concerning Adultery." In *Account of Our Religion, Doctrine and Faith Given by Peter Rideman of the Brothers Whom Men Call Hutterites,* translated by the Society of Brothers, 97–102. Rifton, N.Y.: Plough Publishing House, [1970].

Marriage is a union of two, in which one taketh the other to care for and the second submitteth to obey the first, and thus through their agreement two become one, and are no longer two but one. But if this is to be done in a godly way they must come together not through their own action and choice, but in accordance with God's will and order, and therefore neither leave nor forsake the other but suffer both ill and good together all their days.

Marriage is, however, in three grades or steps. First is that of God with the soul or spirit, then that of the spirit with the body, and thirdly that of one body with another, that is, the marriage of man with woman; which is not the first but the last and lowest grade, and is therefore visible, recognizable and to be understood by all. Now because it is visible, recognizable and to be understood it is a picture, an instruction and indication of what is invisible, that is of the middle and highest grades. For as man is head of the woman, so is the spirit the head of the body, and God is the head of the spirit.

Thus, we see marriage instructeth and leadeth men to God, for if one regardeth and observeth it aright it teacheth us to know God and to cleave to him. Where, however, it is not regarded and observed rightly it leadeth men away from God and bringeth them to death. And since they are few who regard it rightly and many who regard it not aright (still less observe it aright) Paul saith, it is good for a man not to touch a woman lest in their ignorance they lapse and destroy themselves. Therefore we want to speak of marriage insofar as is given us from God to speak.

We say, first, that since woman was taken from man, and not man from woman, man hath lordship but woman weakness, humility and submission, therefore she should be under the yoke of man and obedient to him, even as the woman was commanded by God when he said to her, "The man shall be thy lord." Now, since this is so she should heed her husband, inquire of him, ask him and do all things with and naught without his counsel. For where she doeth this not, she forsaketh the place in the order in which she hath been set by God, encroacheth upon the lordship of the man and forsaketh the command of her Creator as well as the submission that she promised her husband in the union of marriage: to honor him as a wife her husband.

The man, on the other hand, as the one in whom something of God's glory is seen, should have compassion on the woman as the weaker instrument, and in love and kindness go before her and care for her, not only in temporal but also and still more in spiritual things; and faithfully share with her all that he hath been given by God. He should go before her in honesty, courage and all the Christian virtues, that in him she may have a mirror of righteousness, and instigation to blessedness and a leader to God. Where, however, the husband doeth this not or is careless and superficial therein, he forsaketh the glory which was given him by God, as well as God's order....

Marriage is a union of two, in which one taketh the other to care for and the second submitteth to obey the first, and thus through the agreement of both the marriage is confirmed. Contrariwise, where this agreement is broken and transgressed, it mattereth not by whom, the marriage is broken. If the husband preserve not his honor as the glory of God and go before his wife and guide her to blessedness, he hath already broken the marriage with his wife, and if he breaketh it thus with his wife, he soon sinneth in the next grade, namely against his spirit, for he alloweth himself not to be ruled by it but by the flesh, and becometh superficial and forsaketh his lordship; if, however, his spirit is overcome and weakened by the flesh, he falleth in the third grade and breaketh his union with the Creator by whom he is led.

Likewise, if the woman forsake obedience to her husband who faithfully goeth before her, she hath broken and transgressed against the marriage with her husband, that is the union made with him. If she thus sinneth against her husband, she, likewise, goeth on to sin as is said above in all three grades; except where her husband through carelessness hath first broken the marriage with her, become superficial and wanted also to draw her after him. In this case she should let the broken marriage go and hold to that which is unbroken, that is obedience to the Spirit and to God, otherwise she falleth into death, together with her husband.

Where, however, the man doeth his part, but his wife acteth not with but without his counsel, she transgresseth her marriage and union in small things as well as in great things, and taketh from her husband his honor and lordship. If the man permit her to do this he sinneth with her as Adam did with Eve, in that he consented to eat of the forbidden fruit, and both fell to death. For they broke marriage with their Creator and transgressed his order.

The Lord Christ saith concerning adultery, "Whosoever looketh on a woman to lust after her hath committed adultery with her already in his heart." Thirdly, there cometh adultery with the work of the flesh, if one or the other of the partners in marriage go to another man or woman. Where this taketh place, where one committeth adultery in this way, the other should put him or her away and have no more in common with him or her before he or she hath shown real fruits of repentance. For where one mixeth with the transgressor before he or she hath repented, one committeth adultery with the other, even though they were husband or wife before. For it is no longer a marriage, because it is broken until through repentance it is healed, therefore this should be punished by separation as much as the other.

33 ▪ THE MARTYRDOM OF ANABAPTIST ELIZABETH OF LEEUWARDEN

The formal Anabaptist creeds and teachings forbade women to preach, teach, or baptize. Other factors, however, such as Anabaptist theology and political turmoil, worked to provide women with opportunities for considerable participation. They sometimes simply assumed the roles of teacher and prophet when men were imprisoned and executed. One notable example of this kind of female leadership is Elizabeth of Leeuwarden, who was martyred in 1549. She was a dominant figure in Dutch Anabaptism, frequently traveling and working with Menno Simons. When the authorities arrested her she was accused of being a "teacheress," or someone who spoke and taught publicly. During her trial she was questioned about her teaching and leadership functions.

Source: "Elizabeth, A.D. 1549." In *The Bloody Theater or Martyrs Mirror of the Defenseless Christians Who Baptized Only upon Confession of Faith, and Who Suffered and Died for the Testimony of Jesus, Their Saviour, from the Time of Christ to the Year A.D. 1660*, compiled by Thieleman J. van Bragt and translated by Joseph F. Sohm, 481–83. 9th ed. Scottsdale, Pa.: Herald Press, 1972.

Elizabeth was apprehended on the 15th of January, 1549. When those who had come to apprehend her entered the house in which she lived, they found a Latin Testament. Having secured Elizabeth, they said: "We have got the right man; we have now the teacheress"; adding: "Where is your husband, Menno Simons, the teacher?"

They then brought her to the town-house. The following day two beadles took her between them to prison.

She was then arraigned before the council, and asked upon oath, whether she had a husband.

Elizabeth answered: "We ought not to swear, but our words should be Yea, yea, and Nay, nay; I have no husband."

Lords: "We say that you are a teacher, and that you seduce many. We have been told this, and we want to know who your friends are."

Elizabeth: "My God has commanded me to love my Lord and my God, and to honor my parents; hence I will not tell you who my parents are; for what I suffer for the name of Christ is a reproach to my friends."

Lords: "We will let you alone in regard to this, but we want to know whom you have taught."

Elizabeth: "Oh, no, my lords, let me in peace with this, but interrogate me concerning my faith, which I will gladly tell you."

Lords: "We shall make you so afraid, that you will tell us."

Elizabeth: "I hope through the grace of God, that He will keep my tongue, so that I shall not become a traitoress, and deliver my brother into death."

Lords: "What persons were present when you were baptized?"

Elizabeth: "Christ said: Ask them that were present, or who heard it" (John 18:21).

Lords: "Now we perceive that you are a teacher; for you compare yourself to Christ."

Elizabeth: "No, my lords, far be it from me; for I do not esteem myself above the offscourings which are swept out from the house of the Lord."

Lords: "What then do you hold concerning the house of God? do you not regard our church as the house of God?"

Elizabeth: "No, my lords, for it is written: 'Ye are the temple of the living God; as God hath said, I will dwell in them, and walk in them'" (2 Cor. 6:16).

Lords: "What do you hold concerning our mass?"

Elizabeth: "My lords, of your mass I think nothing at all; but I highly esteem all that accords with the Word of God."

Lords: "What are your views with regard to the most adorable, holy sacrament?"

Elizabeth: "I have never in my life read in the holy Scriptures of a holy sacrament, but of the Lord's Supper." (She also quoted the Scripture relating to this.)

Lords: "Be silent, for the devil speaks through your mouth."

Elizabeth: "Yea, my lords, this is a small matter, for the servant is not better than his lord."

Lords: "You speak from a spirit of pride."

Elizabeth: "No, my lords, I speak with frankness."

Lords: "What did the Lord say, when He gave His disciples the Supper?"

Elizabeth: "What did He give them, flesh or bread?"

Lords: "He gave them bread."

Elizabeth: "Did not the Lord remain sitting there? Who then would eat the flesh of the Lord?"

Lords: "What are your views concerning infant baptism, seeing you have been rebaptized?"

Elizabeth: "No, my lords, I have not been rebaptized. I have been baptized once upon my faith; for it is written that baptism belongs to believers."

Lords: "Are our children damned then, because they are baptized?"

Elizabeth: "No, my lords, God forbid, that I should judge the children."

Lords: "Do you not seek your salvation in baptism?"

Elizabeth: "No, my lords, all the water in the sea could not save me; but salvation is in Christ (Acts 4:10), and He has commanded me to love God my Lord above all things, and my neighbor as myself."

Lords: "Have the priests power to forgive sins?"

Elizabeth: "No, my lords; how should I believe this? I say that Christ is the only priest through whom sins are forgiven" (Heb. 7:21).

Lords: "You say that you believe everything that accords with the holy Scriptures; do you not believe the words of James?"

Elizabeth: "Yea, my lords, why should I not believe them?"

Lords: "Does he not say: 'Go to the elder of the church, that he may anoint you, and pray over you'?" (James 5:14).

Elizabeth: "Yea, my lords; but do you mean to say that you are of this church?"

Lords: "The Holy Ghost has saved you already; you need neither confession nor sacrament?"

Elizabeth: "No, my lords, I acknowledge that I have transgressed the ordinance of the pope, which the Emperor has confirmed by decrees. But prove to me that I have transgressed in any article against my Lord and my God, and I will cry woe over me, miserable being."

The foregoing is the first confession.

Afterwards she was again brought before the council, and led into the torture chamber, Hans, the executioner, being present. The lords then said: "We have thus long dealt with you in kindness; but if you will not confess, we will resort to severity with you." The Procurator General said: "Master Hans, seize her."

Master Hans answered: "Oh, no, my lords, she will voluntarily confess."

But as she would not voluntarily confess, he applied the thumbscrews to her thumbs and forefingers, so that the blood squirted out at the nails.

Elizabeth said: "Oh! I cannot endure it any longer."

The lords said: "Confess, and we will relieve your pain."

But she cried to the Lord her God: "Help me, O Lord, Thy poor handmaiden! for Thou art a helper in time of need."

The lords all exclaimed: "Confess, and we will relieve your pain; for we told you to confess, and not to cry to God the Lord."

But she steadfastly adhered to God her Lord, as related above; and the Lord took away her pain, so that she said to the lords: "Ask me, and I shall answer you: for I no longer feel the least pain in my flesh, as I did before."

Lords: "Will you not yet confess?"

Elizabeth: "No, my lords."

They then applied the screws to her shins, one on each.

She said: "O my lords, do not put me to shame; for never a man touched my bare body."

The Procurator General said: "Miss Elizabeth, we shall not treat you dishonorably."

She then fainted away. They said to one another: "Perhaps she is dead."

But waking up, she said: "I live, and am not dead."

They then took off all the screws, and plied her with entreaties.

Elizabeth: "Why do you thus entreat me? this is the way to do with children."

Thus they obtained not one word from her, detrimental to her brethren in the Lord, or to any other person.

Lords: "Will you revoke all that you have previously confessed here?"

Elizabeth: "No, my lords, but I will seal it with my death."

Lords: "We will try you no more; will you voluntarily tell us, who baptized you?"

Elizabeth: "Oh, no, my lords; I have certainly told you, that I will not confess this."

Sentence was then passed upon Elizabeth, on the 27th of March, 1549; she was condemned to death—to be drowned in a bag, and thus offered up her body to God.

34 · THE SISTERS' CHOIR AT EPHRATA

The semimonastic community established at Ephrata in Lancaster County, Pennsylvania, flourished in the 1750s under the leadership of Johann Conrad Beissel (1691–1768). Beissel was originally a member of the German Baptist Brethren (or Dunkers) and retained many of their beliefs and practices, such as nonresistance and love-feasts. The community included a printing press and academy where music and the writing of devotional literature were encouraged. The Chronicon Ephratense *describes the origins of a singing school and the appointment of certain solitaries, or celibate sisters, to a choir to be headed by Beissel as the superintendent. The music became such an enchanting diversion that "one did not know who would perform the outside work."*

Source: "Lamech and Agrippa." In *Chronicon Ephratense; A History of the Community of Seventh-Day Baptists at Ephrata, Lancaster County, Penn'a*, translated by J. Max Hark, 160–65. Lancaster, Pa.: S. H. Zahm & Co., 1889.

Now we will again return to the Solitary. Thus far they had sought self-sacrifice in hard labor but now the Superintendent was urged by his Guide to establish higher schools, of which the singing school was the beginning....

Before the commencement was made, he [the Superintendent] entered upon a strict examination of those things which are either injurious or beneficial to the human voice, in consequence of which he declared all fruit, milk, meat to be viands injurious to the voice.... When bringing all this before the brethren for examination, they observed that he crossed some words with his pen, by which he had declared the love of women as also injurious to the voice. When asked why he did this, he answered that some might take offence at it. But the sentence was retained with full consent of the Brethren, and the writing was added as a preface to the hymn-book. This was but fair, for who does not know that carnal intercourse stains not only the soul, but also weakens the body, and renders the voice coarse and rough; so that the senses of him must be very blunt who cannot distinguish a virgin from a married woman by her voice....

But he also added to the things necessary to be observed in united song, that godly virtue must be at the source of our whole walk, because by it you obtain favor with the spirit of singing, which is the Holy Spirit. It has been observed that the least dissension of spirit in a choir of singers has brought confusion into the whole concert. The singing-school began with the Sisters, lasted four hours, and ended at midnight. Both master and scholars appeared in white habits, which made a singular procession, on which account people of quality frequently visited the school. The Superintendent, animated by the spirit of eternity, kept the school in great strictness and every fault was sharply censured. The whole neighborhood, however, was touched by the sound of this heavenly music, a prelude of a new world and a wonder to the neighbors. . . .

Soon after a choir of Sisters appeared in the meeting, and sang the hymn, "God we come to meet Thee," with five voices, which was so well received in the settlement, that everyone had his name entered for the choir, so that one did not know who should perform the outside work. . . . The Sisters were divided into three choirs, the upper, middle and lower; and in the choruses a sign was made for each choir, when to be silent and when to join in singing. These three choirs had their separate seats at the table of the Sisters during love-feasts, the upper choir at the upper end, the middle at the middle, and the lower at the lower end; in singing antiphonally, therefore, the singing went alternately up and down the table. Not only had each choir to observe its time when to join in, but, because there were solos in each chorale, every voice knew when to keep silent, all of which was attentively observed. And now the reason appeared which induced him to establish such choirs of virgins. It was with him as with Solomon, he was zealous to make manifest the wonderful harmony of eternity, in a country which but lately wild savages had inhabited.

Chapter 5

WOMEN AND CHRISTIANITY
IN THE AMERICAN COLONIES

35 ▪ MORE VIRTUOUS WOMEN

Cotton Mather (1663–1728), one of colonial New England's most prominent ministers, was pastor of Second Church, Boston, and author of over four hundred works on topics ranging from science and philosophy to the evangelism of slaves. His popular Ornaments for the Daughters of Zion, *which went through three editions between 1692 and 1741, is a manual of conduct, of "dos and don'ts," for women who wished to be virtuous. It is a curious blend of the conventional and novel in its approach to the status and role of women. Mather accepts a social order in which women are discreet, submissive, and silent and tries to shape their future behavior accordingly. But, unlike his Puritan ancestors and contemporaries, he speaks highly of women—past and present—who had already demonstrated great virtue and personal piety. Here he draws upon women in the Bible to dismiss any claim that women are evil and to elevate their status.*

Source: Cotton Mather. *Ornaments for the Daughters of Zion.* A facsimile reproduction with an introduction by Pattie Colwell, 25–31. Delmar, N.Y.: Scholars'
Facsimiles & Reprints, 1978.

Fourthly, A *Virtuous Woman* Labours to *Please* and *Serve* the great God,
with the greatest of her Cares[.] The *Fear* of God, is thus described by the
Apostle, in *Heb* 12.28 *Let us serve God acceptably with Reverence and godly
Fear*. And nothing is more *acceptable* to the virtuous Woman, than that she
may *acceptably Serve* her God[.] Let her be of never so *high* Rank, she thinks
it no Stoop for her, to be a *Servant* of that Lord, who has all the Angels
in Heaven for his *Ministers;* nor does her Opinion vary from that of those
Apostles who chose, to be call'd, *The Servants of Jesus Christ*, when they
might have been called, *His Kinsmen;* or of those Emperours, who valued
it as one of their Prerogatives, to subscribe themselves, *the Vassals of the
Lord Jesus Christ!* Let her be of never so *Low* Rank, she will not stoop to
be a *Servant* of the World, or of the Flesh, or of the Devil; nor can she
brook that the Curse of so being a *Servant of Servants*, ever should come

upon her. When she contemplates that Lord, who is *A greater than Solomon*, she cries out, *Happy are thy Servants; Oh that I might be one of them!* And she would always be doing the will of God, in such a Manner, as may be pleasing to Him. We read of One, *he had this Testimony, that he pleased God*. Now, that is the Testimonial to be given of the virtuous Woman; she aspires after the Imitation of the Lord Jesus in, *doing always the Things that please the Father*. It is the Name of a good Man, *the Man that pleaseth God;* and whatever Change the Name of this Woman may undergo, still she keeps that Name, *the Woman that pleaseth God*. How so? Even because she does all she can in and for the *Service* of God; and she would not leave Room for that Expostulation of the Lord, *If I be a Master where is my Fear?* No, as often as she says, *Our Father*, so often does her Heart within her say, *Our Master is in Heaven!* We read in the Bible, concerning, *certain Women that ministered unto Jesus;* and this Woman is ambitious to be of that blessed Company.

Fifthly. *A vertuous Woman* does attend the *Worship of God*, with an unwearied and exemplary Diligence. The *Proselytes*, that of old were brought unto the *Worship* of the true God, are thus distinguished, in Psal. 115.11. *Ye that fear the Lord*. And the virtuous Woman accordingly expresses her *Fear* of God by *worshiping* of him that is *worthy to be feared*[.] It may with only the necessary Variation be said of her, as it was of *Cornelius* long ago, *She is a devout Woman, and one that fears God, and prays to God, always*[.] As the Almighty God was called, *The Fear of Isaac;* because he was *worshiped* by that renowned Man; so may He be called *The Fear of the virtuous Woman;* because this Woman will observe all the Parts of that *Worship* which is due unto the Lord. There is the *natural Worship* of God, whereto she is no less piously *affected* than constantly accustomed. She is a *Woman* full of *Prayer*, and perhaps it may be said concerning every Room of her House, *She has perfum'd it with her Prayer*. *Prayer* is what she will be *early* as well as often at; and she is every Morning jealous, lest like *Origen*, she give the Devil an Advantage by omitting of it. She makes not her *Closet* a Place for meer Trifles and Pictures, but for *Prayers* with devoutest *Meditations*[.] She retires into her *Closet* every Day, that she may there have a Visit from the eternal *Bridgroom* of her Soul; and whatever Exercises may be at any Time upon her Mind, she does as *Hannah* did. *She pours out her Soul unto the Lord, that she may be no more sad*[.] Yea, she is not unacquainted with solemn *Humiliations*, and solemn *Thanksgivings*, upon the just Occasions of them. She is a Woman whom *Scriptures* and *Sermons* are very dear unto: And it is not every Trifle (as the want of a Garment, or a dread of the Weather) that she will make her excuse for her absence from the *Means of Grace*. How fain would she be with *Mary*, always hearing the sweet Admonitions of her Lord, about, *The one Thing needful* and *the good Part which cannot be taken away!* The *Sabbath* she calls *her Delight;* nor will she wast the sacred Hours of it in the *naughty Superfluities* of Diet and Rayment; but be as often as well as she can in the Congregation of, *the People of God;* and there, as her *Voice* makes a sound that shall be no *Base*, for the Musick of the Publick *Psalms*, thus her *Heart* is an *Altar* from whence, during the whole Solemnity, there ascend unto God, *the Sacrifices which he Desires*[.] There is likewise the *appointed Worship* of God, whereto she counts herself most indispensable obliged[.] She cannot bear to be shut out from the *Church* of God, any more than *Miriam* from the *Camp* of old; but whatever *Longings* ever may disturb her, she never has any more craving and raging ones than this, *O God, thou art my God, my Soul thirsteth for thee, my Flesh longeth for thee, to see thy Power and thy Glory in the Sanctuary!* Indeed among the *Turks* the *Woman* do never go to Church; but *Christian Women* would count it *Hell upon Earth* to be so debar'd. She is desirous to *eat* and to *drink*, where she may not *speak;* and having been *baptiz[e]d* she is not satisfied until she come to *eat* among the *Friends*, to *drink* among the *beloved*, of the Lord Jesus Christ. She will not make Part of that *unworthy Crowd*, which throng out of Doors, when the *Supper* of the Lord is going to be administered, as if they were frighted at it; or had Cause to say, *The Table of the Lord is polluted*. She dares not indeed come without a *Wedding-Garment*, but she will not stay away like those, whose only real Apology can be, *They are loth to be at the Pains of putting the Garment on*[.] Altho' she sometimes counts herself as a *Dog*, yet like that *Syrophenician* Woman, she will ask for some *Crumbs from the Table of the Lord*[.] Having had her Soul *purify'd* by *Regeneration*, she brings her *Offerings* to the *Tabernacle*. She presents unto the Church (if it be asked for) a sensible Account, like another *Lydia*, of some never to be forgotten Things which *God has done for her Soul;* or at least, she makes the Church to understand, like *Ruth* of old, *That she would come to rest under the Wings of the God of Israel*. Nor would she let the *Bufferings* of the Devil altogether discourage her from joining herself to some holy Society of Believers, where she may have her *Soul bound up in the Bundle of Life*. She was a noble Woman of *Bohemia*, that left her Friends, her House, her Plate, and all, and because the Gates of the City were guarded, crept through the common Sewer, that she might enjoy the *Institutions* of the Lord Jesus Christ at another Place where they might be had. Such is the Esteem which a *virtuous Woman* has for the *Institutions* of our Lord, she can say, *Lord, I have loved the Place where thy Honour dwells*, and when she can't *go*, yet she'll *creep* to, *the Habitation of his House*.

This is the *virtuous Woman!* It was very cruelly spoken by those two very ancient Poets; the first of which usually (in his Comedies) represented *Women* as *very bad;* but the latter usually represented them, *very good;* saying, *The first represented what they are, the latter what they should be*. I hope I have in this Discourse represented, not only, what *all* Women *should be*, but also, what *very many* of them *are*.

36 ▪ WIVES AS MODEL CHRISTIANS

Benjamin Colman (1673–1747) was one of Boston's leading colonial ministers and an advocate for change in Puritan worship practices. The pastor of Brattle Street Church from 1699 until his death, Colman was active in civic affairs and was offered the presidency of Harvard University. One of his most important publications was a series of discourses on the parable of the ten virgins in Matthew 25. His overall purpose is to remind his audience that death and judgment can strike at any time, and that they must prepare by accepting God's salvation. The bridegroom in the parable represents Jesus, in Colman's eyes, while the wise virgins are those who profess the Christian faith. In the passage below, he compares the marriage relationship to that between Christ and the believer. All Christians are to use good wives as their role models because such women love and honor their husbands and submit themselves in humble obedience.

Source: Benjamin Colman. *Practical Discourses on the Parable of the Ten Virgins: Being a Serious Call and Admonition to Watchfulness and Diligence in Preparing for Death and Judgment*, 8–10. Boston: Rogers and Fowle, 1747.

That the *Relation* wherein Christ proposes and offers himself unto us, agrees in many respects to the conjugal or marriage Relation. As,

First, It is the *nearest*, most intimate and indissoluble. As Marriage makes *Two* to become *One*, so he that *is joined to the Lord is one Spirit*. . . . There is a spiritual Union by Faith and Love[.] . . . The Marriage Covenant gives way to this, and binds not when it comes into Competition. We must *forsake* and *hate* every *Relative* for the sake of Christ. Because there is no higher *Allusion* known among Men, whereby to express the Union of Believers to Christ, therefore has the Holy Ghost used *this*[.] . . . 'We are Members of his Body, of his Flesh, and of his Bones.['] The Reference is to those Words of *Transport* wherewith *Adam* receiv'd and welcom'd *Eve;* charm'd at her Sight he said, *This is now Bone of my Bone*, &c. And as the Marriage Covenant binds till Death, so is our Union to Christ for Life, *for ever:* Death do's but perfect it. *This God is our God for ever and ever.*

Secondly, Our Relation to Christ is by a most sacred and awful *Covenant:* as of Marriage we read, *she is thy Companion and the Wife of thy Covenant.* There is a free Contract: the Choice is mutual, and so is the Obligation.

It is between *two only*, Christ and the Soul; wherein our Faith is plighted, Fidelity engaged, in exclusion of all others.

Thirdly, The *Duties* of this Covenant are like those which a *Wife* engages in her Marriage: for instance, intire, unfeigned, fervent, and perpetual *Love* to Christ. Hence the Church speaks of him in this Style, *Him whom my Soul loveth*. Again, *Subjection and Obedience* are the willing Offering of Love. *As the Church is subject unto Christ, so let the Wife*, &c. This is in Acknowledgment of the Excellency, Preheminence, Authority of Christ, 'For the Husband is the Head of the Wife, even as Christ is the Head of the Church and the Saviour of the Body.[']

Fidelity, Purity, and *Honour* are express'd and evidenc'd in Obedience. All Sin and Disobedience is resented as a defiling our selves with strange and impure Loves. Honour and Worship is due, *as the Wife show'd see that she reverence her Husband*. Constancy in Love and Obedience to the Death, is the grand Engagement of the Covenant; even *as the Wife is bound by the Law as long as her Husband liveth*. All Sin is Treachery and Disloyalty against the Saviour. We are to be perpetual Captives to his Love: *Be thou faithful to the Death!*

Lastly, The *Privileges* of the Covenant in Christ do agree with those to which a Wife is entitled by Marriage. *As*, there is a special Propriety in Christ and in all his Benefits: *My Beloved is mine and I am his*. A Title to his Love, *I am my Beloved's, and his Desire is towards me*. As it is natural and invincible to love our own Bodies; 'for no Man ever yet hated his own Flesh, but loveth and cherisheth it, even as the Lord the Church.[']

The Fruits of this tender Affection are, *Provision, Protection*, and *Conduct* from Christ. Is the Husband to provide for the Wife? 'For if any Man provide not for his own, especially those of his own House, he has denied the Faith,['] &c. So are our Wants supply'd by Christ, who cares for us; 'My God shall supply all your Wants, according to his Riches in Glory by Jesus Christ.['] Is the Husband to *protect* and defend the Wife? So the Lord the Church: God having *put all things under his Feet, and given him to be Head over all things to the Church*. Again, Ought the Husband to counsel and *guide* the Wife, which is the proper Office of the *Head*? So the Church is under the Watch and Influence of the Redeemer, who is the eternal *Wisdom* of God, and *wonderful in Counsel*.

Again, By our Covenant Relation to Christ we partake in his *Honours and Inheritance*; as the Wife shares in the Degree and Possessions of the Husband: *For if the Head be honoured*, so are the Members; the Crown is put on the Head, but it dignifies the whole Body: Now ye are the Body of Christ and Members in particular. We are said to be *Heirs with him*; and he has said, 'The Glory which thou gavest me, I have given them.[']

37 • ANNE HUTCHINSON

In 1635 the public order of the Massachusetts Bay Colony was threatened by a deep division over whether a sanctified life was evidence of conversion and an indispensable part of the salvation process. Leaders of the faction that pressed for a "Covenant of Grace" unrelated to works included Anne Hutchinson (1591–1643) and her brother-in-law, Rev. John Wheelwright. Despite a petition from influential Bostonians on his behalf, Wheelwright was banished from the colony in November 1637, and Hutchinson was shortly thereafter brought to trial before the general court. She was accused not only of advocating false theological ideas but of behaving in a manner inappropriate for a woman. Specifically, she was accused of holding and teaching at meetings in her home and of refusing to submit to her "parents," the magistrates. Hutchinson further frustrated the court by replying to their questions with questions of her own, forcing them to justify their positions from the Bible. She responded to them in a tone of clever defiance rather than submission.

Source: "The Examination of Mrs. Anne Hutchinson at the Court at Newtown." In Thomas Hutchinson, *The History of the Colony and Province of Massachusetts-Bay*. Edited by Lawrence Shaw Mayo, 366–70. Cambridge: Cambridge University Press, 1936.

Mr. Winthrop governor: Mrs. Hutchinson, you are called here as one of those that have troubled the peace of the commonwealth and the churches here; you are known to be a woman that hath had a great share in the promoting and divulging of those opinions that are causes of this trouble, and to be nearly joined not only in affinity and affection with some of those the court had taken notice of and passed censure upon, but you have spoken divers things as we have been informed very prejudicial to the honour of the churches and ministers thereof, and you have maintained a meeting and an assembly in your house that hath been condemned by the general assembly as a thing not tolerable nor comely in the sight of God nor fitting for your sex, and notwithstanding that was cried down you have continued the same, therefore we have thought good to send for you to understand how things are, that if you be in an erroneous way we may reduce you that so you may become a profitable member here among us, otherwise if you be obstinate in your course that then the court may take such course that you may trouble us no further, therefore I would intreat you to express whether you do not assent and hold in practice to those opinions and factions that have been handled in court already, that is to say, whether you do not justify Mr. Wheelwright's sermon and the petition.

Mrs. Hutchinson: I am called here to answer before you but I hear no things laid to my charge.

Gov.: I have told you some already and more I can tell you.

Mrs. H.: Name one Sir.

Gov.: Have I not named some already?

Mrs. H.: What have I said or done?

Gov.: Why for your doings, this you did harbour and countenance those that are parties in this faction that you have heard of.

Mrs. H.: That's matter of conscience, Sir.

Gov.: Your conscience you must keep or it must be kept for you.

Mrs. H.: Must not I then entertain the saints because I must keep my conscience[?]

Gov.: Say that one brother should commit felony or treason and come to his brother's house, if he knows him guilty and conceals him he is guilty of the same. It is his conscience to entertain him, but if his conscience comes into act in giving countenance and entertainment to him that hath broken the law he is guilty too. So if you do countenance those that are transgressors of the law you are in the same fact.

Mrs. H.: What law do they transgress?

Gov.: The law of God and of the state.

Mrs. H.: In what particular?

Gov.: Why in this among the rest, whereas the Lord doth say honour thy father and thy mother.

Mrs. H.: Ey Sir in the Lord.

Gov.: This honour you have broke in giving countenance to them.

Mrs. H.: In entertaining those did I entertain them against any act (for there is the thing) or what God hath appointed?

Gov.: You knew that Mr. Wheelwright did preach this sermon and those that countenance him in this do break a law.

Mrs. H.: What law have I broken?

Gov.: Why the fifth commandment.

Mrs. H.: I deny that for he saith in the Lord.

Gov.: You have joined with them in the faction.

Mrs. H.: In what faction have I joined with them?

Gov.: In presenting the petition.

Mrs. H.: Suppose I had set my hand to the petition what then?

Gov.: You saw that case tried before.

Mrs. H.: But I had not my hand to the petition.

Gov.: You have councelled them.

Mrs. H.: Wherein?

Gov.: Why in entertaining them.

Mrs. H.: What breach of law is that Sir?

Gov.: Why dishonouring of parents.

Mrs. H.: But put the case Sir that I do fear the Lord and my parents, may not I entertain them that fear the Lord because my parents will not give me leave?

Gov.: If they be the fathers of the commonwealth, and they of another religion, if you entertain them then you dishonour your parents and are justly punishable.

Mrs. H.: If I entertain them, as they have dishonoured their parents I do.

Gov.: No but you by countenancing them above others put honour upon them.

Mrs. H.: I may put honour upon them as the children of God and as they do honour the Lord.

Gov.: We do not mean to discourse with those of your sex but only this; you do adhere unto them and do endeavor to set forward this faction and so you do dishonour us.

Mrs. H.: I do acknowledge no such thing neither do I think that I ever put any dishonour upon you.

Gov.: Why do you keep such a meeting at your house as you do every week upon a set day?

Mrs. H.: It is lawful for me so to do, as it is all your practices and can you find a warrant for yourself and condemn me for the same thing? The ground of my taking it up was, when I first came to this land because I did not go to such meetings as those were, it was presently reported that I did not allow of such meetings but held them unlawful and therefore in that regard they said I was proud and did despise all ordinances, upon that a friend came unto me and told me of it and I to prevent such aspersions took it up, but it was in practice before I came therefore I was not the first.

Gov.: For this, that you appeal to our practice you need no confutation. If your meeting had answered to the former it had not been offensive, but I will say that there was no meeting of women alone, but your meeting is of another sort for there are sometimes men among you.

Mrs. H.: There was never any man with us.

Gov.: Well, admit there was no man at your meeting and that you was sorry for it, there is no warrant for your doings, and by what warrant do you continue such a course?

Mrs. H.: I conceive there lyes a clear rule in Titus, that the elder women should instruct the younger and then I must have a time wherein I must do it.

Gov.: All this I grant you, I grant you a time for it, but what is this to the purpose that you Mrs. Hutchinson must call a company together from their callings to come to be taught of you?

Mrs. H.: Will it please you to answer me this and to give me a rule for them I will willingly submit to any truth. If any come to my house to be instructed in the ways of God what rule have I to put them away?

Gov.: But suppose that a hundred men come unto you to be instructed will you forbear to instruct them?

Mrs. H.: As far as I conceive I cross a rule in it.

Gov.: Very well and do you not so here?

Mrs. H.: No Sir for my ground is they are men.

Gov.: Men and women all is one for that, but suppose that a man should come and say Mrs. Hutchinson I hear that you are a woman that God hath given his grace unto and you have knowledge in the word of God I pray instruct me a little, ought you not to instruct this man?

Mrs. H.: I think I may.——Do you think it not lawful for me to teach women and why do you call me to teach the court?

Gov.: We do not call you to teach the court but to lay open yourself.

Mrs. H.: I desire you that you would then set me down a rule by which I may put them away that come unto me and so have peace in so doing.

Gov.: You must shew your rule to receive them.

Mrs. H.: I have done it.

Gov.: I deny it because I have brought more arguments than you have.

Mrs. H.: I say, to me it is a rule.

Mr. Endicot: You say there are some rules unto you. I think there is a contradiction in your own words. What rule for your practice do you bring, only a custom in Boston[?]

Mrs. H.: No Sir that was no rule to me but if you look upon the rule in Titus it is a rule to me. If you convince me that it is no rule I shall yield.

Gov.: You know that there is no rule that crosses another, but this rule crosses that in the Corinthians. But you must take it in this sense that elder women must instruct the younger about their business and to love their husbands and not to make them to clash.

Mrs. H.: I do not conceive but that it is meant for some publick times.

Gov.: Well, have you no more to say but this?

Mrs. H.: I have said sufficient for my practice.

Gov.: Your course is not to be suffered for, besides that we find such a course as this to be greatly prejudicial to the state, besides the occasion that it is to seduce many honest persons that are called to those meetings and your opinions being known to be different from the word of God may seduce many simple souls that resort unto you, besides that the occasion which hath come of late hath come from none but such as have frequented your meetings, so that now they are flown off from magistrates and ministers and this since they have come to you, and besides that it will not well stand with the commonwealth that families should be neglected for so many neighbours and dames and so much time spent, we see no rule of God for this, we see not that any should have authority to set up any other exercises besides what authority hath already set up and so what hurt comes of this you will be guilty of and we for suffering you.

Mrs. H.: Sir I do not believe that to be so.

Gov.: Well, we see how it is we must therefore put it away from you or restrain you from maintaining this course.

Mrs. H.: If you have a rule for it from God's word you may.

Gov.: We are your judges, and not you ours and we must compel you to it.

Mrs. H.: If it please you by authority to put it down I will freely let you for I am subject to your authority.

Mr. Bradstreet: I would ask this question of Mrs. Hutchinson, whether you do think this is lawful? for then this will follow that all other women that do not are in a sin.

Mrs. H.: I conceive this is a free will offering.

Bradst.: If it be a free will offering you ought to forbear it because it gives offence.

Mrs. H.: Sir, in regard of myself I could, but for others I do not yet see light but shall further consider of it.

Bradst.: I am not against all women's meetings but do think them to be lawful.

Mr. Dudley. dep. gov.: Here hath been much spoken concerning Mrs. Hutchinson's meetings and among other answers she saith that men come not there, I would ask you this one question then, whether never any man was at your meeting?

Gov.: There are two meetings kept at their house.

Dep. gov.: How; is there two meetings?

Mrs. H.: Ey Sir, I shall not equivocate, there is a meeting of men and women and there is a meeting only for women.

Dep. gov.: Are they both constant?

Mrs. H.: No, but upon occasions they are deferred.

Mr. Endicot: Who teaches in the men's meetings none but men, do not women sometimes?

Mrs. H.: Never as I heard, not one.

Dep. gov.: I would go a little higher with Mrs. Hutchinson. About three years ago we were all in peace. Mrs. Hutchinson from that time she came hath made a disturbance, and some that came over with her in the ship did inform me what she was as soon as she was landed. I being then in place dealt with the pastor and teacher of Boston and desired them to enquire of her, and then I was satisfied that she held nothing different from us, but within half a year after, she had vented divers of her strange opinions and had made parties in the country, and at length it comes that Mr. Cotton and

Mr. Vane were of her judgment, but Mr. Cotton hath cleared himself that he was not of that mind, but now it appears by this woman's meeting that Mrs. Hutchinson hath so forestalled the minds of many by their resort to her meeting that now she hath a potent party in the country. Now if all these things have endangered us as from that foundation and if she in particular hath disparaged all our ministers in the land that they have preached a covenant of works, and only Mr. Cotton a covenant of grace, why this is not to be suffered, and therefore being driven to the foundation and it being found that Mrs. Hutchinson is she that hath depraved all the ministers and hath been the cause of what is fallen out, why we must take away the foundation and the building will fall.

38 • THE "UNFEMININE ACTIVITIES" OF SARAH OSBORN

After the death of her first husband and the illness of her second, Sarah Osborn (1714–1796) kept her family just above poverty by running a small school in Newport, Rhode Island. In the early 1740s, after a visit from revival preachers George Whitefield and Gilbert Tennent, Osborn was invited to form a society of young women to promote Christian piety, which she led for the rest of her life. In the 1766–1767 revival season, she played an even wider and more controversial role. Her house became a gathering place where large groups—male and female, young and old, slave and free—engaged in devotional exercises almost every evening of the week. In this letter of February 28 and March 7, 1767, to her friend and spiritual adviser Rev. Joseph Fish, Osborn defends her work. She makes it clear that God's work would remain undone if she discontinued her gatherings, because pastor and church remained unmoved. She has no intention of "Moving beyond my Line," however, and is eager to see her slave gatherings as a "school" rather than "meeting." To Fish's suggestion that she use her evenings for the more feminine activities of needlework and meditation, Osborn replies that her social activities were much more refreshing and productive.

Source: "Sarah Osborn to the Reverend Joseph Fish, February 28–March 7, 1767." In Mary Beth Norton, "My Resting Reaping Times: Sarah Osborn's Defense of Her 'Unfeminine' Activities, 1767." *Signs* 2 (Winter 1976): 522–29.

And now believing Zions cause is as dear as ever to my venerable friend, permit me to set my self as a child in the Presence of her Father to Give you the Most Satisfactory account of my conduct as to religious affairs I am capable. I will begin with the Great one respecting the poor Blacks on Lords day Evenings, which above all the rest Has been Exercising to my

Mind. And first Let me assure you Sir it would be the Joy of my Heart to commit it into Superior Hands did any arrise for their Help. My Revd Pastor and Brethren are my wittnesses that I Have earnestly Sought, yea in bitterness of Soul, for their assistance and protection. [I] would Gladly be under inspection of Pastor and church and turn things into a safe channel. O forever blessed be my Gracious God that Has Himself vouchsaft to be my protection Hithertoo by Putting His fear into My Heart and thereby Moving me as far as possible in this surprizing day. To avoid Moving beyond my Line, while I was anxiously desirous the poor creatures should be favrd with some sutable one to pray with them, I was Greatly distresst; but as I could not obtain [help] I Have Given it up and Thay Have not Had above one [prayer] Made with them I believe Sir Since you was here. I only read to them talk to them and sing a Psalm or Hymn with them, and then at Eight o clock dismiss them all by Name as upon List. They call it School and I Had rather it should be calld almost any thing that is good than Meeting, I reluct so much at being that Head of any thing that bears that Name. Pray my dear Sir dont Look upon it as a rejecting your council; that I Have not yet dismist. It is Such a tender point with me while the poor creatures attend with so Much decency and quietness you Might almost Hear as we say the shaking of a Leaf when there is More than an Hundred under the roof at onece (I mean with the young Mens Society in the chamber) for all there was so Many. Yet was not the Net broken Has sometimes been a refreshing thot. They cling and beg for the Priviledge and no weathers this winter stops them from Enjoying it, nor Have I been once prevented from attending them.

I know of no one in the town now that is against me. My dear Mrs. Cheseborough and Mrs. Grant Have both been to see me and thank'd me for persisting Stedily in the path of duty against their discouragements, ownd they were at first uneasy but now rejoicd and wish'd a blessing. Mr. C is quite silent. Every Intimate brother and friend intreats and charges me not to dismiss So Long as things rest as they are, telling me it would be the worst days work that Ever I did if I should, as God Him Self Has thus Employd me. If any disturbance or disorder Should arise Either to the breaking of Public or family Peace, that would immediately Make the path of duty Plain for dismissing *at once*, but on the contrary Ministers and Magistrates send their Servants and approve. And other Masters and Misstresses frequently send me presents in token of gratitude, Express their thanks Speaking of the good Effects that thro the blessing of the Lord it Has Had upon their Servants. And my dear sir what shall I do? Did not onisemus, a servant and once a vile one too, supply that want of a phyleman? Were Phylemon Present onicimus would soon give way....

As to friday Evning friends, my dear Sir I by no means Set up for their instructor. They come indeed for Mutual Edification and Sometimes condescend to direct part of conversation to me and so far I bear a part as to answer etc. but no otherway. They consist of the Brethren of our own church or congregation and Members of Societies Either that Meet at the deacons or our young Men, all I think Except My only one according to the flesh viz my own Brothers Son Mr Haggar, who sits under Doct Styles. That these Gatherings at our House Sir I Imagine no way tend to Separations rents or diversions but are rather a Sweet Sementing bond of union that Holds us together in this critical day. My dear Mr Osborn thro infirmity is unable to Go often to the Deacons on Thursdays Evenings and is very fond of this friday Nights visit, and they are Sweet refreshing Evenings my resting reaping times and as God Has Gatherd I dare not Scatter. In any wise I trust My reasons for Encouraging rather than dispersing will prevent your thinking me Obstinate in bad sence. I dont reject council; dont Let My Honrd Father think I do. The exercises of the Evening Consist in singing, reading Gods word anotation and other Good Books, prayer in turn twice; and Seven or Eight of them are the Most Excelent Men in prayer I believe few private christians Exceeds them. O I trust our God is in the Midst of us, does pour out on us a Spirit of prayer and Supplication—Some of our female Society went frequently to the other female Society on friday Evenings, and as a Means Gradualy to draw them off with out Objecting against their going because they are Baptist, I Have invited such Here with concent of the brethren and we were 20 in Number Last Evening—feb 28 1767[.] . . .

Thursday afternoon and Evening after catechising (Except the Last thursday in Every Month on which our Society Meets) is reserved for transient visiters business or what Ever providence allots. Satterday afternoon is my dear Miss Susa's particular time to visit me. Satterday Evening is reserv'd to ourselves. Now sir, if my Evenings were not thus improved I could not spend them to so much advantage that I know of any other way, for indeed I am not so capable after the Exercises of the day of working at my Needle; that overpowers me vastly more than the duties I am Engagd in. I could not retire the Evening as I could not Endure cold etc. nor can I Long attain to clost fixt Meditation or any Clearness of thot tho I Labour Ever so much for it; I am at that Season Much more capable of social duties then any other. These seem then to refresh recruit and enliven my Exhausted spirits, and companys Most of them are dismist before Nine o clock [so] that I have some time Left for other duties. My family Has the advantage of all these seasons, Except the wensday Evenings *only* Mr Osborn with draws a Little while before they break up, I mean from the young ones. And if my Evenings were not thus filld up they doubtless would be with trancient visiters, and some chat Less to Edification Especialy in this *critical day* would break in, which is by this Means *shut out*, [so] that at present I do acquiese in my time being thus taken up. Thus Sir I have given you the best account of My time I am capable of, but after all, while others are wondring, I find cause daily to bemoan before God the Misspence of precious time and oft appear to my self a very Loiterer a very snail. I fly with Haste from all my poor narrow Scanty performances and bless God I Have a perfect rightiousness to Plead and Hope to Escape to Heaven after all by the way of a free Pardon—I would now Humbly beg Leave Just to Speak a word as to Jethros advice, which I own to be very Good, but Here my dear Sir Lies the difference. Moses was Head of the people and So Had it in His power to comply with Jethros advice by appointing Elders etc. to take part with Him, but I am rather as a Servant that Has a Great work assignd Him and However unworthy and unequal he may think Himself, and others may think Him, and However ardently He may wish it was in Superior Hands or that His Master would at Least Help Him, yet if He declines He dares not tell Him, well if you dont do it your self it shall go undone for I will not, but rather trys to do what He can till God in his providence point out a way for it to be better done. And God did uphold Moses til He pointed out that way of relief He could comply with. Dont think me obstinate then Sir if I dont know How to Let Go these shoals of fish (to which My dear Susa compares them) that we Hope God [h]as Gatherd ready to be caught in the Gospel Net when Ever it shall please Him to shew His dear Ministers on which side the ship to Let it down for advanight—the Harvest truely appears to be Plenteous but the Labourers are few. O that the Lord of the Harvest may send forth Labourers into His Harvest and crown their Labours with success —

39 · SARAH EDWARDS'S RELIGIOUS ECSTASY

In 1742 Sarah Edwards (1710–1758) experienced nine days of extraordinary religious emotion as part of the Great Awakening, which was sweeping Northampton, Massachusetts. Her first-person narrative of this ecstatic interlude in her life as wife of the minister and theologian Jonathan Edwards has been preserved by her grandson. Known for her beauty, wit, piety, and skillful household management, Edwards had come to realize through careful introspection that she continued to be anxious about her esteem in the eyes of her husband and community. She also harbored deep resentment of the success a visiting minister, Samuel Buell, was experiencing while her husband was away from his Northampton church. These feelings melt away, however, as the love and beauty of God infuse her soul and produce fits of exaltation and joy.

Source: "Mrs. Edwards . . . Her Uncommon Discoveries of the Divine Perfections and Glory. . . . " In Sereno Edwards Dwight, *The Life of President Edwards*, 176–78. New York: Carvell, 1830.

When I came home, I found Mr. Buell, Mr. Christophers, Mr. Hopkins, Mrs. Eleanor Dwight, the wife of Mr. Joseph Allen, and Mr. Job Strong, at the house. Seeing and conversing with them on the Divine goodness, renewed my former feelings, and filled me with an intense desire that we might all arise, and, with an active, flowing and fervent heart, give glory to God. The intenseness of my feelings again took away my bodily strength. The words of one of Dr. Watts's Hosannas powerfully affected me; and, in the course of the conversation, I uttered them, as the real language of my heart, with great earnestness and emotion.

> "Hosanna to King David's Son,
> Who reigns on a superior throne," &c.

And while I was uttering the words, my mind was so deeply impressed with the love of Christ, and a sense of his immediate presence, that I could with difficulty refrain from rising from my seat, and leaping for joy. I continued to enjoy this intense, and lively and refreshing sense of Divine things, accompanied with strong emotions, for nearly an hour; after which, I experienced a delightful calm, and peace and rest in God, until I retired for the night; and during the night, both waking and sleeping, I had joyful views of Divine things, and a complacential rest of soul in God. I awoke in the morning of Thursday, June 28th, in the same happy frame of mind, and engaged in the duties of my family with a sweet consciousness, that God was present with me, and with earnest longings of soul for the continuance, and increase, of the blessed fruits of the Holy Spirit in the town. About nine o'clock, these desires became so exceedingly intense, when I saw numbers of the people coming into the house, with an appearance of deep interest in religion, that my bodily strength was much weakened, and it was with difficulty that I could pursue my ordinary avocations. About 11 o'clock, as I accidentally went into the room where Mr. Buell was conversing with some of the people, I heard him say, "O that we, who are the children of God, should be cold and lifeless in religion!" and I felt such a sense of the deep ingratitude manifested by the children of God, in such coldness and deadness, that my strength was immediately taken away, and I sunk down on the spot. Those who were near raised me, and placed me in a chair; and, from the fulness of my heart, I expressed to them, in a very earnest manner, the deep sense I had of the wonderful grace of Christ towards me, of the assurance I had of his having saved me from hell, of my happiness running parallel with eternity, of the duty of giving up all to God, and of the peace and joy inspired by an entire dependence on his mercy and grace. Mr. Buell then read a melting hymn of Dr. Watts, concerning the loveliness of Christ, the enjoyments and employments of heaven, and the christian's earnest desire of heavenly things; and the truth and reality of the things mentioned in the hymn, made so strong an impression on my mind, and my soul was drawn so powerfully towards Christ and heaven, that I leaped unconsciously from my chair. I seemed to be drawn upwards, soul and body, from the earth towards heaven; and it appeared to me that I must naturally and necessarily ascend thither. These feelings continued while the hymn was reading, and during the prayer of Mr. Christophers, which followed. After the prayer, Mr. Buell read two other hymns, on the glories of heaven, which moved me so exceedingly, and drew me so strongly heavenward, that it seemed as it were to draw my body upwards, and I felt as if I must necessarily ascend thither. At length my strength failed me, and I sunk down; when they took me up and laid me on the bed, where I lay for a considerable time, faint with joy, while contemplating the glories of the heavenly world. After I had lain a while, I felt more perfectly subdued and weaned from the world, and more fully resigned to God, than I had ever been conscious of before. I felt an entire indifference to the opinions, and representations and conduct of mankind respecting me; and a perfect willingness, that God should employ some other instrument than Mr. Edwards, in advancing the work of grace in Northampton. I was entirely swallowed up in God, as my only portion, and his honour and glory was the object of my supreme desire and delight. At the same time, I felt a far greater love to the children of God, than ever before. I seemed to love them as my own soul; and when I saw them, my heart went out towards them, with an inexpressible endearedness and sweetness. I beheld them by faith in their risen and glorified state, with spiritual bodies re-fashioned after the image of Christ's glorious body, and arrayed in the beauty of heaven. The time when they would be so, appeared very near, and by faith it seemed as if it were present. This was accompanied with a ravishing sense of the unspeakable joys of the upper world. They appeared to my mind in all their reality and certainty, and as it were in actual and distinct vision; so plain and evident were they to the eye of my faith, I seemed to regard them as begun. These anticipations were renewed over and over, while I lay on the bed, from twelve o'clock till four, being too much exhausted by emotions of joy, to rise and sit up; and during most of the time, my feelings prompted me to converse very earnestly, with one and another of the pious women, who were present, on those spiritual and heavenly objects, of which I had so deep an impression. A little while before I arose, Mr. Buell and the people went to meeting.

40 · EULOGY FOR GEORGE WHITEFIELD

When a young child, Phillis Wheatley (1753–1784) was purchased as a household servant by wealthy Boston merchant John Wheatley. Her intelligence and precocity won her the attention of the family, who encouraged her to study and write verse. Both her poetry and her conversational skills made her a favorite in Boston society. Her publications were celebrated by antislavery factions, who saw in them evidence for the argument that African Americans could rise to great heights through education. She enjoyed similar acclaim in England where she was the guest of the Countess of Huntingdon, to whom George Whitefield had been chaplain. In 1770 the countess probably played a role in having Wheatley's poem on Whitefield published. The poem mourns the loss of the preacher who brought the blessing of revival to America and praises the redemptive power of an impartial savior who died for African Americans as well as Americans. It was later incorporated into a collection of Wheatley's works entitled Poems on Various Subjects, Religious and Moral, *which was prefaced by a statement from eighteen prominent Massachusetts men testifying to the poems' authenticity.*

Source: Phillis Wheatley. "On the Death of the Rev. Mr. George Whitefield (1770)." In *Phillis Wheatley: Poems and Letters*, edited by Chas. Fred. Heartman, 36–37. Reprint. Miami: Mnemosyne Publishing Co., 1969.

Hail, happy saint, on thine immortal throne,
Possest of glory, life and bliss unknown;
We hear no more the music of thy tongue,
Thy wonted auditories cease to throng.
Thy sermons in unequall'd accents flow'd,
And ev'ry bosom with devotion glow'd;
Thou didst in strains of eloquence refin'd
Inflame the heart and captivate the mind.
Unhappy we the setting sun deplore,
So glorious once, but ah! it shines no more.
    Behold the prophet in his tow'ring flight!
He leaves the earth for heav'n's unmeasur'd height,
And worlds unknown receive him from our sight.
There *Whitefield* wings with rapid course his way,
And sails to *Zion* through vast seas of day.
Thy pray'rs, great saint, and thine incessant cries
Have pierce'd the bosom of thy native skies.
Thou moon hast seen, and all the stars of light,
How he has wrestled with his God by night.

He pray'd that grace in ev'ry heart might dwell,
He long'd to see America excel:
He charg'd its youth that ev'ry grace divine
Should with full lustre in their conduct shine;
That Saviour, which his soul did first receive,
The greatest gift that ev'n a God can give,
He freely offer'd to the num'rous throng,
That on his lips with list'ning pleasure hung.
"Take him, ye wretched, for your only good,
"Take him, ye starving sinners, for your food.
"Ye thirsty, come to this life-giving stream,
"Ye preachers, take him for your joyful theme;
"Take him my dear *Americans*, he said,
"Be your complaints on his kind bosom laid;
"Take him, ye *Africans*, he longs for you,
"*Impartial Saviour* is his title due;
"Washed in the fountain of redeeming blood,
"You shall be sons and kings, and priests to God."
     Great *Countess*, we *Americans* revere
Thy name, and mingle in thy grief sincere;
New England deeply feels, the *Orphans* mourn,
Their more than father will no more return.
But, though arrested by the hand of death,
Whitefield no more exerts his lab'ring breath,
Yet let us view him in th' eternal skies,
Let ev'ry heart to this bright vision rise;
While the tomb safe retains its sacred trust,
Till life divine re-animates his dust.

41 ▪ QUAKER WOMEN MAY SPEAK

Margaret Fell (1614–1702) played a decisive role in the successful Quaker struggle for survival amid religious and political hostility. In addition to being a prolific writer and correspondent, she tirelessly petitioned the English government for tolerance, funded traveling ministers, and made her home, Swarthmoor Hall, a secure place of refuge and worship. She wrote Womens Speaking Justified *in 1666 during one of her periodical imprisonments for holding unauthorized meetings. The pamphlet is a vindication of female preaching. It makes the point that man and woman were created as equals. Furthermore, the redemptive power of Jesus puts enmity between woman and sin, freeing her to speak with divine authority. This redemptive power was given concrete expression when Jesus commissioned women to spread the message that he had risen from the dead.*

Source: Margaret Fell. *Womens Speaking Justified, Proved and Allowed of by the Scriptures*, 1–3, 6–9. London: Pythia Press, 1989.

But first let me lay down how God himself hath manifested his Will and Mind concerning Women, and unto Women.

And first, when *God created Man in his own Image; in the Image of God created he them, Male and Female; and God blessed them; and God said unto them, Be fruitful, and multiply: and God said, Behold, I have given you of every Herb, etc.* Gen. 1. Here God joins them together in his own Image, and makes no such distinctions and differences as men do; for though they be weak, he is strong; and as he said to the Apostle, *His Grace is sufficient, and his strength is made manifest in weakness*, 2 Cor. 12.9. And such hath the Lord chosen, even the weak things of the world, to confound the things which are mighty; and things which are despised, hath God chosen, to bring to nought things that are, 1 Cor. 1. And god hath put no such difference between the Male and Female as men would make.

It is true, *The Serpent that was more subtle then any other Beast of the Field*, came unto the Woman, with his Temptations, and with a lie; his subtly discerning her to be more inclinable to harken to him, when he said, *If ye eat, your eyes shall be opened;* and the Woman saw that *the Fruit was good to make one wise;* there the temptation got into her, and *she did eat, and gave to her Husband, and he did eat also*, and so they were both tempted into the transgression and disobedience; and therefore God said unto Adam, when that he hid himself when he heard his voice, *Hast thou eaten of the Tree which I commanded thee that thou shouldst not eat?* And Adam said, *The Woman which thou gavest me, she gave me of the Tree, and I did eat.* And the Lord said unto the Woman, *What is this that thou hast done?* and the Woman said, *The Serpent beguiled me, and I did eat.* Here the Woman spoke the truth unto the Lord: see what the Lord saith, verse 15 after he had pronounced Sentence on the Serpent; *I will put enmity between thee and the Woman, and between the Seed and her Seed; it shall bruise his heel*, Genesis 3.

Let this Word of the Lord, which was from the beginning, stop the mouths of all that oppose Womens Speaking in the Power of the Lord; for he hath put enmity between the Woman and the Serpent; and if the Seed of the Woman speak not, the Seed of the Serpent speaks; for God hath put enmity between the two Seeds, and it is manifest, that those that speak against the Woman and her Seeds Speaking, speak out of the enmity of the old Serpents Seed; and God hath fulfilled his Word and his Promise, *When the fullness of time was come, he hath sent forth his Son, made of a Woman, made under the Law, that we might receive the adoption of Sons,* Gal. 4.4,5. . . .

Thus we see that Jesus owned the Love and Grace that appeared in Women, and did not despite it; and by what is recorded in the Scriptures, he received as much love, kindness, compassion, and tender dealing towards him from Women, as he did from any others, both in his life time, and also after they had exercised their cruelty upon him; for Mary Magdalene, and Mary the Mother of Jesus, beheld where he was laid; And when the Sabbath was past, Mary Magdalene, and Mary the Mother of James and Salom, had *brought sweet spices that they might anoint him: And very early in the morning, the first day of the week, they came unto the Sepulchre at the rising of the Sun; and they said among themselves, Who shall roll us away the stone from the door of the Sepulchre? And when they looked, the stone was rolled away, for it was very great;* Mark 16.1,2,3,4. Luke 24.1,2. and they went down into the Sepulchre; and as Matthew saith, *The Angel rolled away the stone; and he said unto the Women, Fear not, I know whom ye seek, Jesus which was Crucified; he is not here, he is risen,* Mat. 28. Now Luke saith thus, That *there stood two men by them in shining apparel, and as they were perplexed and afraid, the men said unto them, He is not here; remember how he said unto you when he was in Galilee, That the Son of Man must be delivered into the hands of sinful men, and be crucified, and the third day rise again; and they remembered his words, and returned from the Sepulchre, and told all these things to the eleven, and to all the rest.*

It was Mary Magdalene, and Joanna, and Mary the Mother of James, and the other Women that were with them, which told these things to the Apostles, *And their words seemed unto them as idle tales, and they believed them not.* Mark this, ye despisers of the weakness of Woman, and look upon your selves to be so wise; but Christ Jesus doth not so, for he makes use of the weak: for when he met the Women after he was risen, he said unto them, All Hail, and they came and held him by the Feet, and worshipped him; then said Jesus unto them, *Be not afraid; go tell my Brethren that they go into Galilee, and there they shall see me,* Mat. 28.10 Mark 16.9. And John saith, when Mary was weeping at the Sepulchre, that Jesus said unto her, *Woman, why weepest thou? what seekest thou? And when she supposed him to be the Gardener, Jesus saith unto her, Mary; she turned her self, and saith unto him Rabboni, which is to say Master; Jesus saith unto her, Touch me not, for I am not yet ascended to my Father, but go to my Brethren, and say unto them, I ascend unto my Father, and your Father, and to my God, and your God,* John 20.16,17.

Mark this, you that despise and oppose the Message of the Lord God that he sends by Women; what had become of the Redemption of the whole Body of Man-kind, if they had not believed the Message that the Lord Jesus sent by these Women, of and concerning his Resurrection? And if these Women had not thus, out of their tenderness and bowels of love, who had received Mercy, and Grace, and forgiveness of sins, and Virtue, and Healing from him; which many men also had received the like, if their hearts had not been so united and knit unto him in love, that they could not depart as the men did, but sat watching, and waiting, and weeping about the Sepulchre until the time of his Resurrection, and so were ready to carry his Message, as is manifested; else how should his Disciples have known, who were not there?

Oh! blessed and glorified be the Glorious Lord; for this may all the whole body of man-kind say, through the wisdom of man, that never knew God, is always ready to except against the weak; but the weakness of God is stronger than men, and the foolishness of God is wiser than men.

42 ▪ QUAKER WOMEN AS MISSIONARIES

Patience Brayton (b. 1733) played an active role among Rhode Island Quakers for much of her life. In 1771 she was moved to travel south on behalf of the Friends, leaving behind her husband and large family. Her journey lasted for several months and was followed, twelve years later, by a visit to Britain to support Quaker women there in a plea for their own London Yearly Meeting. It is clear from her journal entries that Brayton did not find her ministry easy. She suffered from feelings of inadequacy, physical ailments, and bouts of homesickness for her family. She sees her ability to speak as a direct result of the movement of God within her soul. The journal entries tell us much about the day-to-day circumstances surrounding the work of the traveling Quaker women.

Source: Patience Brayton. *A Short Account of the Life and Religious Labours of Patience Brayton, Late of Swansey, in the State of Massachusetts, Mostly Selected from Her Own Minutes,* 18–20, 42–43. New York: Isaac Collins, 1801.

Having been confined several days in Philadelphia with a bad cold, until second-day, 30th of 9th month, I then attended the select meeting, where we were comforted together, and on the 1st of 10th month my esteemed friend Hannah Foster from New-Jersey, accompanying me, we left Philadelphia, and taking Chester meeting, we were favoured with divine assistance therein, and came to Wilmington and lodged at David Ferris's, who was gone to New-England with Samuel Neal, on a religious visit; but oh! the discouragement I was under at times, which made me cry in my heart to God, that he would strengthen me, more and more to give up to his will: I was low in bodily health, and my spirits seemed to sink within me; notwithstanding I have been strengthened day by day, that I have reason to bless my God, and say in truth it is marvellous, he is the Lord and will do all things for them that put their trust in him; he weans from husband and children, house and land, for his name's sake, and these shall receive an hundred fold: nothing less than the love of God and his peace in our minds, enables us to submit; and when I behold the goodness of the Almighty, I am encouraged to invite all, to come taste and see how good the Lord is. On the 4th we went to John Churchman's at Nottingham, and attended monthly meeting; and the sixth and seventh days following, the yearly meeting, which was to our comfort. On the 8th of 10th month we rode eighteen miles to the house of one, not belonging to friends, and many people coming, I was comforted in an opportunity with them, and thought the Lord heard my prayers, and I hope it will prove of service to some of the company. Taking Sassafras meeting, came to the meeting of ministers and elders at Cecil; but so poor I felt, that oh! thought I, if my Master would only let me return home, pleading that there were many better qualified for that work than I was, for I feared I should dishonour God, and bring grief on all my friends; but in this trial I endeavoured after stillness, and was inwardly comforted, and brought to say as Peter did, "not only wash my feet, but my hands and my head also." Next day, being first of the week, we went to meeting again, which was a good meeting, and the day following light broke forth in the meeting, in a wonderful manner, to our comfort. On third-day the 15th, we attended the select meeting, and I was silent until the men withdrew, and the women's meeting came on; then my mouth was opened, and it pleased the Lord still to cause the light more and more to break forth. Oh! how I felt the love of God to this people, if they would be faithful to what is made known to them. . . .

2d of 5th mo. I went to the select meeting, in the city, and the Lord gave me some strength to perform his will, for the will of man never wrought the righteousness of God: but the will of God, is the righteousness of our poor souls. Next day being 1st-day, I went to Pine Street meeting, wherein a degree of light broke forth, and I felt love still to increase in me, to the cause of truth. In the afternoon, went to the Bank meeting, where I sat under much exercise, thinking with the apostle, oh wretched man that I am, who shall deliver me from this body of death? but trusting in the Lord for strength, I arose in much love, and was carried through to my relief: and in the evening meeting I still felt a concern to be inwardly cleansed; knowing that without that my preaching would be in vain, and under a weight of spirit I arose, without a word in my mouth, and after standing a while in much poverty, my mouth was opened with these words; Lord help all those weak ones, who are bowed before thee; and it pleased the God and Father of all our mercies to own me, a poor drooping and unworthy child, and the meeting ended in a solid manner, my heart being filled with praise to him alone, who worketh miracles in his poor depending children, at times. The next day was their quarterly meeting, in which I was silent; but many good testimonies were borne, which were sweet to my taste.

Chapter 6

WOMEN ORGANIZING
FOR MISSION AND REFORM

43 ▪ THE CULT OF TRUE WOMANHOOD

Aptly illustrating the mid-Victorian "cult of true womanhood," these excerpts are from a series of public lectures given to audiences of men and women and first published in 1840 by George Washington Burnap (1802–1850). Burnap was pastor of the First Unitarian Church in Baltimore and a distinguished man of letters who frequently contributed to literary journals and lectured in cities along the East Coast. He makes it plain that the domestic sphere is the domain for which women were "originally intended," but he wants to compensate for this by assuring them that they are really the architects of human society and government. Husbands are only able to make the most of their skills in the workplace if they are comforted and cared for at home. Sons can only take their part on the stage of national life if their characters have been carefully molded by a diligent mother.

Source: George W. Burnap. *The Sphere and Duties of Woman.* 5th ed. Baltimore: John Murphy, 1854.

We now see woman in that sphere for which she was originally intended, and which she is so exactly fitted to adorn and bless, as the wife, the mistress of a home, the solace, the aid, and the counsellor of that ONE, for whose sake alone the world is of any consequence to her. If life be increased in cares, so is it also enriched by new satisfactions. She herself, if she be inspired by just sentiments and true affection, perceives that she has attained her true position. Delivered from that tastelessness, which sooner or later creeps over a single life, every power and faculty is called into energetic exercise, and she feels the current of existence to flow in a richer, deeper stream. . . .

The good wife! How much of this world's happiness and prosperity is contained in the compass of these two short words! Her influence is immense. The power of a wife, for good or for evil, is altogether irresistible.

Home must be the seat of happiness, or it must be for ever unknown. A good wife is to a man wisdom, and courage, and strength, and hope, and endurance. A bad one is confusion, weakness, discomfiture, despair. No condition is hopeless when the wife possesses firmness, decision, energy, economy. There is no outward prosperity which can counteract indolence, folly, and extravagance at home. No spirit can long resist bad domestic influences. Man is strong, but his heart is not adamant. He delights in enterprise and action, but to sustain him he needs a tranquil mind, and a whole heart. He expends his whole moral force in the conflicts of the world. His feelings are daily lacerated to the utmost point of endurance by perpetual collision, irritation, and disappointment. To recover his equanimity and composure, home must be to him a place of repose, of peace, of cheerfulness, of comfort; and his soul renews its strength and again goes forth with fresh vigor to encounter the labors and troubles of the world. But if at home he find no rest, and there is met by a bad temper, sullenness, or gloom; or assailed by discontent, complaint, and reproaches, the heart breaks, the spirits are crushed, hope vanishes, and the man sinks into total despair.

Let woman know then, that she ministers at the very fountain of life and happiness. It is her hand that lades out with overflowing cup its soul refreshing waters, or casts in the branch of bitterness which makes them poison and death. Her ardent spirit breathes the breath of life into all enterprise. Her patience and constancy are mainly instrumental in carrying forward to completion the best human designs. Her more delicate moral sensibility is the unseen power which is ever at work to purify and refine society. And the nearest glimpse of heaven that mortals ever get on earth is that domestic circle, which her hands have trained to intelligence, virtue, and love; which her gentle influence pervades, and of which her radiant presence is the centre and the sun....

We come in the next place to speak of woman in the most important and responsible relation which she sustains, as the mother. In this relation Providence fully makes up to her the inferiority of her physical powers, the narrowness of her sphere of action, and the alleged inferiority of her intellectual endowments. In the influence she has in forming the character of the young, and training up each rising generation as it comes forward, and assumes the control of the destinies of the world, she has her full share in that power which sways and governs mankind, which makes nations, families, individuals great, prosperous, virtuous, happy,—or mean, degraded, vicious, and wretched. Woman is mistress of the fortunes of the world, by holding in her plastic hand the minds and hearts of those who are to mould the coming age, at that decisive period when the character is determined and fixed in good, or irrecoverably bent on vice and mischief. She governs the world in the capacity of mother, because in the forming period of life, the cords of love and gentleness are stronger and more prevailing than all the chains which mere force has ever forged. She sways the world, because her influence is on the whole paramount in the primary element of all society, the domestic circle. Men go forth to act their parts on the great stage of life, the most gifted to exert vast influence over its affairs, but it is only to act out the character that has been formed at home. Woman then, whose control over the character is almost absolute, presides at the very fountainhead of power.

44 ▪ EXTENDING WOMAN'S SPHERE

In his position as pastor of the First Presbyterian Church in Augusta, Georgia, Ebenezer Platt Rogers (1817–1881) was called upon to address the students of the Washington Female Seminary, established by the congregation in 1839, on the occasion of its tenth anniversary. Rogers chose to focus on the ways in which Christianity had elevated the status of women wherever it was given free reign and the "peculiar claims" it had upon them as a result. The first part of this selection from his speech reminds women that Christianity placed them in an "almost omnipotent" position as mistresses of the home, a position for which they had God-given talents. The second section comes from a general discussion of the ways in which women can repay their debt. It is interesting that while Rogers is certain that women have a "sphere," he does not want them cloistered and encourages them to move outside of the home to relieve poverty and illness.

Source: Ebenezer P. Rogers. *The Obligations and Duties of the Female Sex to Christianity. An Address Delivered at the Annual Examination of the Washington Female Seminary . . .* , 5–7, 13–15. Augusta, Ga.: James McCafferty, 1849.

Christianity, too, assigns to woman her appropriate place in the social circle, and crowns her as the lawful queen of the little world of home. The bosom of the family is her undisputed empire. Her sceptre is the most potent which is wielded on earth—it is the sceptre of Love! In that most interesting and important place, the family where love, tenderness, refinement of thought and feeling, and all that can exalt and purify, and adorn the world, centres—she is acknowledged as supreme. This is her place, the cherished companion and friend of her husband, not a play-thing, nor merely one in whose society he may spend his leisure hours, but his other and dearer self, whose judgment and counsel he seeks in all matters seriously affecting his interest, and whose constant and devoted affection is the day-star of his existence, the ever beaming bow of promise and of hope; she is the guide and companion of her children, whose influence shapes their characters and directs their destiny—the depository of their cares, their sorrows and their joys—their blessing and their pride. This is emphatically woman's place, a place fitted for the display of those peculiar talents and graces with which God has invested the female character, a place for the wielding of that unseen, unostentatious, but almost omnipotent influence which is like the sunshine and the dew to earth, indispensable to its beauty and its productiveness. But where does she occupy this sphere, but in a Christian land? Philosophy in her best days never gave her such a place. Heathen morality, ancient refinement and learning, never thus exalted her; for what she is now in our land, and among all truly enlightened nations, she is a debtor to Christianity alone.

But if woman owes so much to the influence of the Gospel, in the elevation of her sex, then, has not the Gospel peculiar claims upon her? If it has done so much for her, in raising her from the degradation into which heathenism and paganism plunges her, and placing her in a position where her influence is the most potent which the world acknowledges, is she not bound by peculiarly weighty obligations, to be the friend and advocate of true religion? Let the measure of your own indebtedness, be the measure of your obligation and the standard of your duty, and I ask no more.

Again: Christianity has peculiar claims upon woman, because, through its influence only can she be enabled to fulfil her mission in the important relations of life. In the accomplishment of those moral and religious ends intended by God to be secured by his first and most sacred institution, the family, the part of woman is one of transcendant importance. She may exert, and she has exerted, an elevating and refining influence upon society, in the walks of literature and science; but this is not her great mission. As before remarked, her realm is the domestic circle—she is the priestess of its sacred shrine, "the gentle and lovely minister of whatever of purity and brightness sheds its lustre there." A group of young immortals, their budding energies to be unfolded and guided to the attainment of noble ends, their fervent aspirations to be cherished and directed to the purest and worthiest objects, are given to her, to train for life, and on the manner in which she discharges this solemn duty, depend not only the welfare of her family, but the best interests of society, the prosperity of the state, the progress of the world. Her mission is the greatest that earth can know. She does not move amid the halls of legislation; she does not lead on armies to the shock of battle; she does not sway the public mind from the platform or the forum. But her influence is felt even here: the mind of the statesman whose word is a nation's law, has been under a mother's culture; the energies of the hero were developed and fostered by a mother's hand; those master springs of human action, which, in the results of their working, astonish men and thrill the world, were first adjusted and moved by her, and the first impulse which sent forth a great and gifted mind to call its generation to a loftier life, has been communicated by a mother's hand. How needs she then the aid of Christianity, in the fulfilment of her noble destiny! It is Christianity, alone, which has opened for her this glorious path. Shall she, then, shut out from her journey its illuminating radiance? It is Christianity, alone, which has put these wonderful elements of dignity and power within her grasp. Shall she not learn from its heavenly teachings, how to wield them with a master hand? If, "in communicating eternal principles of truth to minds destined for immortality, she is doing what can never cease to be felt, and if when the kingdoms and empires of earth have melted away and are forgotten, when the eloquence and wisdom of statesmen, and the achievements of heroes have passed away, then her labors will be known and acknowledged, and be seen eternally unfolding in new and glorious results,"—is she not under peculiar obligations to that Christianity, which has furnished for her such a sphere, and made it possible for her to secure so noble a destiny? . . .

Having made her first and noblest offering to God—herself—let then that offering be made daily till life shall close. Let her faith be shown by her works. Woman has a sphere in which to move, and in which her influence is to tell mightily upon the world. She was not made to be secluded from life, and shut up within the narrow limits of a cloister. They little understand the nature of her mission, who would immure her thus. As well might you shut up the flowers that bloom in the meadow, and rob the earth of their fragrance or their loveliness. As well might you ask that the star light should be concentrated within some dungeon cell, and not watch the slumbers of a sleeping world. As well might you wall up the sun-beams and not pour their gladsome rays upon a living creation. No! With a due regard for that delicacy which is one of woman's highest ornaments, would we beg her to retire from the crowded and bustling scenes and noisy strifes of the ex-change or the forum; but we would not exclude her from the actual world, nor rob life of her softening, humanizing, refining, and purifying influence. I would not have her "a sweet enthusiast, whose element is solitude, and whose luxury is emotion." I would not have her seem to belong to another world, in her sympathies, and associations, and have nothing in common with this "diurnal sphere." There is work for her to do here in the actual world. There are children of want and sorrow to be sought out, and cheered and fed and taught, and lifted from their degradation; and woman can do this, and she seems most like an angel of mercy as she stoops beside the bed of suffering in the cottage of the poor and sorrow laden, yea, far more angel like than when she is threading the mazes of the dance, or receiving the heartless homage of a crowd of brainless admirers.

Those who have given us the most beautiful illustrations of the power of religion, have not been interesting recluses, or pensive sisters of the cloister, but warm hearted, active, zealous women, who went abroad on errands of mercy to the sick and the destitute, and were the benefactresses of the children of misfortune and sorrow. They might say, in the beautiful language of Job, "When the ear heard me then it blessed me, and when the eye saw me it gave witness to me, Because I delivered the poor that cried, and the fatherless and him that had none to help him. The blessing of him that was ready to perish came upon me and I caused the widow's heart to sing for joy." The constant and engrossing pursuits of business, often prevent the other sex from discharging the duties of active personal benevolence. But woman can go on these errands of love to bless with her comforting presence many an abode of sorrow, and minister joy to many a desponding sufferer. I know that this path is an unobtrusive and noiseless one; that it is not seen by the world, and its labors neither known or appreciated; but in the day of revelation, and of judgment, it will then appear how much the world has owed to woman's labors and self-denial, and verily she shall not lose her reward.

That Saviour who said, "In as much as ye have done it unto one of the least of these my brethren ye have done it unto me," will crown her with a crown of heavenly radiance, and place her as one of the most brilliant gems, in his eternal coronet.

You see, then, my youthful hearers, what is the noble mission of your sex. Be ye faithful to it. Let the light of your piety illumine with a serener radiance your own loved home; let your influence upon father, mother, sister, brother, husband, son, be yet more elevating and purifying. Pour out the streams of your benevolence into the abodes of poverty and sickness. Be an ornament and a blessing to your native land, and your mission is fulfilled, your work is done. Then, each of you having been one of God's richest gifts to earth, you shall shine as one of the brighter stars, in an eternal Heaven.

45 · THE CAUSE OF MORAL REFORM

The circular reprinted here was drawn up at the organizational meeting of the New York Female Moral Reform Society on May 12, 1834. The society hoped not only to convert New York's prostitutes to Protestant Christianity but also to launch a women's crusade against sexual license in general and the double standard in particular. The circular reveals much about motives and strategies linked to this second grand goal of sexual purity. The crusade is seen clearly as part of God's work of reform in preparation for the coming millennium. Possibly remembering the criticism heaped upon New York's earlier Magdalen Society for dealing with "obscene" issues, the writers urge women not to shy away from speaking out on delicate subjects of great social consequence. They are, however, challenged to go beyond general disapproval. They are to unmask the libertines in their social circles and shun their company. The circular conveys a sense of anger and determination (licentious men are called "vipers" against which the "sisterhood" should fight) that is echoed in Carroll Smith Rosenberg's argument that these women, frustrated by male domination, wished to define and limit male sexual behavior.[1]

Source: *The Constitution and Circular of the New York Female Moral Reform Society; with the Addresses Delivered at Its Organization*, 16–18. New York: J. N. Bolles, 1834.

To the Ladies of the United States of every Religious Denomination.

BELOVED SISTERS:—Suffer a word of exhortation on a subject of vital interest to the entire sisterhood: we refer to the sin of LICENTIOUSNESS.

We need not inform you that this sin prevails to an alarming extent in our land. The fact is obvious to all. A moment's reflection will show you that it has woven itself into all the fibres of society, shaping its opinions, modifying its customs, and in one form or other spreading an atmosphere of corruption and death throughout the entire community. Not that all are impure—far from it; but, unconsciously to ourselves even, we breathe the atmosphere of pollution. Sentiments are afloat, customs are in vogue—the creatures of this sin—which strike at the vitals of all that is lovely in female purity and innocence, and so doing, strike at all that is precious in the most endeared and sacred relations of life. If this be not so, whence, we ask, is that sense of danger, that at times and in certain circumstances, so oppresses the mind of the virtuous female? Whence the fact, that the libertine, known to be such, is welcomed to the society of the chaste? Whence that corrupt public sentiment, that pervades all classes of society—the high and the low, the good and the bad, the pure and the impure—and that storms and rages at the least intimation of exposure, and sends forth, as on the wings of the wind, the cry, "hush," "hush," "indelicate," "indelicate," "you will only corrupt the virtuous";—that in effect, blots out the 7th commandment from the decalogue, and proscribes other portions of the word of God, as too gross and indecent for this age of refinement, and thus practically puts the ban of silence on the pulpit and the press?—Whence all this; whence, especially, this unwonted unity of sentiment, among persons of every description and character? Strange alliance! And what does it evince

---

1. Carroll Smith Rosenberg, "Beauty, the Beast and the Militant Woman: A Case Study in Sex Roles and Social Stress in Jacksonian America," *American Quarterly* 23 (October 1971): 564–65.

but the fearful fact, that while men slept the enemy has sowed tares—that these have sprung up unnoticed, to rank maturity, and have thrown a poisonous atmosphere over the entire field. So we believe; and so believing, we feel that it is time for *us*, in common with others, to take our stand on the side of virtue and God, and do what we can to turn back the tide of pollution that is sweeping over the land, and bearing its victims onward, by thousands, to the chambers of death.

And now, beloved sisters, we ask you to take your stand with us. The evil we know is great, and the public sentiment it has created for itself, and behind which it entrenches itself, is mighty. Nevertheless, we have confidence in the gospel; that it is mighty through God, to the pulling down of strong holds. And we believe that its efficacy will not fail in this case. The evil, great as it is, *can be reached*, and the public sentiment behind which it is entrenched, mighty as it is, CAN BE MET AND CHANGED. Already, if we mistake not, is the change begun. The press is beginning to speak. The pulpit, to a greater extent than ever before, is beginning to break its guilty silence. The ministers of God are ceasing to be any longer "partial in the law." It is matter of rejoicing, of encouragement, and of unfeigned gratitude to God that it is so.

But this sin, we are persuaded, is one in respect to which it is emphatically true, that a radical reform can never be effected without the co-operation of woman. Here, if we mistake not, her influence may be most powerful and efficacious. She may wield a power that can be wielded by no one else. Ask you how?

The answer is—1st. Let her do what she can to disseminate light on the subject—by conversation—by the circulation of such papers and tracts as are fitted to be a discerner of the thoughts and intents of the heart, and, at the same time, to show the enormity and guilt, and fatal tendencies and results of this sin—though it be only the sin of the heart.

2d. Let her take the ground, so obviously in accordance with truth, that the libertine is no less guilty than his victim, and as such, shall be at once excluded from her society. This you will perceive by the annexed Constitution, is the ground that your sisters in New-York have taken. We ask you—we entreat you—to take the same. We point you to the whole sex, the entire sisterhood, and we say that demon in human shape, that fixed his lascivious eye upon your sister, and wrought her ruin, is the enemy of your sex. Exclude him then at once from all society with you—in self-defence—in defence of the sex, exclude him. He wants but the opportunity, and he will as soon make you his victim as that erring, fallen sister. Some of you, perhaps, are mothers. God has blessed you with a family of lovely children—daughters, pure, innocent, the joy of your heart, the objects of your purest, sweetest, strongest affections. But see, the demon has marked your first born as his victim. His wanton eye is already on her. Mothers, away with him—in defence of your beloved children, away with him, we entreat you, from your families, and from the society of your children. Teach them to shun him as they would a viper. He wants but the opportunity, and he will not hesitate to seize upon his victim, and thereby plunge a dagger to your heart. In self-defence—in defence of your families, and we may add, in defence of the whole community, away with such a one from all society and intercourse with you. This done, and the work of Moral Reform is done, and the virtue and peace of the community secured.

Beloved Sisters, we are persuaded that in this simple way, we may wield an influence on this subject that cannot be resisted. If we will but organize ourselves into associations on this principle, and have the moral courage thus to stand up for injured and outraged innocence, not heeding the reproach that may, for a little season, be heaped upon us, we verily believe, that in God, we shall triumph. God seems in a special manner, to have committed this work to our hands; and without arrogance, it is not too much to say, that, if we will, we may, by this simple process, put such a brand of infamy upon the licentious man—we may gather upon him such a withering frown of virtuous indignation, as to save not only the victim, but the destroyer also, and thus put an effectual check to the tide of pollution that is now sweeping us away.

And now, sisters, what say you? Under God, the privilege and the responsibility of this holy and blessed work, is yours. It is for you, in a special manner, to say, what shall be done. Oh! then show, we do intreat you, that you have the virtue, the principle, the moral courage, to breast a corrupt and mighty public sentiment, in defence of virtue and religion.

46 ▪ EQUAL RIGHTS AND MORAL DUTIES

In 1837 Sarah Grimké (1792–1873) accompanied her sister Angelina on a tour of New England on behalf of the antislavery movement. Both women attracted large audiences of men and women wherever they spoke, partly because they were former slaveholders and women who, in public lecturing, were stepping beyond conventional boundaries. They were viciously attacked for their unwomanly behavior in a pastoral letter issued by the Congregational Ministerial Association of Massachusetts. Sarah Grimké responded head-on in a series of letters to Mary Parker, president of the Boston Female Anti-slavery Society. Eventually published as a single tract, the letters chronicle the condition of women throughout the world, analyze their legal position, and examine the inequities they suffer in education and employment. The letter reproduced here responds specifically to the pastoral letter. Using the New Testament as her basis,

Grimké argues that women can be neither excused nor prevented from carrying out their moral responsibilities because of human notions of propriety.

Source: Sarah Grimké. *Letters on the Equality of the Sexes and the Condition of Woman.* Edited with an introduction by Elizabeth Ann Bartlett, 37–41. New Haven: Yale University Press, 1988.

Haverhill, 7th Mo. 1837

Dear Friend,

When I last addressed thee, I had not seen the Pastoral Letter of the General Association. It has since fallen into my hands, and I must digress from my intention of exhibiting the condition of women in different parts of the world, in order to make some remarks on this extraordinary document. I am persuaded that when the minds of men and women become emancipated from the thraldom of superstition and "traditions of men," the sentiments contained in the Pastoral Letter will be recurred to with as much astonishment as the opinions of Cotton Mather and other distinguished men of his day, on the subject of witchcraft; nor will it be deemed less wonderful, that a body of divines should gravely assemble and endeavor to prove that woman has no right to "open her mouth for the dumb," than it now is that judges should have sat on the trials of witches, and solemnly condemned nineteen persons and one dog to death for witchcraft.

But to the letter. It says, "We invite your attention to the dangers which at present seem to threaten the FEMALE CHARACTER with wide-spread and permanent injury." I rejoice that they have called the attention of my sex to this subject, because I believe if woman investigates it, she will soon discover that danger is impending, though from a totally different source from that which the Association apprehends,—danger from those who, having long held the reins of *usurped* authority, are unwilling to permit us to fill that sphere which God created us to move in, and who have entered into league to crush the immortal mind of woman. I rejoice, because I am persuaded that the rights of woman, like the rights of slaves, need only be examined to be understood and asserted, even by some of those, who are now endeavoring to smother the irrepressible desire for mental and spiritual freedom which glows in the breast of many, who hardly dare to speak their sentiments.

"The appropriate duties and influence of women are clearly stated in the New Testament. Those duties are unobtrusive and private, but the sources of *mighty power*. When the mild, *dependent*, softening influence of woman upon the sternness of man's opinions is fully exercised, society feels the effects of it in a thousand ways." No one can desire more earnestly than I do, that woman may move exactly in the sphere which her Creator has assigned her; and I believe her having been displaced from that sphere has introduced confusion into the world. It is, therefore, of vast importance to herself and to all the rational creation, that she should ascertain what are her duties and her privileges as a responsible and immortal being. The New Testament has been referred to, and I am willing to abide by its decisions, but must enter my protest against the false translation of some passages by the MEN who did that work, and against the perverted interpretation by the MEN who undertook to write commentaries thereon. (I am inclined to think, when we are admitted to the honor of studying Greek and Hebrew, we shall produce some various readings of the Bible a little different from those we now have.)

The Lord Jesus defines the duties of his followers in his Sermon on the Mount. He lays down grand principles by which they should be governed, without any reference to sex or condition.—"Ye are the light of the world. A city that is set on a hill cannot be hid. Neither do men light a candle and put it under a bushel, but on a candlestick, and it giveth light unto all that are in the house. Let your light so shine before men, that they may see your good works, and glorify your Father which is in Heaven" (Matt. 5:14-16). I follow him through all his precepts, and find him giving the same directions to women as to men, never even referring to the distinction now so strenuously insisted upon between masculine and feminine virtues: this is one of the anti-christian "traditions of men" which are taught instead of the "commandments of God." Men and women were CREATED EQUAL; they are both moral and accountable beings, and whatever is *right* for man to do, is *right* for woman.

But the influence of woman, says the Association, is to be private and unobtrusive; her light is not to shine before man like that of her brethren; but she is passively to let the lords of the creation, as they call themselves, put the bushel over it, lest peradventure it might appear that the world has been benefitted by the rays of *her* candle. So that her quenched light, according to their judgment, will be of more use than if it were set on the candlestick. "Her influence is the source of mighty power." This has ever been the flattering language of man since he laid aside the whip as a means to keep woman in subjection. He spares her body; but the war he has waged against her mind, her heart, and her soul, has been no less destructive to her as a moral being. How monstrous, how anti-christian, is the doctrine that woman is to be dependent on man! Where, in all the sacred Scriptures, is this taught? Alas! she has too well learned the lesson, which MAN has labored to teach her. She has surrendered her dearest RIGHTS, and been satisfied with the privileges which man has assumed to grant her; she has been amused with the show of power, whilst man has absorbed all the reality into himself. He has adorned the creature whom God gave him as a companion, with baubles and gewgaws, turned her attention to personal attractions, offered incense to her vanity, and made her the instrument of his selfish gratification, a plaything to please his eye and amuse his hours of leisure. "Rule by obedience and by submission sway," or in other words, study to be a hypocrite, pretend to submit, but gain your point, has been the code of household morality which woman has been taught. The poet has sung, in sickly strains, the loveliness of woman's dependence upon man, and now we find it reechoed by those who profess to teach the religion of the Bible. God says, "Cease ye from man whose breath is in his nostrils, for wherein is he to be accounted of?" Man says, depend upon me. God says, "HE will teach us of his ways." Man says, believe it not, I am to be your teacher. This doctrine of dependence upon man is utterly at variance with the doctrine of the Bible. In that book I find nothing like the softness of woman, nor the sternness of man: both are equally commanded to bring forth the fruits of the Spirit, love, meekness, gentleness, &c.

But we are told, "the power of woman is in her dependence, flowing from a consciousness of that weakness which God has given her for her protection." If physical weakness is alluded to, I cheerfully concede the superiority; if brute force is what my brethren are claiming, I am willing to let them have all the honor they desire; but if they mean to intimate, that mental or moral weakness belongs to woman, more than to man, I utterly disclaim the charge. Our powers of mind have been crushed, as far as man could do it, our sense of morality has been impaired by his interpretation of our duties; but no where does God say that he made any distinction between us, as moral and intelligent beings.

"We appreciate," say the Association, "the *unostentatious* prayers and efforts of woman in advancing the cause of religion at home and abroad, in leading religious inquirers TO THE PASTOR for instruction." Several points here demand attention. If public prayers and public efforts are necessarily ostentatious, then "Anna the prophetess, (or preacher,) who departed not from the temple, but served God with fastings and prayers night and day," "and spake of Christ to all them that looked for redemption in Israel," was ostentatious in her efforts. Then, the apostle Paul encourages women to be ostentatious in their efforts to spread the gospel, when he gives them directions how they should appear, when engaged in praying, or preaching in the public assemblies. Then, the whole association of Congregational ministers are ostentatious, in the efforts they are making in preaching and praying to convert souls.

But woman may be permitted to lead religious inquirers to the PASTORS for instruction. Now this is assuming that all pastors are better qualified to give instruction than woman. This I utterly deny. I have suffered too keenly from the teaching of man, to lead any one to him for instruction. The Lord

Jesus says,—"Come unto me and learn of me" (Matt. 2:29). He points his followers to no man; and when woman is made the favored instrument of rousing a sinner to his lost and helpless condition, she has no right to substitute any teacher for Christ; all she has to do is, to turn the contrite inquirer to the "Lamb of God which taketh away the sins of the world" (John 1:29). More souls have probably been lost by going down to Egypt for help, and by trusting in man in the early stages of religious experience, than by any other error. Instead of the petition being offered to God,— "Lead me in thy truth, and TEACH me, for thou art the God of my salvation" (Ps. 25:5),—instead of relying on the precious promises—"What man is he that feareth the Lord? him shall HE TEACH in the way that he shall choose" (Ps. 25:12)—"I will instruct thee and TEACH thee in the way which thou shalt go—I will guide thee with mine eye" (Ps. 27:2)—the young convert is directed to go to man, as if he were in the place of God, and his instructions essential to an advancement in the path of righteousness. That woman can have but a poor conception of the privilege of being taught of God, what he alone can teach, who would turn the "religious inquirer aside" from the fountain of living waters, where he might slake his thirst for spiritual instruction, to those broken cisterns which can hold no water, and therefore cannot satisfy the panting spirit. The business of men and women, who are ORDAINED OF GOD to preach the unsearchable riches of Christ to a lost and perishing world, is to lead souls to Christ, and not to Pastors for instruction.

The General Association say, that "when woman assumes the place and tone of man as a public reformer, our care and protection of her seem unnecessary; we put ourselves in self-defence against her, and her character becomes unnatural." Here again the unscriptural notion is held up, that there is a distinction between the duties of men and women as moral beings; that what is virtue in man, is vice in woman; and women who dare to obey the command of Jehovah, "Cry aloud, spare not, lift up thy voice like a trumpet, and show my people their transgression" (Isa. 58:1), are threatened with having the protection of the brethren withdrawn. If this is all they do, we shall not even know the time when our chastisement is inflicted; our trust is in the Lord Jehovah, and in him is everlasting strength. The motto of woman, when she is engaged in the great work of public reformation should be,—"The Lord is my light and my salvation; whom shall I fear? The Lord is the strength of my life; of whom shall I be afraid?" (Ps. 27:1). She must feel, if she feels rightly, that she is fulfilling one of the important duties laid upon her as an accountable being, and that her character, instead of being "unnatural," is in exact accordance with the will of Him to whom, and to no other, she is responsible for the talents and the gifts confided to her. As to the pretty simile, introduced into the "Pastoral Letter," "If the vine whose strength and beauty is to lean upon the trellis work, and half conceal its clusters, thinks to assume the independence and the overshadowing nature of the elm," &c. I shall only remark that it might well suit the poet's fancy, who sings of sparkling eyes and coral lips, and knights in armor clad; but it seems to me utterly inconsistent with the dignity of a Christian body, to endeavor to draw such an anti-scriptural distinction between men and women. Ah! how many of my sex feel in the dominion, thus unrighteously exercised over them, under the gentle appel-lation of *protection*, that what they have leaned upon has proved a broken reed at best, and oft a spear.

Thine in the bonds of womanhood,

Sarah M. Grimké

47 ▪ WOMAN'S INFLUENCE MUST BE UNOBTRUSIVE

This selection from Catharine Beecher's An Essay on Slavery and Abolitionism *argues forcefully that while women might band together in societies to improve their benevolent, maternal, and domestic skills, abolition societies were inappropriate. Beecher (1800–1878) devoted her life as an educator and writer to the conviction that women, if properly trained, would find happiness and power in the domestic sphere. Their power rested in the promotion of peace and love, yet the abolitionists would make them public combatants in an effort to coerce the South to free its slaves. She claims here that even signatures on a petition would denigrate women and erode their domestic power, which was enormous if they would but seize it. Her essay began as a letter to a friend telling him why he should not join an abolition society but was expanded to include her beliefs on the duties of American females when Angelina Grimké's* Appeal to the Christian Women of the South *appeared in 1836.*

Source: Catharine E. Beecher. *An Essay on Slavery and Abolitionism, with Reference to the Duty of American Females*, 98–105. Philadelphia: Henry Perkins, 1837.

It is the grand feature of the Divine economy, that there should be different stations of superiority and subordination, and it is impossible to annihilate this beneficent and immutable law. . . . In this arrangement of the duties of life, Heaven has appointed to one sex the superior, and to the other the subordinate station, and this without any reference to the character or conduct of either. It is therefore as much for the dignity as it is for the interest of females, in all respects to conform to the duties of this relation. And it is as much a duty as it is for the child to fulfil similar relations to parents, or subjects to rulers. But while woman holds a subordinate relation in society to the other sex, it is not because it was designed that her duties or her influence should be any the less important, or all-pervading. But it was designed that the mode of gaining influence and of exercising power should be altogether different and peculiar. . . .

Woman is to win every thing by peace and love; by making herself so much respected, esteemed and loved, that to yield to her opinions and to gratify her wishes, will be the free-will offering of the heart. But this is to be all accomplished in the domestic and social circle. There let every woman become so cultivated and refined in intellect, that her taste and judgment will be respected; so benevolent in feeling and action, that her motives will be reverenced;—so unassuming and unambitious, that collision and competition will be banished;—so "gentle and easy to be entreated," as that every heart will repose in her presence; then, the fathers, the husbands, and the sons, will find an influence thrown around them, to which they will yield not only willingly but proudly. A man is never ashamed to own such influences, but feels dignified and ennobled in acknowledging them. But the moment woman begins to feel the promptings of ambition, or the thirst for power, her aegis of defence is gone. All the sacred protection of religion, all the generous promptings of chivalry, all the poetry of romantic gallantry, depend upon woman's retaining her place as dependent and defenceless, and making no claims, and maintaining no right but what are the gifts of honour, rectitude and love.

A woman may seek the aid of co-operation and combination among her own sex, to assist her in her appropriate offices of piety, charity, maternal and domestic duty; but whatever, in any measure, throws a woman into the attitude of a combatant, either for herself or others—whatever binds her in a party conflict—whatever obliges her in any way to exert coercive influences, throws her out of her appropriate sphere. If these general principles are correct, they are entirely opposed to the plan of arraying females in any Abolition movement; because it enlists them in an effort to coerce the South by the public sentiment of the North; because it brings them forward as partisans in a conflict that has been begun and carried forward by measures that are any thing rather than peaceful in their tendencies; because it draws them forth from their appropriate retirement, to expose themselves to the ungoverned violence of mobs, and to sneers and ridicule in public places; because it leads them into the arena of political collision, not as peaceful mediators to hush the opposing elements, but as combatants to cheer up and carry forward the measures of strife.

If it is asked, "May not woman appropriately come forward as a suppliant for a portion of her sex who are bound in cruel bondage?" It is replied, that, the rectitude and propriety of any such measure, depend entirely on its probable results. If petitions from females will operate to exasperate; if they will be deemed obtrusive, indecorous, and unwise, by those to whom they are addressed; if they will increase, rather than diminish the evil which it is wished to remove; if they will be the opening wedge, that will tend eventually to bring females as petitioners and partisans into every political measure that may tend to injure and oppress their sex, in various parts of the nation, and under the various public measures that may hereafter be enforced, then it is neither appropriate nor wise, nor right, for a woman to petition for the relief of oppressed females.

The case of Queen Esther is one often appealed to as a precedent. When a woman is placed in similar circumstances, where death to herself and all her nation is one alternative, and there is nothing worse to fear, but something to hope as the other alternative, then she may safely follow such an example. But when a woman is asked to join an Abolition Society, or to put her name to a petition to congress, for the purpose of contributing her measure of influence to keep up agitation in congress, to promote the excitement of the North against the iniquities of the South, to coerce the South by fear, shame, anger, and a sense of odium to do what she has determined not to do, the case of Queen Esther is not at all to be regarded as a suitable example for imitation.

In this country, petitions to congress, in reference to the official duties of legislators, seem, IN ALL CASES, to fall entirely without the sphere of female duty. Men are the proper persons to make appeals to the rulers whom they appoint, and if their female friends, by arguments and persuasions, can induce them to petition, all the good that can be done by such measures will be secured. But if females cannot influence their nearest friends, to urge forward a public measure in this way, they surely are out of their place, in attempting to do it themselves.

48 · THE GATHERING OF WOMEN FOR MISSIONS

On October 9, 1800, fourteen Baptist and Congregationalist women formed an association for prayer and fund-raising to aid the mission work of their denominations. The constitution for the Boston Female Society for Missionary Purposes stated clearly that the women were free to make donations as they saw fit, and they soon were purchasing Testaments, supporting the translation of the Bible into foreign languages, and contributing to the deployment of home and foreign missionaries. In order to muster more support for their work, the members, who numbered more than 250 by 1818, published an account of the origins and history of the group. The selection below is a description of the society's efforts to turn its attention to the needy inhabitants of Boston. The women planned to hire two men to work in poverty-stricken neighborhoods of the city.

They also sought community cooperation to begin an asylum in which women "who have forfeited their good name and reputation" could be counseled and trained for a more respectable life. Apparent in the report are both a confidence in the value of their work and a strong sense of solidarity with like-minded sisters.

Source: *A Brief Account of the Origin and Progress of the Boston Female Society for Missionary Purposes. With Extracts from the Reports of the Society in May, 1817 and 1818, and Extracts from the Reports of Their Missionaries Rev. James Davis, and Rev. Dudley D. Rosseter,* 4–5. Boston: Lincoln & Edmands, 1818.

During the past season the attention of the Society has been particularly turned to the state of *our own town.* The multiplied exertions in favor of more distant objects have at length led us to look *at home* (where charity is usually said to begin). Viewing the destitute situation of a certain class of inhabitants, whose poverty forbids their appearing decent at public worship and of others who have abandoned themselves to every species of vice, and are totally disinclined to go where the gospel is dispensed; and especially considering how few, comparatively, can be accommodated in our houses of worship, free of expense; we have thought it our duty to try the practicability of a new plan; and have accordingly appropriated the whole income of the year, which closes this day, to the support of two missionaries (for a few months, as an experiment) to visit and labour with the above description of people. May the Lord raise up and eminently qualify men for this important undertaking. We trust we have not gone thus far without deliberation, nor without prayer. And every soul, who has an interest at a throne of grace, should earnestly supplicate a divine blessing. We know that Paul may plant and Apollos water, but God alone can give the increase. We know that we cannot make one hair white or black; but we are taught to "sow our seed in the morning, and in the evening not to withhold our hand, not knowing which shall prosper, or whether both shall be alike good." The Lord has wonderfully blessed the exertions of his people; and he has promised to be with his faithful ministers even to the end of the world. We therefore cherish the animating hope that some real good will result from this attempt, and that habitations which now echo with profanity and discord, will ere long resound with the mild accents of the gospel, and the voice of prayer and praise will be heard.

Should *only one immortal being* reap essential advantage from these labors, it will be an ample reward. But on the contrary, should they all, with one consent, put these things from them, and judge themselves unworthy of eternal life; we may conscientiously turn to some other object: and the ministers of Jesus may shake off the dust of their feet for a testimony against them.

It will be recollected by those who were present at our last meeting, that another important subject was brought forward. The question had been agitated—Should any of those poor unhappy females, who have wandered into the paths of vice and folly, and forfeited their good name and reputation, be disposed by means of missionary labors to reform and become correct in their lives,—*what is to become of them?* respectable persons would feel it unsafe to take them into their families; and their connections (if they have any) probably would have too little confidence in their reformation to receive them to their homes. To remain where they are, would expose them not only to sufferings, but to a liability of relapsing into sin. What then can be done? It was suggested, that if proper exertions should be made, an Asylum might be provided, to which those pitiable objects might resort, where they should be suitably employed, and the proceeds of their labour go to their support. Here they might be favoured with religious instruction and wholesome advice, until proof be given that their repentance is sincere. They might then be able to obtain an honest and reputable living for themselves. It was resolved that a close box, with an aperture in the lid, be kept in the Society for the purpose of receiving voluntary contributions for this object, should the attempt be made. This is indeed a small beginning, but the Lord is able to provide a sufficiency. The society by no means proposes to take a work of such magnitude into its own hands; but most sincerely and ardently recommends it to the consideration and patronage of the benevolent and virtuous; and would cheerfully help as far as consistent. Without boasting, it may be asserted, that many thousands of dollars have been raised in this town to spread the gospel in regions not favoured with its heavenly influence; we may therefore conclude that the friends of religion and virtue in other places would cheerfully contribute to an undertaking like this; particularly when it is considered, that but a small proportion of these unhappy creatures are natives of this place. They are collected from almost all parts of the country, and some even from foreign climes. The calamity is a *public* calamity; the cause of virtue is a *public cause*, and if good is done it will be felt by the community. There are several institutions of this kind in Europe, which have proved a blessing to many. To check the torrent of vice, which is flowing with increasing impetuosity, and restore the wanderer to her father's house, must be truly gratifying to the benevolent mind. And if the *great Redeemer* condescended to notice and reclaim such characters, his disciples must view it a privilege and an honour to follow his example. "The disciple is not above his master."

In answer to a Circular to similar societies, proposing a correspondence by letter and concert in prayer; communications have been received from ninety-seven societies; and from information otherwise received, we find that many more have united in the prayer meeting. Thus, while the female of the metropolis rejoices to retire from her usual avocations, her sisters in the country also feel it their privilege on THE FIRST MONDAY IN THE MONTH, (a day favored of the Lord;) to assemble with the thousands of Israel, and pour out their united supplications before the mercy seat.

49 ▪ MISSIONARY WOMEN STEP BEYOND THEIR SPHERE

Baptist lay leader Helen Barrett Montgomery (1861–1934) was one of this century's most active speakers, writers, and organizers on behalf of women's foreign missions. The causes to which she devoted herself and her approach to missions were both determined by her passion to break down the "caste of sex" at home and abroad. Among other achievements, she served as the first female president of the Northern Baptist Convention and translated the New Testament from the Greek to create a popular English study edition. In 1910 she wrote Western Women in Eastern Lands *to mark the fiftieth anniversary of women's boards of missions in America. It celebrates their achievements and points to challenges they will be forced to face. Montgomery reminds readers that women physicians played a shining role in advancing the kingdom of God abroad, although they had to battle prejudice from many sources at home. She also speaks directly to the efforts to merge men's and women's mission boards in several denominations. Montgomery objects to this, citing among other concerns the need for men to always be in charge and the possibility that women and children in foreign lands would be neglected as funds shifted to ministerial training and maintenance.*

Source: Helen Barrett Montgomery. *Western Women in Eastern Lands: An Outline Study of Fifty Years of Woman's Work in Foreign Missions*, 117–19, 122–29, 268–72. New York: Macmillan, 1910.

One of the striking developments of the woman's century was the entrance of women into the practice of medicine. Their first step in this direction met with bitter opposition. In 1849 Elizabeth Blackwell was admitted to study medicine in Geneva, after knocking in vain at the doors of twelve medical colleges. This great woman, looking out over the few overcrowded avenues of employment open to women, had resolved to "open a new door, to tread a fresh path." The story of her resolute overcoming of hateful persecution and terrible obstacles, of her conquest for herself of the best medical education, is one of the romances of biography. Those who are inclined to give the clergy a monopoly in conservatism and blind opposition to progress, should read the story of the obstacles put in the way of

pioneer women physicians by the medical profession. In 1859 the Philadelphia Medical Society passed a resolution of excommunication against
any doctor who lectured or taught in the Women's Medical College, and
against every graduate of that institution. Yet, in spite of opposition, within
six years after Elizabeth Blackwell graduated at Geneva, the first Women's
Hospital in all the world had been founded by Dr. Sims in New York, and
the first permanent Woman's College of Medicine had been organized in
Philadelphia.

We cannot pursue the story of this chapter in the expanding life of
women further than to note its bearing on foreign missions. These lion-
hearted pioneers in the field of medicine were blazing a trail whose importance they little dreamed. If the contracted ideas of propriety held by the
vast majority of men and women in the civilized world of that time had tri-
umphed, one of the most powerful agencies in the Christian conquest of the
world would have been wanting. Whether there were to be women physicians was a question of interest in America: but in Asia it was a question of
life and death. The women of half the world were shut out from medical
assistance unless they could receive it at the hands of women. So with God
and nature leading them, the women pioneers pressed out into the untried
path; hundreds of more timid souls followed them, and the protesting old
world settled back grumbling to get used to the new situation. . . .

While volumes might be written in regard to the evils, absurdities, and
cruelties of the medical systems of the non-Christian world, the full horror
of the situation would only be reached when the sufferings of women and
children were told. Thousands of women die annually because such help as
might be given them cannot be had on account of the restricted conditions
of their lives. A physician walking in the streets of a city in India recently
heard the screams of a woman coming from a fine native house. He asked
a servant to say to the master of the house that a physician was passing by
who would gladly be of service. The man returned answer that he would
rather his wife should die than be relieved by a male physician. . . .

The need for women physicians to relieve the physical sufferings of
their own sex was first perceived and first emphasized by missionaries. Both
men and women united in the demand which they began to urge upon the
home churches; the men found themselves barred from practising among
women by caste and custom; the women, teachers and missionaries, had
daily pressing upon them the throngs of women and little children who
came to get help from the missionary medicine closet that was a part of the
equipment of every station. These women often acquired considerable skill
in prescribing for minor ailments, and in caring for wounds and burns; but
found themselves helpless before the cases that demanded the services of a
fully trained physician. . . .

The first response came from a woman, Sarah J. Hale, of Philadelphia. The editor of *Godey's Lady's Book* was the prophet who saw from afar this marvellous movement in the coming kingdom, to which the men and women of her generation were utterly blinded by prejudice and indifference. In 1851 she organized a Ladies' Medical Missionary Society whose object was "to aid the work of foreign missions by sending out young women qualified as physicians to minister to the wants of women in heathen lands." She wrote editorials in the *Lady's Book*,—the *Ladies' Home Journal* of those days—corresponded with influential people, and held parlor meetings. A few clergymen expressed themselves in sympathy; two young ladies just graduated from the Women's Medical College were ready and anxious to go, but the time had not yet come. The project aroused a storm of opposition and ridicule. At that time the old superstitious division between the "spiritual" and the "secular" was rigidly maintained. It was felt to be a waste of precious time and money to send missionaries to deal with anything but the perishing souls of men. The intimate connection between the soul and the body was not fully appreciated. And the example of the Master in the time he devoted to relieving bodily distress was apparently overlooked. Then there was that awful bogy of a woman going out of her *sphere*, even for the saving of life. So Mrs. Hale, after repeated efforts to storm the fort of public prejudice, was forced to postpone the desire of her heart to a better day. For twenty years she waited to see the church begin tardily and timidly the task that should have been begun in 1851.

Nothing further was done for seventeen years; then in India itself a medical missionary, Dr. J. L. Humphrey, began to deliver a course of lectures to a class of young women in the orphanage at Bareilly. The initiative in this case came from an educated Hindu gentleman, Pundit Nund Kishore, who knew the dreadful suffering of women in childbirth under the malpractice of ignorant midwives. He offered to defray half the expenses of training these young women if the government could be induced to help. The governor of the province regarded the matter favorably, but so much opposition came from physicians that the project seemed likely to fall through. Then a noble English official became personally responsible for the amount asked from the government, and the first class of nine women was opened at Naini Tal, May 1, 1869, a day that ought to be celebrated by the women of India. A two years' course of study was given to these women; and then four of them were sent up to stand the government examination. So much hung upon their success! Every one said that the scheme was a wild one; that women had neither the brains nor the judgment to successfully pass tests framed for men. But the four timid Indian women stood bravely before the Board of English Physicians (one of them the Inspector-general of Hospitals), answered correctly the questions, bore themselves so quietly, showed such thorough knowledge, that they won the Board and their coveted certificates at the same time. They were certificated in "Anatomy, Midwifery, Pharmacy, and the management of minor surgical cases, including the more common kinds of fractures and dislocations." The Board testified that these young women "answered questions with quickness and precision" and had a knowledge of medicine and surgery "quite equal to the generality of locally entertained native doctors."

At the time that this "lively experiment" was being made in India, Mrs. Thomas of Bareilly was writing to Mrs. Gracey asking her to interest the Philadelphia Branch of the Woman's Union Missionary Society in sending out a "medical lady." Mrs. Gracey read the letter which described the experiment with the native class at Naini Tal at one of the regular meetings of the Branch. We can well imagine the joy of Mrs. Hale, who was at the time president of the Society, when she heard the plan which she had cherished for nearly twenty years proposed and seemingly about to be realized. Inquiries were made at the Woman's Medical College to see if there was a graduate ready to go to India as a medical missionary. The name of Clara Swain of Castile, New York, was given. A letter was written to her which resulted in her accepting the call, after three months of thought and prayer. Meanwhile the women of the Methodist Church had organized, and the Union Missionary Society most generously surrendered all claim to Miss Swain (who was herself a Methodist), and relinquished the honor of sending the first woman physician to the women of non-Christian lands. This beautiful deed of generous courtesy on the part of the pioneer Woman's Board has never been forgotten by the Methodist women. Miss Swain sailed with Miss Thoburn, the first missionaries to be sent out by the Methodist women of America. . . .

Would it not be better to have one great organization of the entire church to which both men and women contributed? This is the question that is most agitated to-day. Some of the brethren say: "Let the women collect, they are such splendid collectors. We will spend it far more wisely than they can." Others say, "Let us all work together, have men and women on the Board, men and women in the work."

The first plan will commend itself to few women. The opportunity for self-expression and the development that comes through responsibility are as necessary to women as to men. It is not the united wisdom of the men of the church which would be available for this sacred office of direction, but simply that of some individual secretary or secretaries. The modern educated woman has ideas not only on the way to collect money but on the way to spend it, and the purposes for which it should be spent.

The second plan is very attractive. It looks ideal to have one tremendous organization with men and women working side by side. Perhaps the day will come in the growth of the kingdom when this can be, but let us look at all sides of the argument before hastening out of organizations which have been so blessed of God.

In the first place, are men ready for it? Are they emancipated from the caste of sex so that they can work easily with women, unless they be head and women clearly subordinate? Certain facts seem to indicate that in spite of the rapid strides undoubtedly made in this direction we have still a long stretch of unexplored country to be traversed before the perfect democracy of Jesus is reached. When the Religious Education Association was formed, for example, although for years almost the only really scientific work in the Sunday school had been done by women in the primary department, no woman was asked to speak, and none was among the body of officers and backers of the movement. To have two or three women on a Board who are assigned to unimportant committees would hardly be satisfactory to the women. But in the present state of civilization could we look for much more?

Again, would the plan of consolidation work well for the interests of the work? For years the general Boards tried the lump method in gathering their funds; but all of them are supplementing that method to-day. When people were asked to give to some great, intangible faraway thing labelled Foreign Missions, the sense of responsibility was feeble, and the response feeble. To-day we have the "living link" by which a church agrees to become responsible to send one, the "missionary pastor," by which a church supports not only its home pastor but also its pastor on the field, the "substitute" idea, by which a man keeps his substitute working on the other side of the world while he sleeps. There are "station plans" and "specifics" innumerable. The result is dollars for dimes. The Word had to tabernacle among us that we might touch Him; so do causes. Now if we were to give up that intimate, near appeal made by work for women and homes and little children upon the women of the church, would the cause gain or lose? The experience of denominations which have tried consolidation of causes has not been particularly successful. Take cases where domestic and foreign missions are handled by one organization, and compare the per capita gifts with those where separate appeals on the merits of the case are made. Again, suppose that the same plan were tried in other lines. Would it be a gain to combine the Young Women's Christian Association and the Young Men's Christian Association in one vast organization which should jointly collect? Is it not true that in the startling diversity of human interests we must allow causes to make their appeal, and select their supporters by some inner law of affinity? Neither are they rivals. Each supports and furthers the other. Philanthropies depend on the cultivation of the spirit of philanthropy, and each helps to enrich the soil from which good deeds spring. So long as our national bill for chewing gum exceeds our gifts to foreign missions, and our ostrich feather and candy outputs could float the missionary benevolences like skiffs on a river, we need not fear impoverishing the churches by too much importunity.

Again, is there not a distinctive place for this distinctive work? There is always a danger that in the pressing demands of the wider work the women's interests might be overlooked, unless there were organizations specifically formed to care for them. It is only natural and right that the work of establishing churches, training ministers, educating the future leaders, should absorb the energies of men. The constant pressure for funds is so great, the opportunities for reaching the men of the non-Christian community so striking, that it is little wonder if, in the multiplicity of demands, the work for women and children should not be pressed. Men have seen this need of distinctive women's work clearly and have urged it persistently. One missionary now on the field said recently: "Never give up your separate women's organizations; the work for women is sure to suffer if you do. It needs some one continually pushing on that one point."

Once more, is there not a distinctive contribution that the women's organizations may make? We are not like men, but diverse. There is a feminine viewpoint which, to be sure, is only partial, but it is different. Certain methods are tried out, certain experiments made that would not appeal to men, but do to women. Cannot we coöperate all the better in joint undertakings, for having the separate work which each does better alone? Have women no contribution to add to missionary wisdom?

Chapter 7

NINETEENTH-CENTURY PREACHERS AND SCHOLARS

50 ▪ A DEFENSE OF FEMALE PREACHING

The Wesleyan Methodists combined intense revivalism with radical social reform, believing that obedience to the gospel was not genuine unless linked with abolitionism and temperance. Luther Lee (1800–1889) became a prominent leader and architect of this denomination after careers as a preacher and antislavery agent. His support of temperance led him to become an outspoken supporter of a woman's right to speak publicly on behalf of the movement. It was probably through temperance channels that he met Antoinette Brown and was invited to preach at the service of her ordination in 1853 in the First Congregational Church, Butler, New York. Lee's sermon hinges on the idea that the church, living in the light of Pentecost, had experienced the fulfillment of Joel's promise that God's spirit would someday lead men and women to prophesy. Lee argues that since the Bible contains a multitude of examples that women in Israel and the early church spoke publicly with God's blessing, the prohibitions in 1 Corinthians 14 and 1 Timothy 2 must be local and specific in their application.

Source: Luther Lee. "Woman's Right to Preach the Gospel." In *Five Sermons and a Tract by Luther Lee*, edited with an introduction by Donald W. Dayton, 92–95. Chicago: Holrad House, 1975.

This discourse would be defective, should I not pay some attention to those scriptures which some suppose forbade females to exercise their gifts in public. There are, so far as I know, but two texts, that are, or can be relied upon as proof against the right of females to improve in public. They are as follows:

"Let your women keep silence in the churches: for it is not permitted unto them to speak; but they are commanded to be under obedience, as also saith the law. And if they will learn any thing, let them ask their husbands at home: for it is a shame for woman to speak in the church" (1 Cor. 14:34, 35).

"Let the women learn in silence with all subjection. But I suffer not a woman to teach, nor to usurp authority over the man, but to be in silence" (1 Tim. 2:11, 12).

These two texts, I believe, are all the proof there is to offset the array of texts and arguments which have been adduced in proof of the right of females to preach the gospel. If I were to say, "I do not know what they mean," they could never disprove the fact that females did prophesy and pray in the church, and if explained at all, they must be so explained as to harmonize with that fact. Let us then examine the matter.

If these texts are to be understood as a general prohibition of the improvement of female gifts in public, it must be entire and absolute, and must cut females off from all vocal part in public worship. It will preclude them from singing and vocal prayer. The expression, "Let your women keep silence in the churches," if it touches the case at all, forbids singing and vocal prayer. Can a woman sing and keep silence at the same time? Can she pray vocally, and keep silence at the same time? Such then is the true issue, and as we must meet the issue before the people, it is important that it be presented to them in its true light. Singing is as much a violation of the command to keep silence as praying or preaching. We must then put locks upon the lips of the sisterhood in time of prayer, and compel them to let their harps hang in silence while we, the lords of creation, chant Zion's songs, and leave the song itself devoid of the softer melodies which flow from woman's soul.

Such a construction of these texts most clearly makes them conflict with other portions of divine truth. Glance for a moment at the weight of evidence on the other side. My text affirms, as a broad foundation on which to stand, "There is neither male nor female; for ye are all one in Christ Jesus." Miriam was a prophetess and led the host of women in Israel forth, and when the men sun[g] of Jehovah's triumph, she responded loudly and gloriously in the face of all Israel. Deborah was a prophetess and was a judge of all Israel. Huldah was a prophetess, and dwelt in the College at Jerusalem, and prophesied in the name of the Lord, to king Josiah. "Thus saith the Lord God of Israel." Anna prophesied concerning Christ in the temple to all them that looked for redemption in Jerusalem. The prophet Joel foretold that daughters should prophesy under the New Dispensation; and God did pour out his Spirit on females and they spake with other tongues. Philip "had four daughters which did prophesy," sixty years after the birth of Christ. Paul the author of this supposed law of silence imposed upon females, tells us that Phebe was a deaconess or minister of the Church which was at Cenchrea; and commends several other females in the same chapter, who labored in the Lord. Paul also wrote to the church at Philippi, and told them to "help those women that labored in the gospel." And all antiquity agrees that women were set apart to some church office by the imposition of a bishop's hands.

Now, in the face of all this, are we to understand Paul as issuing a command, covering all countries and all ages, absolutely requiring all women to keep silence in the churches, and not to speak a word within the walls of the sanctuary? Those must believe it who can, but I cannot believe it with the light I now have, and must seek some explanation, which will, in my view, make a better harmony in the word of God.

Every writer should be so construed, if it be possible, as to make him agree with himself, and to do this, Paul must be so understood in these two texts, as to make the sense accord with what he has so plainly taught in other places, that females might and did exercise their gifts in public. Compare with 1 Corinthians 11:5, 6, 13, 14, 15.

"But every woman that prayeth or prophesieth with her head uncovered, dishonoreth her head; for that is even all one as if she were shaven. For if the woman be not covered, let her be covered. Judge in yourselves: is it comely that a woman pray unto God uncovered? Doth not even nature itself teach you, that, if a man have long hair, it is a shame unto him? But if a woman have long hair, it is a glory to her: for her hair is given her for a covering."

Here the apostle most clearly gives directions how women are to pray and prophesy in public, and are we to understand him as first giving directions how females should pray and prophesy, and then in the same letter, absolutely forbid the thing he had given directions how to perform? I cannot believe this, and must seek another exposition. It is clear that women did pray and prophesy in that church, and the apostle told them it must be done with their heads covered, that is wearing the customary veil. This was founded upon the customs of the times, to which it was necessary to conform in order to success, as to appear in public without a veil, in that community, subjected a female to suspicions of a want of virtue. What the apostle calls nature was only the prejudice of education, which has now ceased to exist, or rather never existed among us. The Greek word, *phusis*, here translated *nature*, signifies not only nature, but "constitution, disposition, character, custom, habit, use." We have no such nature in this country, and as the rule grew out of the then existing customs and prejudices of society, it is no longer binding, and females may appear with or without veils as may suit their taste or convenience. But the point is, that as Paul gives instructions for women to pray and prophesy with their heads covered, he cannot be understood as forbidding them to pray and prophesy under any and all circumstances. But what does the apostle mean when he says it is not permitted for women to speak?

It is certain that he does not speak of female teachers or preachers, as such, for he comprehends the entire membership of the church. The twenty-third verse says, "If therefore the whole church be come together into some place, and all speak with tongues," &c. This proves that the apostle is not treating of teachers as officers, as a distinct class, nor of the eligibility of persons to the office [of] teacher, as distinguished from the membership generally, but of the duties, rights and privileges of the membership in common, as members. If, therefore, the text precludes women from speaking in the church as a general rule, it precludes them, not merely as authorized teachers, but from the right of speaking as common or unofficial members of the church.

In view of the numerous and unanswerable proofs that God did employ females, under the Old and New Covenants, as public instrumentalities of spreading truth, all who hold the doctrine of the absolute equality of males and females, under all circumstances, and in all relations, will as a matter of course, regard these two texts as local and specific in their application, founded upon some peculiarity in the circumstances of the community at that time and in those places, and as having no general bearing on the question. It will be much easier for them to believe that there were circumstances, which were then understood, calling for such a rule, thus specific and local in its bearing, and constituting an exception to the general rule, that women had a right to, and did prophesy; than to believe that the facts that they did teach, scattered, as they are, through a period of more than fifteen centuries, are proved by these two texts to be the exceptions to, and in violation of, a positive law of God, the foundation of which he has laid in nature. The simple admission of such numerous and wide spread exceptions to what is claimed to the law of God, having its foundation in nature, must come but little short of nullification.

51 ▪ BIBLICAL EXAMPLES OF PREACHING WOMEN

Catherine Booth (1829–1890) is best known as the cofounder of the Salvation Army. She was also, however, an outspoken advocate for women's rights in society, politics, and religious institutions and did much to shape the Salvation Army's tradition of female equality. Booth was outraged by an attack on American Holiness leader Phoebe Palmer after Palmer had preached in Newcastle-Upon-Tyne. Booth responded by letter to Palmer's opponent, who claimed that female preaching was unscriptural, and subsequently expanded the letter into a pamphlet, Female Ministry, *which was published in 1859. Her objective is to show that not only is the preaching of women not forbidden in the Bible, but it is "enjoined by precept and example." Booth cites examples of many women in the history of Israel and the early church who spoke publicly according to the leading of the Spirit. Such women could be sure of their calling because of the fruits of their labors. Notice her reference to the realization of Joel's promise at Pentecost that both men and women would prophesy when the Spirit was bestowed.*

Source: Catherine Booth. *Female Ministry; or, Woman's Right to Preach the Gospel*, 14–18. Reprint. New York: The Salvation Army Supplies Printing and Publishing Department, 1975.

We commend a few passages bearing on the ministrations of women under the old dispensation to the careful considerations of our readers. *"And Deborah, a prophetess, the wife of Lapidoth, she judged Israel at that time,"* etc. (Judg. 4:4-10). There are two particulars in this passage worthy of note. First, the authority of Deborah as a prophetess, or revealer of God's will to Israel, was acknowledged and submitted to as implicitly as in the cases of the male judges who succeeded her. Secondly, she is made the military head of ten thousand men, Barak refusing to go to battle without her.

Again, in 2 Kings 22:12-20, we have an account of the king sending the high-priest, the scribe, etc., to Huldah, the prophetess, the wife of Shallum, who dwelt at Jerusalem, in the college, to enquire at her mouth the will of God in reference to the book of the law which had been found in the House of the Lord. The authority and dignity of Huldah's message to the king does not betray anything of that trembling diffidence or abject servility which some persons seem to think should characterise the religious exercises of woman. She answers him as the prophetess of the Lord, having the signet of the King of Kings attached to her utterances.

"The Lord gave the word, and great was the company of those that published it" (Ps. 68:11). In the original Hebrew it is, "Great was the company of women publishers, or women evangelists." Grotius explains this passage, "The Lord shall give the word ... so that he would call those which follow the great army of preaching women, victories, or female conquerors." How comes it that the feminine word is actually excluded in this text? That it is there as plainly as any other word no Hebrew scholar will deny. It is too much to assume that as our translators could not *alter* it, as they did "Diaconon" when applied to Phebe, they preferred to leave it out altogether rather than give a prophecy so unpalatable to their prejudice. But the Lord gives the word, and He will choose whom He pleases to publish it, notwithstanding the condemnation of translators and divines.

"For I brought thee up out of the land of Egypt, and redeemed thee out of the house of servants; and I sent before thee Moses, Aaron, and Miriam" (Mic. 6:4). God here classes Miriam with Moses and Aaron, and declares that *He*

sent her before His people. We fear that had some of our friends been men of Israel at that time, they would have disputed such a leadership.

In the light of such passages as these, who will dare to dispute the fact that God did, under the old dispensation, endow His handmaidens with the gifts and calling of prophets answering to our present idea of preachers. We are thankful to find abundant evidence that the *"spirit of prophecy which is the testimony of Jesus,"* was poured out on the female as fully as on the male disciple, and "His daughters and His handmaidens" prophesied. We commend the following texts from the New Testament to the careful consideration of our readers.

"And she (Anna) was a widow of about fourscore and four years, which departed not from the temple, but served God with fastings and prayers night and day. And she coming in at that instant, gave thanks likewise unto the Lord, and spake of Him to all them that looked for redemption in Jerusalem" (Luke 2:37, 38). Can any one explain wherein this exercise of Anna's differed from that of Simeon, recorded just before? It was in the same public place, the temple. It was during the same service. It was equally public, for she *"spake* of Him to all who looked for redemption in Jerusalem."

Jesus said to the two Marys, *"All hail! And they came and held Him by the feet, and worshipped Him. Then said Jesus unto them, Be not afraid: go, tell my brethren that they go before me into Galilee"* (Matt. 28:9, 10). There are two or three points in this beautiful narrative to which we wish to call the attention of our readers.

First, it was the *first* announcement of the glorious news to a lost world and a company of forsaking disciples. *Second*, it was as *public* as the nature of the case demanded; and intended ultimately to be published to the ends of the earth. *Third*, Mary was expressly commissioned to reveal the fact to the Apostles; and thus she literally became their teacher on that memorable occasion. Oh, glorious privilege, to be allowed to herald the glad tidings of a Saviour risen! How could it be that our Lord chose a *woman* to this honour? Well, one reason might be that the male disciples were all missing at the time. They all forsook Him and fled. But woman was there, as she had ever been, ready to minister to her risen, as to her dying, Lord—

> "Not she with traitorous lips her Saviour stung;
> Not she denied Him with unholy tongue;
> She, whilst Apostles shrunk, could danger brave;
> Last at the cross, and earliest at the grave."

But surely, if the dignity of our Lord or His message were likely to be imperilled by committing this sacred trust to a woman, He who was guarded by legions of angels could have commanded another messenger; but, as if intent on doing her honour and rewarding her unwavering fidelity, He reveals Himself *first* to her; and, as an evidence that He had taken out of the way the curse under which she had so long groaned, nailing it to His cross, He makes her who had been first in the transgression, first also in the glorious knowledge of complete redemption.

Refer to Acts 1:14, and 2:1, 4. We are in the first of these passages expressly told that the women were assembled with the disciples on the day of Pentecost; and in the second, that the cloven tongues sat upon them *each*, and the Holy Ghost filled them *all*, and they spake as the Spirit gave them utterance. It is beside the point to argue that the gift of tongues was a miraculous gift, seeing that the Spirit was the primary bestowment. The tongues were only emblematical of the office which the Spirit was henceforth to sustain to His people. The Spirit was given alike to the female as to the male disciple, and this is cited by Peter [Acts 2:16-18], as a peculiar speciality of the latter dispensation. What a remarkable device of the Devil that he has so long succeeded in hiding this characteristic of the latter day glory! *He* knows, whether the Church does or not, how eminently detrimental to the interests of his kingdom have been the religious labours of woman; and while her Seed has mortally bruised his head, he ceases not to bruise her heel; but the time of her deliverance draweth nigh. . . .

Notwithstanding, however, all this opposition to female ministry on the part of those deemed authorities in the Church, there have been some in all ages in whom the Holy Ghost has wrought so mightily, that at the sacrifice of reputation and all things most dear, they have been compelled to come out as witnesses for Jesus and ambassadors for His Gospel. As a rule, these women have been amongst the most devoted and self-denying of the Lord's people, giving indisputable evidence by the purity and beauty of their lives, that they were led by the Spirit of God. Now, if the Word of God forbids female ministry, we would ask how it happens that so many of the most devoted handmaidens of the Lord have felt themselves constrained by the Holy Ghost to exercise it? Surely there must be some mistake somewhere, for the Word and the Spirit cannot contradict each other. Either the Word does not condemn women preaching, or these confessedly holy women have been deceived. Will anyone venture to assert that such women as Mrs. Elizabeth Fry, Mrs. Fletcher of Madeley, have been deceived with respect to their call to deliver the Gospel messages to their fellow-creatures? If not, then God does not call and qualify women to preach, and His Word, rightly understood, cannot forbid what His Spirit enjoins.

Further, it is a significant fact, which we commend to the consideration of all thoughtful Christians, that the public ministry of women has been eminently owned of God in the salvation of souls and the edification of His people. Paul refers to the *fruits* of his labours as evidence of his Divine commission (1 Cor. 9:2). *"If I am not an Apostle unto others, yet doubtless I am to you: for the seal of mine Apostleship are ye in the Lord."* If this criterion be allowed to settle the question respecting woman's call to preach, we have no fear as to the result.

52 · AMANDA SMITH'S CALL TO PREACH

Amanda Berry Smith (1837–1915), evangelist and missionary, occupies a position of preeminence among African American female preachers. Embracing the Holiness movement and experiencing entire sanctification, she began her preaching ministry in 1869. Nine years later she left for a decade of missionary work in England, India, and Monrovia. In this selection from her autobiography she receives a clear call from God to preach in Salem, New Jersey; she receives this call while worshiping in the Fleet Street A.M.E. Church in Brooklyn. She is wearied by the local male A.M.E. preachers who question the validity of her call, discouraged by physical deprivation, and plagued by doubts about her ability to accomplish her task. God, however, provides her with a message and the strength to deliver it. The result is a dramatic two-week revival that restores her confidence.

Source: Amanda Smith. *An Autobiography: The Story of the Lord's Dealings with Mrs. Amanda Smith the Colored Evangelist,* 147–48, 152–59. New York: Oxford University Press, 1988.

We went early, and went into the Sabbath School. At the close of the Sabbath School the children sang a very pretty piece. I do not remember what it was, but the spirit of the Lord touched my heart and I was blessed. My bad feelings had gone for a few moments, and I thought, "I guess the Lord wanted to bless me here." But when we went upstairs I began to feel the same burden and pressure as I had before. And I said, "Oh, Lord, help me, and teach me what this means." And just at that point the Tempter came with this supposition: "Now, if you are wholly sanctified, why is it that you have these dull feelings?"

I began to examine my work, my life, every day, and I could see nothing. Then I said, "Lord, help me to understand what Thou meanest. I want to hear Thee speak."

Brother Gould, then pastor of the Fleet Street Church, took his text. I was sitting with my eyes closed in silent prayer to God, and after he had been preaching about ten minutes, as I opened my eyes, just over his head I seemed to see a beautiful star, and as I looked at it, it seemed to form into the shape of a large white tulip; and I said, "Lord, is that what you want me to see? If so, what else?" And then I leaned back and closed my eyes.

Just then I saw a large letter "G," and I said: "Lord, do you want me to read in Genesis, or in Galatians? Lord, what does this mean?"

Just then I saw the letter "O." I said, "Why, that means go." And I said "What else?" And a voice distinctly said to me "Go preach."

The voice was so audible that it frightened me for a moment, and I said, "Oh, Lord, is that what you wanted me to come here for? Why did you not tell me when I was at home, or when I was on my knees praying?" But His paths are known in the mighty deep, and His ways are past finding out. On Monday morning, about four o'clock, I think, I was awakened by the presentation of a beautiful, white cross—white as the driven snow— similar to that described in the last chapter. It was as cold as marble. It was laid just on my forehead and on my breast. It seemed very heavy; to press me down. The weight and the coldness of it were what woke me; and as I woke I said: "Lord, I know what that is[.] It is a cross."

I arose and got on my knees, and while I was praying these words came to me: "If any man will come after Me let him deny himself and take up his cross and follow Me." And I said, "Lord, help me and I will. . . . "

I had all the work I could do, and more, at one dollar and twenty-five cents to two dollars a day, until October, 1870, when I left my home at God's command, and began my evangelistic work. I did not know then that it meant all that it has been. I thought it was only to go to Salem, as the Lord had showed me. Shortly after this I was off to Salem. Got as far as Philadelphia, where I purposed leaving my little girl with her grandfather, while I went on to Salem. But strange to say, notwithstanding all the light, and clear, definite leading of the Lord, my heart seemed to fail me. I said to myself, "After all, to go on to Salem, a stranger, where I don't know a minister, or anybody. No, I will do some work here in Philadelphia."

So I got some tracts, went away down in the lower part of town, on St. Mary's street, and Sixth, and Lombard, and all in that region. I went into saloons and gave tracts; gave tracts to people on the corners; spoke a word here and there; some laughed and sneered; some took a tract. Then I went to the meetings, and sang and prayed and exhorted. I went about among the sick, and did all I could. And I said, "After all, the Lord may not want me to go to Salem."

After spending a week in Philadelphia I thought I would go home. Friday came, and I thought to myself, "Well, I will go home Saturday." But, Oh! there came such an awful horror and darkness over me. On Friday night, after I had come home from an excellent meeting, I could not sleep, all night. Oh! how I was troubled. I did not know what to do, for I had spent all my money; father did not have much means, and when Mazie and I were at home I generally provided, not only for ourselves, but for all the family; so that my means went almost before I knew it; I had not much, anyhow. But it seemed to me I would die. So I told the Lord if He would spare me till morning, though I had not any money, I would go and see my sister, and if she could lend me a dollar so as to get on to Salem, I would go.

Saturday morning came. I borrowed a dollar, came home, and spent twenty-five cents of it for breakfast; then with what it cost me to ride down to get on the boat, in all about fifteen cents, I had left about sixty cents. My ticket on the boat was fifty cents; I had had some little hymns struck off; we colored people were very fond of ballads for singing.

A little while after I got on the boat, who should come in but Brother Holland, who used to be my pastor eight years before, in Lancaster, Pa. All this had come to pass in the years after I had known him; so that he did not know anything at all about it. He was very glad to see me, and asked me where I was going. I told him the Lord had sent me to Salem. Then I began to tell him my story. How the Lord had led me. How He had called me to His work. Dear old man, he listened to me patiently, and when I had got through he said:

"Well, Sister Smith, you know I don't believe in women preaching. But still, honey, I have got nothing to say about you. You go on. The Lord bless you."

I was dumbfounded; for I thought he was in the greatest sympathy with woman's work, though I had never heard him express himself with regard to it. But I was glad of the latter part of what he said.

It was quite a cool day, and the boat got in about two o'clock in the afternoon. There were no street cars then, as there are now. There was a big omnibus. They didn't let colored people ride inside an omnibus in those days. So I took my carpet bag and had to sit outside on the top of the omnibus.

They didn't let colored people off till all the white people were off, even if they had to go past where they wanted to stop; so I had to ride round on the omnibus at least three-quarters of an hour before I was taken to where I wanted to go.

The woman's name, where I had been told to go, was Mrs. Curtis. She was a widow, and owned her own house and grounds; she had quite a nice, comfortable little house. But she was a queer genius. Old Father Lewis, who had once been pastor of the A.M.E. Church at Salem, and at this time was pastor of the church at Jersey City Heights, N.J., had recommended me to Sister Curtis, because she was alone and had plenty of room, and he thought it would be so nice for me. It was more than a half mile from the locality in which the colored church was situated, and in which the majority of the colored people lived. But Sister Curtis seemed as though she was frightened at me. I told her who had sent me to her house, and how the Lord had called me to His work, and all my story of the Lord's doing. She listened, but was very nervous. Then she said she didn't know what in the world she would do, for she hadn't anything but some hard bread to give me to eat, and she hadn't any sugar; and I said, "Well, no matter for that. I can eat hard bread, and I can drink tea without sugar, if you can only accommodate me till Monday, at least."

Well, she said she could keep me all night, but she didn't like to leave any one in the house on Monday, because she generally went away to wash; and she generally had the cold pieces given her from the hotel where she went to wash dishes, and that was all she could give me to eat.

She knew how we colored people are about eating; we do like to eat; so I think she told me that thinking she would frighten me; but I agreed to everything. Then I asked her if she could tell me where Brother Cooper, who was then pastor, lived. She said, "Yes, it is about a mile and a half."

I asked her if she would show me which way to go. She did so, but did not give me anything to eat. I was very hungry, but I did not ask her for anything. So I started off about three o'clock, or a little after, and went to see Brother Cooper.

I was tired, and walked slowly, and it was about half-past four when I got up to the little village above. I inquired my way, and was told that Sister Johnson lived right close by Brother Cooper's, and if I would go to her house she could tell me, for it was just through her yard to Brother Cooper's house. So I went. I knocked at the door. The sister was in; several nice looking little children were playing around, and an elegant pot of cabbage was boiling over the fire. My! how nice it did smell; and I did wish and pray that the Lord would put it into her heart to ask me to have something to eat. I hinted all I knew how, but she did not take the hint. I knew by the sound of it that it was done and ought to come off!

I told her my story; told her about Brother Lewis; she was very glad to hear from him. I asked her if I could stay all night, because I felt so tired that I thought I could not walk back to Sister Curtis'. She said at once she could not possibly have me stay all night. Her mother had been dead about three months, and she had taken down the bedsteads, and she was so overburdened with her grief she had never put them up, and they were all lying on the floor.

I told her no matter for that; I could sleep on the floor just as well. No, she did not have room. She could not possibly do it.

Well, I stayed till it was pretty dark[.] It was after six o'clock. The more I talked the more she gave me to see that she was not going to ask me to have any cabbage, or to stay all night.

So I said to her, "Will you tell me where Brother Cooper, the minister, lives?"

"Oh, yes," she said, "I will send one of the children with you."

When I got to Brother Cooper's I knocked, and Brother Cooper came to the door; he was an awful timid man; so he stood at the door, holding it half open and leaning out a little ways, and asked me who I was. I told him that I was Amanda Smith; that the Lord sent me to Salem. Then I went on, standing at the door, telling him how the Lord had led me, and all about it. His wife, who was a little more thoughtful than he, heard me, and she called out to him, and said, "Cooper, why don't you ask the sister to come in." So then he said, "Come in, Sister."

I was awful glad, so I went in. Sister Cooper was getting supper. The table was set, and I thought, "Maybe, I will get something to eat now."

So I went on and finished my story, and they seemed to be greatly interested; and when the supper was quite ready, she said, "Will you have some supper, Sister Smith?" I thanked her, and told her I would.

While I was eating my supper who should come in but good Brother Holland, that had been on the boat. He said to Brother and Sister Cooper, "I am glad you have Sister Smith here. You needn't be afraid of her, she is all right; I have known her for years. I have not seen her since I was pastor at Lancaster."

Then they brightened up a little bit, and seemed to be a little more natural. My heart was glad. It was quarterly meeting, and Brother Holland was to preach in the morning and Brother Cooper in the afternoon. So Brother Holland said, as he was Presiding Elder, I might speak at night and tell my story[.]

"All right," I said.

After a little talk, Brother Holland left. Sister Cooper said she would be very glad to have me stay all night, but they had no room. They had not been long there, and had only fitted up one room for their own use. They thought they would make out with that for the winter. So then I was obliged to walk a mile and a half back to Sister Curtis'. I did hate to do it, but the Lord helped me.

So I stayed that night at Sister Curtis', and she gave me a little breakfast on Sunday morning, but it was mighty skimpy! But I found out that a good deal of praying fills you up pretty well when you cannot get anything else! On Sunday morning we went to Love Feast, and had a good time. Prior to this I had been asking the Lord to give me a message to give when I went to Salem. I said, "Lord, I don't want to go to Salem without a message. And now you are sending me to Salem, give me the message. What shall I say?"

Two or three times I had gone before the Lord with this prayer, and His word was, "It shall be made known to you when you come to the place what you shall say." And I said, "All right, Lord." So I didn't trouble Him any more till this Sunday morning. The Lord helped Brother

Holland preach. When he got through preaching and the collection was taken, Brother Cooper made the announcement that I was there; he said, "There is a lady here, Mrs. Amanda Smith" (he had never seen me before or heard of me, and he was a rather jovial kind of a man, and in making this announcement he said, in a half sarcastic and half joking way), "Mrs. Smith is from New York; she says the Lord sent her"; with a kind of toss of the head, which indicated that he did not much believe it. Oh, my heart fell down, and I said, "Oh! Lord, help. Give me the message."

The Lord saw that I had as much as I could stand up under, and He said, "Say, 'Have ye received the Holy Ghost since ye believed?' " (Acts 9:2). That was the message; the first message the Lord gave me. I trembled from head to foot.

A good sister took me home with her to dinner. The people all seemed very kind. I felt quite at home when I got with them. We came back in the afternoon and had a wonderful meeting.

At night after Brother Holland had preached a short sermon, he called me up to exhort. As I sat in the pulpit beside him, he saw I was frightened. He leaned over and said, "Now, my child, you needn't be afraid. Lean on the Lord. He will help you."

And He did help me. There was a large congregation. The gallery was full, and every part of the house was packed. I stood up trembling. The cold chills ran over me. My heart seemed to stand still. Oh, it was a night. But the Lord gave me great liberty in speaking. After I had talked a little while the cold chills stopped, my heart began to beat naturally and all fear was gone, and I seemed to lose sight of everybody and everything but my responsibility to God and my duty to the people. The Holy Ghost fell on the people and we had a wonderful time. Souls were convicted and some converted that night. But the meeting did not go on from that.

Thursday night was the regular prayer meeting night. Brother Cooper said I was there, and would preach Thursday night. He was going to give me a chance to preach, and he wanted all the people to come out.

There was no snow, but Oh! it was cold. The ground was frozen. The moon shone brightly, and the wind blew a perfect gale. One good thing, I did not have to go back to Sister Curtis'. Another good sister asked me to her house to stay. She made me very comfortable, but said I would have to be alone most of the day, as she was going to some of the neighbors to help with the butchering, as they do in the country. I was very glad of that, for it gave me a chance to pray. So I fasted and prayed and read my Bible nearly all day. Oh, I had a good time. And then I thought I would visit a neighbor near by, another friend. So I did; and this was a good old mother in Israel. I told her a little of my experience, and then I told her the message the Lord had given me to speak about, and how it would lead to the subject of sanctification.

"My child," she at once said, "don't you say a word about sanctification here. Honey, if you do, they will persecute you to death. My poor husband used to preach that doctrine, and for years he knew about this blessing. But, Oh! honey, they persecuted him to death. You must not say a word about it."

Well, there I was again! So I went home, and the next day I prayed to God all day. I asked Him to give me some other message. If this message was going to do so much damage, I did not want it. But no, the Lord held me to it. Not a ray of light on anything else but that. I didn't know what to do, but I made up my mind it was all I ever would do, so I would obey God and take the consequences. I thought sure from what the dear old mother told me that the results would be fatal; I didn't know but I would be driven out. But not so. "Obedience is better than sacrifice, and to hearken than the fat of rams." Thursday was a beautiful, bright day; but Oh! cold, bitterly cold. So I got down and prayed and said, "Lord, Thou hast sent me to Salem, and hast given me the message. Now for an evidence that Thou hast indeed sent me, grant to cause the wind to cease blowing at this fearful rate. Thou knowest Lord, that I want people to hear Thy message that Thou hast given me. They will not mind the cold, but the wind is so terrible. Now cause the wind to cease to blow, and make the people come out."

The wind blew all day; all the afternoon. I started to go across the field, about a half mile from where I was, to talk and pray with a friend. On my way back, about five o'clock, as I was crossing a ditch which ran through the field, bordered on either side by a row of hedge trees, and a little plank across it for a kind of a foot bridge, the wind wrapped me round and took me down into the ditch. I could not hold on, could not control myself. I expected to be thrown up against the trees, and I cried out to Him all alone, "Oh! Lord, Thou that didst command the wind to cease on the Sea of Galilee, cause this wind to cease and let me get home."

Just then there came a great calm, and I got up out of that ditch and ran along to the house. By the time we went to church it was as calm as a summer evening; it was cold, but not a bit windy—a beautiful, moonlight night.

The church was packed and crowded. I began my talk from the chapter given, with great trembling. I had gone on but a little ways when I felt the spirit of the Lord come upon me mightily. Oh! how He helped me. My soul was free. The Lord convicted sinners and backsliders and believers for holiness, and when I asked for persons to come to the altar, it was filled in a little while from the gallery and all parts of the house.

A revival broke out, and spread for twenty miles around. Oh! what a time it was. It went from the colored people to the white people. Sometimes we would go into the church at seven o'clock in the evening. I could not preach. The whole lower floor would be covered with seekers—old men, young men, old women, young women, boys and girls. Oh! glory to God! How He put His seal on this first work to encourage my heart and establish my faith, that He indeed had chosen, and ordained and sent me. I do not know as I have ever seen anything to equal that first work, the first seal that God gave to His work at Salem. Some of the young men that were converted are in the ministry. Some have died in the triumph of faith. Others are on the way. I went on two weeks, day and night. We used to stay in the church till one and two o'clock in the morning. People could not work. Some of the young men would hire a wagon and go out in the country ten miles and bring in a load, get them converted, and then take them back.

53 ▪ PAUL PROHIBITS THE PREACHING OF WOMEN

Nineteenth-century clergyman Cyrus Cort argues that Paul was an outstanding champion of evangelical freedom, yet he clearly opposed preaching by women in gender-mixed assemblies. Paul makes his position clear in 1 Corinthians 14 and 1 Timothy 2. Contradictory passages cited by Cort's opponents could only be construed to support female preaching by violating the meaning of the texts and the integrity of Paul's powers of reasoning.

Source: Cyrus Cort. "Woman Preaching Viewed in the Light of God's Word and Church History." *The Reformed Quarterly Review* 29 (1882): 124–26.

If Christianity was to mark a new departure from the established customs of the Jewish Church on this subject St. Paul would have been pre-eminently the one to enunciate and emphasize the new departure. But where do we find the great Apostle of the Gentiles ranging himself on this question? Not in favor of the right of women to preach or pray in public religious services. On the other hand his epistles furnish the classic passages on the opposite side.

Nothing could be more explicit and emphatic than the teachings of St. Paul on this subject. "Let your women keep silence in the churches; for it is not permitted unto them to speak. . . . It is a shame for women to speak in the church." "Let the women learn in silence with all subjection. I suffer not a woman to teach or usurp authority over the man but to be in silence" (see 1 Cor. 14:34, &c. 1 Tim. 2:11, &c.). We could not prohibit women from preaching in language more plain and positive than that here employed by the Apostle Paul.

He positively forbids women from preaching or speaking in public promiscuous assemblies of the church. If we believe in the inspiration of St. Paul and that the New Testament must be taken as our infallible guide in matters of Christian faith and practice we must oppose woman preaching as a dangerous innovation. Few have the hardihood to call in question the plain meaning of the passages just quoted as they stand by themselves and in their connexion. But there are some professing Christians who try to break the force of these passages by quoting others, which they suppose relate to the same subject. They violate fundamental rules of scriptural interpretation and throw discredit upon the Apostolic teaching by striving to prove that St. Paul allows in one place what he repeatedly forbids in other places. Distinct and positive passages must always rule the meaning of passages that are vague, indirect and doubtful in their meaning and application.

Thus when Paul tells us in the eleventh chapter of First Corinthians that "every woman that prayeth or prophesieth with her head uncovered dishonoreth her head," we are not to infer as some do that Paul admits the right of woman to pray and prophesy or preach provided she has proper covering for her head. If that were a correct and necessary inference then St. Paul would flatly contradict, in the fourteenth chapter of this epistle, what he taught or permitted in the eleventh, and the whole question would be involved in confusion.

Paul was not so careless or unsound a reasoner as that. His writings, on this point especially, are in all respects logical and consistent. If we read the eleventh chapter carefully we will see that he nowhere teaches or admits that it is right and proper for woman to pray or prophesy in public promiscuous assemblies either with or without a veil or covering to her head. He says that even nature teaches that it is unbecoming for her to pray or prophesy with uncovered head, but he does not say or admit that she has a right to pray or prophesy at all in the church. He is there discussing more particularly the matter of dress and the relation of the sexes and not the matter of preaching itself. It was an utter violation of the rules of modesty and female subordination for a woman to pray or prophesy publicly in that manner. Afterwards in the fourteenth chapter, when he comes to the subject of preaching itself and the conduct of public worship, he emphatically forbids woman to speak in the church at all, and declares in the next verse that "It is a shame for woman to speak in the church."

Calvin compares 1 Cor. 11:4, with 1 Cor. 14:34, &c., and significantly remarks *apostolus unum improbando alterum non probat*. In condemning the one thing the Apostle does not approve of the other. In censuring particularly the form and manner of the act he does not thereby necessarily say or admit that the act itself would be right and proper under any circumstances. For instance, a minister might say that it is very unbecoming for a set of men or boys to come stalking along the church aisle engaged in boisterous conversation with their hats on during divine service. By such a remark he would not admit that it would be right and proper for them to engage in such conversation with their hats off. So St. Paul, in condemning women for praying and preaching with uncovered head, does not admit their right to pray or preach at all in promiscuous assemblies.

The passage in the eleventh chapter does not contradict or modify the emphatic and distinct deliverance in the fourteenth chapter.

54 ▪ METHODIST DEACONESSES

In 1888 the Methodist Episcopal Church began to license women as deaconesses set apart for medical and social work. The Chicago Training School, launched by Lucy Ryder Meyer (1849–1922), was the church's first home for deaconesses. Meyer saw the position of deaconess as a liberating life for women, freeing them from domestic concerns so that they could pursue work as teachers, nurses, and social workers. Her 1893 address on the movement describes deaconesses as unsalaried, costumed, and trained women who, because of their community life, were free to put the gospel into action in America's cities. She seems anxious to distinguish the deaconesses from women in Catholic orders, stressing that they take no vows, adopt a special costume only because it is economical, and share an open, natural communal existence.

Source: Lucy Ryder Meyer. "Deaconesses and Their Work." In *Woman in Missions: Papers and Addresses Presented at the Woman's Congress of Missions, October 2–4, 1893 in the Hall of Columbus, Chicago*, compiled by E. M. Wherry, 189–92. New York: American Tract Society, 1893.

But notice further. Deaconesses are volunteers, and this simple fact at once places our work on a plane which raises it above whole classes of motives appealing to ordinary workers. Our women come when they will—provided they will submit themselves to the requirements of training, etc.—they go when they please. That is, theoretically they "go"—actually they stay. The work has been established in our church now more than six years, and it numbers more than three hundred women, and one of the great surprises in connection with it has been that, while some have resigned on account of health, so few have left. Some have gone home to care for dependent parents, four have been married in our parlors or chapels, but most of them stay by the work. We ask but one question of importance, of women desiring to become deaconesses, and that is, "Do you believe God has called you to the work?" And if God calls them they will stay. I used to fear that money inducements would affect our workers, especially our nurses; but, though offers of salaried positions have frequently been made them, very rarely has there been a response, even when the position has been associated with other philanthropic work. Our women use money mostly to give it away, and the longer they remain with us the more fully does the power of money as a motive seem to vanish from their lives.

This brings me to the subject of unsalaried work. As I have before stated, deaconesses are entirely and comfortably supported in their work; they have the guarantee of support and all needed care in sickness or old age; they have their allowance for pin-money; but they are entirely un-salaried. Much might be said in favor of our support coming as it does. It entirely relieves us of all questions concerning dress—how our garments are to be obtained and paid for, and how they are to be made. We give the matter not a single thought. Blessed relief! One might almost be tempted to become a deaconess from this motive alone. We have that thing most necessary for our work,

> "A heart at leisure from itself
> To soothe and sympathize."

It gives us accessibility to the poor. We take no vows of poverty—we take no vows of any kind—but we must be simple and humble in our manner of life if we would reach the poor and simple people around us. It would require half our life to convince them of our sincerity and sympathy if we were to go to them in ordinary social ways. Benevolent work in great cities has peculiar difficulties. We meet many who have never felt one touch of brotherliness from Christians, and who have become embittered by the hard experiences of life. As they learn our errand they inevitably suspect us of mercenary motives. Professional religious and benevolent workers have in the past so uniformly worked *with* money that these poor people have the dreadful perversion firmly fixed in their minds that they work *for* money. Alas, alas, that Christian workers have become so sadly associated in the minds of the masses with money loving and money getting! "How much do you get a head," is their blunt question, "for getting our children into the Sunday-school?" "Who pays you for nursing our sick and cleaning our houses?" And nothing so surprises them into confidence and love as our simple answer, "No one pays us, we come only because we love you and want to help you if we may." It is recompense better than any thing earth has to offer that we may disarm prejudice and succeed in our work by the insignificant self-denial of working without a salary. We are unsalaried that there may be more laborers in the field. There is no such demand for phil-anthropic effort today in civilized lands as exists in great cities, and shame would be to us if in this great emergency we women should stand back on our "rights" and refuse to do what we can.

Then there is another consideration: there has never been any money to pay salaries with. Every missionary society is constantly working up to the full measure of its financial ability in paying its regular missionaries. It has been from the first not a question of salary or no salary, but no salary or no existence.

I must devote a few moments to the consideration of our community life, for, while living in a community is not a necessary condition of dea-coness work, the fact is that, since great cities are the principal scenes of deaconess work, deaconesses usually live in a community. It is exceedingly economical, and is exceedingly pleasant. It solves the problem of helpful and congenial companionship. It is said that it will foster a tendency to an introverted and unnatural life; but we cannot think so, so long as continued residence is entirely voluntary, and so long as our workers are constantly in healthful contact with the outside world in their daily activities. Bear in mind also that there is no secrecy or mystery in our Deaconess Homes. This thing is not done in a corner. We do not even have "visiting days"; all our days are visiting days. We are modelled after the family. Absolute freedom in correspondence, such social life as does not interfere with our peculiar calling, and the privilege of leaving the Home at any time—these guard against any possible tendency to danger. The happiest place on earth is doubtless the family, where the father and mother gather the little ones about their knees and each finds his highest joy in living for others; but the next happiest place ought to be our Homes, out from which congenial souls go, day by day, to the joy of working for others, coming back at night to sympathetic converse with each other, and, if need be, to wise and loving counsel from their superintendent. One of the most touching testimonies I have ever heard came from the lips of a deaconess who had long lived in crowded but lonely boarding-houses, but who was now rejoicing that God had "set the solitary in a family."

55 · WOMEN RE-VISION THE BIBLE

Toward the end of her life, Elizabeth Cady Stanton (1815–1902) came to believe that the Bible was the greatest obstacle to women's rights in America. In response she organized a committee of learned women to write commentaries on those portions of the Bible that deal with women. The result was The Woman's Bible, *published in two parts in 1895 and 1898. The commentaries draw attention to the patriarchal character of much of the material while appropriating some of it for feminism. Both commentaries below are from the pen of Cady Stanton. Vashti is presented to the reader as a "grand type of woman" who valued her dignity and modesty above obedience to her husband. The thoughts on Jesus' parable of the wise and foolish virgins reject the traditional tendency to see this as a story about eternal salvation and final judgment in favor of the claim that foolish virgins are women who have failed to develop their own minds and spirits.*

Source: Elizabeth Cady Stanton, ed. *The Woman's Bible.* Part 2:84–86, 123–26. Reprint. Edinburgh: Polygon Books, 1985.

Comments on Esther

The kingdom of Ahasuerus extended from India to Ethiopia, consisting of one hundred and twenty-seven provinces, an overgrown kingdom which in time sunk by its own weight. The king was fond of display and invited subjects from all his provinces to come by turns to behold his magnificent palaces and sumptuous entertainments.

He gave two great feasts in the beginning of his reign, one to the nobles and the princes, and one to the people, which lasted over a hundred days. The king had the feast for the men spread in the court under the trees. Vashti entertained her guests in the great hall of the palace. It was not the custom among the Persians for the sexes to eat promiscuously together, especially when the king and the princes were partaking freely of wine.

This feast ended in heaviness, not as Balshazzar's with a handwriting on the wall, nor like that of Job's children with a wind from the wilderness, but by the folly of the king, with an unhappy falling out between the queen and himself, which ended the feast abruptly and sent the guests away silent and ashamed. He sent seven different messages to Vashti to put on her royal crown, which greatly enhanced her beauty, and come to show his guests the majesty of his queen. But to all the chamberlains alike she said, "Go tell the king I will not come; dignity and modesty alike forbid."

This vanity of a drunken man illustrates the truth of an old proverb, "When the wine is in, the wit is out." Josephus says that all the court heard his command; hence, while he was showing the glory of his court, he also showed that he had a wife who would do as she pleased.

Besides seven chamberlains he had seven learned counsellors whom he consulted on all the affairs of State. The day after the feast, when all were sober once more, they held a cabinet council to discuss a proper punishment for the rebellious queen. Memucan, Secretary of State, advised that she be divorced for her disobedience and ordered "to come no more before the king," for unless she was severely punished, he said, all the women of Medea and of Persia would despise the commands of their husbands.

We have some grand types of women presented for our admiration in the Bible. Deborah for her courage and military prowess; Huldah for her learning, prophetic insight and statesmanship, seated in the college in Jerusalem, where Josiah the king sent his cabinet ministers to consult her as to the policy of his government; Esther, who ruled as well as reigned, and Vashti, who scorned the Apostle's command, "Wives, obey your husbands." She refused the king's orders to grace with her presence his revelling court. Tennyson pays this tribute to her virtue and dignity:

> "Oh, Vashti! noble Vashti!
> Summoned forth, she kept her state,
> And left the drunken king to brawl
> In Shushan underneath his palms. . . . "

Comments on Matthew

In this chapter we have the duty of self-development impressively and repeatedly urged in the form of parables, addressed alike to man and to woman. The sin of neglecting and of burying one's talents, capacities and powers, and the penalties which such a course involve, are here strikingly portrayed.

This parable is found among the Jewish records substantially the same as in our own Scriptures. Their weddings were generally celebrated at night; yet they usually began at the rising of the evening star; but in this case there was a more than ordinary delay. Adam Clarke in his commentaries explains this parable as referring chiefly to spiritual gifts and the religious life. He makes the Lord of Hosts the bridegroom, the judgment day the wedding feast, the foolish virgins the sinners whose hearts were cold and dead, devoid of all spiritual graces, and unfit to enter the kingdom of heaven. The wise virgins were the saints who were ready for translation, or for the bridal procession. They followed to the wedding feast; and when the chosen had entered *"the door was shut."*

This strikes us as a strained interpretation of a very simple parable, which, considered in connection with the other parables, seems to apply much more closely to this life than to that which is to come, to the intellectual and the moral nature, and to the whole round of human duties. It fairly describes the two classes which help to make up society in general. The one who, like the foolish virgins, have never learned the first important duty of cultivating their own individual powers, using the talents given to them, and keeping their own lamps trimmed and burning. The idea of being a helpmeet to somebody else has been so sedulously drilled into most women that an individual life, aim, purpose and ambition are never taken into consideration. They ofttimes do so much in other directions that they neglect the most vital duties to themselves.

We may find in this simple parable a lesson for the cultivation of courage and of self-reliance. These virgins are summoned to the discharge of an important duty at midnight, alone, in darkness, and in solitude. No chivalrous gentleman is there to run for oil and to trim their lamps. They must depend on themselves, unsupported, and pay the penalty of their own improvidence and unwisdom. Perhaps in that bridal procession might have been seen fathers, brothers, friends, for whose service and amusement the foolish virgins had wasted many precious hours, when they should have been trimming their own lamps and keeping oil in their vessels.

And now, with music, banners, lanterns, torches, guns and rockets fired at intervals, come the bride and the groom, with their attendants and friends numbering thousands, brilliant in jewels, gold and silver, magnificently mounted on richly caparisoned horses—for nothing can be more brilliant than were those nuptial solemnities of Eastern nations. As this spectacle, grand beyond description, sweeps by, imagine the foolish virgins pushed aside, in the shadow of some tall edifice, with dark, empty lamps in their hands, unnoticed and unknown. And while the castle walls resound with music and merriment, and the lights from every window stream out far into the darkness, no kind friends gather round them to sympathize in their humiliation, nor to cheer their loneliness. It matters little that women may be ignorant, dependent, unprepared for trial and for temptation. Alone they must meet the terrible emergencies of life, to be sustained and protected amid danger and death by their own courage, skill and self-reliance, or perish.

Woman's devotion to the comfort, the education, the success of men in general, and to their plans and projects, is in a great measure due to her self-abnegation and self-sacrifice having been so long and so sweetly lauded by poets, philosophers and priests as the acme of human goodness and glory.

Now, to my mind, there is nothing commendable in the action of young women who go about begging funds to educate young men for the ministry, while they and the majority of their sex are too poor to educate themselves, and if able, are still denied admittance into some of the leading institutions of learning throughout our land. It is not commendable for women to get up fairs and donation parties for churches in which the gifted of their sex may neither pray, preach, share in the offices and honors, nor have a voice in the business affairs, creeds and discipline, and from whose altars come forth Biblical interpretations in favor of woman's subjection.

It is not commendable for the women of this Republic to expend much enthusiasm on political parties as now organized, nor in national celebrations, for they have as yet no lot or part in the great experiment of self-government.

In their ignorance, women sacrifice themselves to educate the men of their households, and to make of themselves ladders by which their husbands, brothers and sons climb up into the kingdom of knowledge, while they themselves are shut out from all intellectual companionship, even with those they love best; such are indeed like the foolish virgins. They have not kept their own lamps trimmed and burning; they have no oil in their vessels, no resources in themselves; they bring no light to their households nor to the circle in which they move; and when the bridegroom cometh, when the philosopher, the scientist, the saint, the scholar, the great and the learned, all come together to celebrate the marriage feast of science and religion, the foolish virgins, though present, are practically shut out; for what know they of the grand themes which inspire each tongue and kindle every thought? Even the brothers and the sons whom they have educated, now rise to heights which they cannot reach, span distances which they cannot comprehend.

The solitude of ignorance, oh, who can measure its misery!

The wise virgins are they who keep their lamps trimmed, who burn oil in their vessels for their own use, who have improved every advantage for their education, secured a healthy, happy, complete development, and entered all the profitable avenues of labor, for self-support, so that when the opportunities and the responsibilities of life come, they may be fitted fully to enjoy the one and ably to discharge the other.

These are the women who to-day are close upon the heels of man in the whole realm of thought, in art, in science, in literature and in government. With telescopic vision they explore the starry firmament, and bring back the history of the planetary world. With chart and compass they pilot ships across the mighty deep, and with skilful fingers send electric messages around the world. In galleries of art, the grandeur of nature and the greatness of humanity are immortalized by them on canvas, and by their inspired touch, dull blocks of marble are transformed into angels of light. In music they speak again the language of Mendelssohn, of Beethoven, of Chopin, of Schumann, and are worthy interpreters of their great souls. The poetry and the novels of the century are theirs; they, too, have touched the keynote of reform in religion, in politics and in social life. They fill the editors' and the professors' chairs, plead at the bar of justice, walk the wards of the hospital, and speak from the pulpit and the platform.

Such is the widespread preparation for the marriage feast of science and religion; such is the type of womanhood which the bridegroom of an enlightened public sentiment welcomes to-day; and such is the triumph of the wise virgins over the folly, the ignorance and the degradation of the past as in grand procession they enter the temple of knowledge, and *the door is no longer shut*.

Chapter 8

AMERICAN WOMEN
IN CATHOLICISM
AND SECTARIANISM

56 ▪ THE VATICAN ON THE ROLE OF WOMEN

The encyclical "On Christian Marriage" was published on December 31, 1930,
in response to what the Vatican saw as a new and perverse morality trampling
Christian marriage underfoot. Among the most pernicious changes were the
proliferation of abortion and the use of contraception as well as a general
cultural acceptance of divorce and adultery as "free from reproach and infamy."
The remedy was obedience to the church. The Vatican early in the letter affirms
all the points of Leo XIII's encyclical "Arcanum," which restated the church's
position that marriage is indissoluble in the face of civil legislation to make
divorce more readily available. "On Christian Marriage" warns women that
they are in danger of losing their regal throne as wives and mothers if they
pursue their own affairs outside the home. They are also reminded that in their
dignified and noble state they are still subject to their husbands.

Source: "On Christian Marriage: Encyclical Letter of His Holiness Pope Pius XI."
The Catholic Mind 29 (January 22, 1931): 29–30, 44–45.

Domestic society being confirmed therefore by this bond of love, it is necessary that there should flourish in it "order of love," as St. Augustine calls
it. This order includes both primacy of the husband with regard to the wife
and children, and the ready subjection of the wife and her willing obedience which the Apostle commends in these words: "Let women be subject
to their husbands as to the Lord, because the husband is the head of the
wife, as Christ is the head of the Church."

This subjection, however, does not deny or take away the liberty which
fully belongs to the woman both in view of her dignity as a human person,
and in view of her most noble office as wife and mother and companion;
nor does it bid her obey her husband's every request even if not in harmony
with right reason or with the dignity due to wife; nor, in fine, does it imply

163

that the wife should be put on a level with those persons who in law are called minors, to whom it is not customary to allow free exercise of their rights on account of their lack of mature judgment, or of their ignorance of human affairs. But it forbids that exaggerated license which cares not for the good of the family; it forbids that in this body which is the family, the heart be separated from the head to the great detriment of the whole body and the proximate danger of ruin. For if the man is the head, the woman is the heart, and as he occupies the chief place in ruling, so she may and ought to claim for herself the chief place in love.

Again, this subjection of wife to husband in its degree and manner may vary according to the different conditions of persons, place and time; in fact, if the husband neglect his duty, it falls to the wife to take his place in directing the family. But the structure of the family and its fundamental law established and confirmed by God, must always and everywhere be maintained intact.

With great wisdom Our predecessor Leo XIII, of happy memory, in the Encyclical which We have already mentioned on Christian marriages, teaches with regard to this order to be maintained between man and wife:

> The man is the ruler of the family, and the head of the woman, but because she is flesh of his flesh and bone of his bone, let her be subject and obedient to the man not as a servant but as a companion, so that nothing be lacking of honor or of dignity in the obedience which she pays. Both in him who rules and in her who obeys, since each bears the image, the one of Christ, the other of the Church, let Divine charity be the constant guide of their mutual relations.

These, then, are the elements which compose the blessing of conjugal faith: unity, chastity, honorable, noble obedience, which are at the same time an enumeration of the benefits which are bestowed on husband and wife in their married state; benefits by which the peace, the dignity and the happiness of matrimony are securely preserved and fostered. Wherefore it is not surprising that this conjugal faith has always been counted amongst the most priceless and special blessings of matrimony....

The same false teachers who try to dim the luster of conjugal faith and purity do not scruple to do away with the honorable and trusting obedience which the woman owes to the man. Many of them even go further and assert that such a subjection of one party to the other is unworthy of human dignity, that the rights of husband and wife are equal, wherefore, they boldly proclaim, the emancipation of women has been or ought to be effected. This emancipation in their ideas must be threefold, in the ruling of the domestic society, in the administration of family affairs and in the rearing of the children. It must be social, economic, physiological, that is to say the woman is to be freed at her own good pleasure from the burdensome duties properly belonging to a wife as companion and mother (We have already said that this is not an emancipation but a crime); social, inasmuch as the wife being freed from the cares of children and family, should, to the neglect of these, be able to follow her own bent and devote herself to business and even public affairs; finally, economic, whereby the woman even without the knowledge and against the wish of her husband may be at liberty to conduct and administer her own affairs, giving her attention chiefly to these rather than to children, husband and family.

This, however, is not the true emancipation of woman, nor that rational and exalted liberty which belongs to the noble office of a Christian woman and wife. It is rather the debasing of the womanly character and the dignity of motherhood and indeed of the whole family, as a result of which the husband suffers the loss of his wife, the children of their mother, and the home and the whole family of an ever-watchful guardian. More than this, this false liberty and unnatural equality with the husband is to the detriment of the woman herself, for if the woman descends from her truly regal throne to which she has been raised within the walls of the home by means of the Gospel, she will soon be reduced to the old state of slavery, if not in appearance, certainly in reality, and become as amongst the pagans the mere instrument of man.

This equality of rights which is so much exaggerated and distorted must indeed be recognized in those rights which belong to the dignity of the human and which are proper to the marriage contract and inseparably bound up with wedlock. In such things undoubtedly both parties enjoy the same rights and are bound by the same obligation. In other things there must be a certain inequality and due accommodation, which is demanded by the good of the family and the right ordering and unity and stability of home life. As, however, the social and economic conditions of the married woman must in some way be altered on account of the changes in social intercourse, it is part of the office of the public authority to adapt the civil rights of the wife to modern needs and requirements, keeping in view what the natural disposition and temperament of the female sex, good morality, and the welfare of the family demand, and provided always that the essential order of the domestic society remain intact, founded as it is on something higher than human authority and wisdom, namely, on the authority and wisdom of God, and so not changeable by public laws or at the pleasure of private individuals. These enemies of marriage go further, however, when they substitute for that true and solid love, which is the basis of conjugal happiness, a certain vague compatibility of temperament. This they call sympathy and assert that since it is the only bond by which husband and wife are linked together, when it ceases the marriage is completely dissolved. What else is this than to build a house upon sand? A house that, in the words of Christ, would forthwith be shaken and collapse as soon as it was exposed to the waves of adversity: "And the winds blew and they beat upon that house, and it fell. And great was the fall thereof." On the other hand, the house built upon a rock, that is to say, on mutual conjugal chastity and strengthened by a deliberate and constant union of spirit, will not only never fall away but will never be shaken by adversity.

57 • CATHOLIC SISTERS AS AMERICA'S EDUCATORS

Born into a wealthy Bavarian family, Mother Caroline Friess (1824–1892) joined the School Sisters of Notre Dame when she was sixteen. The order had been established by Mother Teresa Gerhardinger to engage in the work of parochial education. In 1847, in response to a request from the Redemptorist priests in America, Friess traveled to the United States with a small party of sisters to relieve the urgent need of teachers for German Catholic immigrants. Friess was eventually charged with establishing a motherhouse in Milwaukee and overseeing the order's American missions, which included by the time of her death over two hundred schools. Friess had to contend with a variety of prejudices that impeded the work of the sisters. Their teaching methods and pragmatic curriculum, however, won them praise among Catholic and Protestant parents alike. She also had to confront—and summon her courage to change—the church's requirement that all consecrated virgins be cloistered.

Source: [Sister Dympna.] *Mother Caroline and the School Sisters of Notre Dame in North America.* Volume 1:36–41, 46–49. Saint Louis: Woodward and Tiernan Co., 1928.

The months of July and August, 1848, were spent by the sisters in the convent in Baltimore in preparation for their work in the schools, especially in the study of English, for which Father Neumann provided teachers. On the nineteenth of August, Sister Caroline began the work assigned her by Mother Teresa, that of opening new schools and superintending those already established. Taking with her Sister Edmund and three candidates, she proceeded to Philadelphia where she opened St. Peter's School, August 21, 1848. The Redemptorist Fathers, at whose invitation they had come, gave them a cordial welcome and promised the kindly interest and aid of their parishioners. On the opening day one hundred seventy girls were enrolled; the boys numbered one hundred sixty-two. The latter were taught by lay teachers until 1853 when Brothers of the Christian Schools were obtained for them. In the beginning the sisters in St. Peter's School endured many hardships; poverty and even hunger were borne unflinchingly for several weeks. Conditions were such that they were not permitted to wear their religious garb for some time....

This agitation extended from 1834 to 1844 through several dioceses in a most frightful manner, and in Philadelphia resulted in a civil war. Through the pulpit and the press, fanatics spread inflammatory reports anent the horrors committed in convents, the tortures nuns are subjected to when they would escape, and many other common calumnies. New England provided a fertile soil for the growth of this noxious weed. The mob of Boston attacked the Ursuline Convent of Mt. Benedict August 11, 1834, and destroyed it by fire and pillage, ransacking even the sacred graves of the dead.

In Philadelphia, a band of lawless men identifying themselves as Native Americans brought things to a crisis in May, 1844, and again in July of the same year. Their spirit was the spirit of "Knownothingism," rampant in Philadelphia and directed especially against foreigners and Catholics. Fanatical mobs committed ravages and outrages of all kinds. They attacked Catholic citizens and drove them from their homes, which they pillaged and burned. St. Michael's Church and presbytery adjoining, were destroyed by these firebrands. St. Augustine's Church, rectory, and the newly built convent of the Sisters of Charity of the Blessed Virgin Mary, also fell a prey to the flames. The precious library of the Hermits of St. Augustine was plundered, the books piled up and burned. This loss can never be repaired.

The Augustinian rectory that was burned had at the time been converted by the Reverend Father Hurley, O.S.A., into a hospital for the victims of cholera. Out of three hundred and sixty-seven patients whom he helped to nurse, only forty-eight were Catholics; the others were professing Protestants. On the blackened walls of St. Augustine's Church there remained only the inscription

"The Lord Seeth"

Such were the religious riots in Philadelphia, the smouldering fires of which were ready to flame up anew when Sister Caroline introduced the sisters to the Redemptorist Fathers of St. Peter's Church. The sisters were insulted on the streets, pelted with mud. They lived in unvarying dread of being molested at night, kept valises packed within easy reach, and slept in especially prepared robes, that they might appear respectable, if driven into the street by fire or marauders. During the last week of September, Sister Caroline was obliged to leave the sisters a prey to these anxieties, as her presence was required at the opening of St. Philomena's School in Pittsburgh, where the sisters were to enter the ranks of the fast increasing pioneers of Bishop O'Connor's diocese. . . .

Father Starke, C.SS.R., and the other Redemptorist Fathers of St. Philomena's Church, welcomed the sisters as cordially as their confreres had done in Philadelphia. Bishop O'Connor blessed the school building, and, at the mass, preached to a large congregation, many of whom were parents and relations of the pupils confided to the care of the new teachers. Fortunately, better conditions prevailed here, and the sisters were spared the hardships and sufferings borne by their companions in the city of Brotherly Love! Sister Caroline divided her time among the six schools now established: St. Mary's in Pennsylvania, St. James', St. Michael's and St. Alphonsus' in Baltimore, St. Peter's in Philadelphia, and St. Philomena's in Pittsburgh. Happily, the blessing of the God of peace and love rested intimately on the indefatigable labors of the Redemptorist Fathers and the School Sisters of Notre Dame. Sister Caroline returned to Philadelphia before Christmas to find that the sisters, who had at first lived in a private house at some distance from the school, now occupied a part of the church basement as a dwelling. Here they were blessed with at least conventual privacy, and with a sense of protection. Sister Caroline devoted no little attention to the class of first communicants. She instructed them in Christian Doctrine, devotional practices, in the virtues of the Christian home, in habits of neatness and clean living, and so successfully that her name and those of her devoted companions became household words among the parishioners, who gladly testified to the happy change wrought in their children during the first year spent in the sisters' school. . . .

The sisters had been in America nearly three years and had borne many sufferings and privations. They had successfully surmounted all obstacles save one—the restriction imposed by the rule of enclosure, rigidly enforced by Mother Teresa, and on which she had insisted in every letter written to the American sisters. Mother Seraphine and her advisers were in sympathy with Mother Teresa, preferring to forgo the founding of new schools rather than submit to constitutional modifications. Mother Seraphine, and those of the same opinion were actuated by the noblest motives of adhering to the spirit and the letter of the constitutions. Mother Teresa was justified in her stand because the Church required all consecrated virgins to be protected by the rule of enclosure, which permitted communication with the outside world only through grills, and because the Holy See would not sanction the rule of a community lax in observing the cloister regulations.

It will be seen from the following incident that Mother Teresa had been accustomed from earliest childhood to the requirements of cloistered life. When she attended the school of the Sisters of St. Peter Fourier, in Stadtamhof, as a very young child, her father carried her to school every morning, placed her in the convent "turn," and waited till the bell announced that his daughter had been taken safely in by one of the sisters. When he called for her every evening she was returned to him in the same manner.

Sister Caroline and her advisers and fellow teachers, having had more opportunity to try out the letter of the constitutions, had, from experience, obtained broader vision, and thus felt assured that, in this instance, the letter of the law ought to be modified to preserve its spirit. They had learned by experience that the poverty of bishops, priests and people in this country was so great that it was an impossibility to have the school and convent built adjacent to the church. Without this arrangement, the sisters might not accompany their pupils to church, nor assist at mass on week days. For the privilege of hearing mass on Sundays and of receiving the sacraments in the parish church, dispensation had to be obtained from the religious superiors and from the bishop of the diocese. They knew also that it was impossible to confer with parents or with externs, only through the grate. This would oblige the sisters to leave their pupils unattended in the classrooms while escorting callers to the convent parlor. Sister Caroline had studied the question thoroughly before joining the community, and had been advised by bishops and priests to choose the newly established congregation because its founders had expressly stated that the new constitutions would have to be adapted to the exigencies of the times. She knew of the efforts made by St. Francis de Sales to have the Sisters of the Visitation founded as an active order, and that for five years they worked unhampered among the children of the poor before he was obliged to withdraw and place them within the cloister. St. Peter Fourier met with powerful opposition when he insisted that the Sisters of Notre Dame should teach children who came to them in the morning and returned to their homes in the evening. Like the Carmelites in Baltimore, when for twenty years, 1831–1851, they taught school on Aisquith Street—Archbishop Carroll having obtained a dispensation for them from the Holy See—the sisters who taught these poor children were permitted to speak to them only in the classrooms; they were bound to restrict themselves in instructing them. In neither case were the teachers permitted to speak to their companions within the cloister concerning pupils or their parents. That conditions such as these militated against the Congregation of the School Sisters in America, was quite apparent. Besides, the sisters were permitted to wear their religious habit only when within the convent walls. The Redemptorists, especially Father Neumann and Father Helmprecht, both of whom were enlightened and practical men, had often urged the sisters to seek a modification of the constitutions. Correspondence had effected nothing, except misunderstanding and misinterpretation of the sisters' motives. Mother

Teresa ignored their letters, and for a year communication with the Mother House in Europe ceased.

In this predicament, Mother Seraphine determined to assume the responsibility of taking the initiative, in hope of securing a definite decision. It was decided that Sister Caroline should go to Europe to confer with Mother Teresa and Father Siegert and solicit a favorable settlement of this important question.

It required great heroism on the part of the young sister to undertake a voyage to Europe on such an errand. Not only was she obliged to travel without a companion or a maid, but without credentials of any kind, for Mother Seraphine had failed to write a letter of explanation to Mother Teresa, nor had she announced Sister Caroline's visit. How would she convince the sisters in Europe that she had crossed the ocean in obedience to the command of her lawful superior, and that she had been commissioned to represent the American sisters in a matter of supreme importance?

She sailed from New York, July 31, 1850, on the third anniversary of her arrival in America. She became very ill from the effects of the voyage during which violent storms whipped the sea and threatened to submerge the vessel. Word went round among the passengers that the sister on board was too ill to speak to any one, and because she kept her cabin door locked, no one could go to her assistance. A Catholic bishop was on board and went to inquire as to the truth of the rumor. Sister Caroline, after being assured that he was really a prelate of the Church, admitted him, gratefully received advice about accepting the care of the stewardess, and was much encouraged by his fatherly interest in her. He was the Right Reverend Bernard O'Rielly, D.D., of Hartford, Connecticut, on a visit to Rome. Returning from one of these visits he perished at sea, January, 1856.

Sister Caroline reached the Mother House on the Feast of the Assumption, three years from the day of the sisters' arrival at St. Mary's. Her apprehensions were realized; she was received with mistrust by the sisters, who supposed she had run away from America. Father Siegert was the first to accord her full and honest recognition. Mother Teresa did not relent. She assigned Sister Caroline to rooms in the guests' quarters and forbade communication with any of the sisters. This was a sore trial to a person of Sister Caroline's honest and loyal disposition. Finally, she asked for an interview with Archbishop Reisach who had been her friend and director for many years, and who now became her support and comforter in this painful ordeal. Her uncle, Father Friess, assured her that the cause for which she had been sent to plead tended to the glory of God and the good of souls, and must eventually prevail.

In the archbishop and Father Siegert she had two powerful advocates, who succeeded in convincing Mother Teresa that she must either withdraw her sisters from America or avail herself of the provisions made by Bishop Wittmann and Father Job in the constitutions for such emergencies: "If branch houses be established wherein you have no chapel, nor service of your own, there will be no other alternative than to cross your threshold, in order to attend divine service in your parish church. Love of religious modesty that should everywhere accompany you, will then serve as a substitute for the enclosure." These two holy founders had always insisted that the constitutions of the re-established congregation must be adapted to the changed conditions of the times, if the sisters were to accomplish all that the Church expected in the reclaiming of the masses through the education of children.

The negotiations were eminently successful. Not only was the enclosure for the sisters in America mitigated for all practical purposes, but the decision was made to appoint Sister Caroline to the full charge of the American branch of the congregation, with the title of Vicar to the Superior General.

58 · CATHOLIC SISTERS AS CIVIL WAR NURSES

In May of 1862 the surgeon in charge of the massive Satterlee Military Hospital in West Philadelphia requested the services of twenty-five Daughters of Charity. He showed a deliberate preference for the sisters over other women involved in benevolent work, perhaps because of their reputed nursing skills, perhaps because of their vow of celibacy. Ninety-one sisters were involved at one time or another at Satterlee until the war ended. Their service is recorded in the journal of Sister Gonzaga, part of which forms the first section of this document, and in the detailed diary entries of a group of unnamed sisters. We learn from the sisters that they earned the respect of physicians, clergy, and patients through their efficient and compassionate nursing. We also learn that they did not hesitate to teach the Catholic faith to the curious and uninformed, sometimes dispelling a lifetime of preconceived ideas.

Source: "Notes on the Satterlee Military Hospital, West Philadelphia, Penna.: From 1862 until Its Close in 1865." *American Catholic Historical Society of Philadelphia. Record* 8 (1897): 403–7, 429–32, 439–40.

In May of 1864, the Jubilee was celebrated at Satterlee Hospital. Our poor sufferers were most happy to have it in their power to obtain this great indulgence. Many received the Sacraments who had not approached them for ten, fifteen, and some for twenty-five years. One had been forty years without going to Confession. He had lived on bad terms with his wife, but he sent for her that they might be reconciled before finishing the Jubilee.

The soldiers wore with the greatest confidence the Scapular, Miraculous Medal and Agnus Dei, and many attributed their preservation from injury to one or the other of these. A pale young man came one evening to the door of Sister N_____'s room for medicine, and, appearing to suffer as he placed his hand on his breast, Sister asked him if the wound was very painful. He answered no, but he knew it would have been mortal but for a pair of Scapulars his mother had placed on his neck before he left home. The bullet had passed through his uniform coat, battered his watch to pieces and lodged in his Scapular, leaving nothing more serious than a little soreness. He now wished to be instructed in regard to them, so that he might be invested with them by the chaplain before he returned to his regiment. Another—a Protestant—said that a friend of his had put the Scapulars on his neck the morning he left home, telling him that the Blessed Virgin would protect him and bring him safe through all dangers if he said a prayer to her every day. He had done so, and although his comrades had fallen on all sides of him, and a shell tore up the ground quite near his feet, he remained unharmed and even fearless. He said to Sister N_____: "I wish to be instructed and baptized." But as he was ordered to his regiment there was no time for it. We distributed a great number of medals and Agnus Deis; even Protestants asked for them before returning to the field, promising to wear them with respect and to say their prayers every day, "because," they said, "the Catholic soldiers who wear them escape so many dangers."

Cases of small-pox had occurred in the Hospital from time to time, but the patients were removed as soon as possible to the Small-pox Hospital, which was several miles from the city. The poor fellows were more distressed on account of their being sent away from the Sisters to be nursed than they were on account of the disease. It was heart-rending when the ambulance came to hear the poor fellows begging to be left, even if they had to be entirely alone, provided the Sisters would be near them to have the Sacraments administered in the hour of danger. We offered our services several times to attend these poor sick, but were told that the Government had sent them away to avoid contagion. At last, however, the Surgeon in Charge obtained permission to keep the small-pox patients in the camp some distance from the Hospital. The tents were made very comfortable, with good large stoves to heat them, and "flys" (double covers) over the tops. The next thing was to have the Sisters in readiness, in case their services were required. Every one was generous enough to offer herself for the duty, but it was thought more prudent to accept one who had had the disease. As soon as the soldiers learned that a Sister had been assigned to the camp, they said: "Well, if I get the small-pox now, I don't care, because one of our Sisters will take care of me." From November, 1864, until

May, 1865, we had upward of ninety cases—of whom nine or ten died. Two had the Black Small-pox. They were baptized before they died. We had, I may say, entire charge of the poor sufferers, as the physician who attended them seldom paid them a visit, but allowed us to do anything we thought proper for them. The patients were very little marked, and much benefitted by drinking freely of tea made from Saracenia Purpura, or Pitcher Plant. When the weather permitted, I visited those poor fellows almost every day. Like little children, at these times they expected some little treat of oranges, cakes, jellies, apples and such things, which we always had for them. They often said it was the Sisters who cured them and not the doctors, for they believed they were afraid of the disease. Our small-pox patients appeared to think that the Sisters were not like other human beings, or they would not attend such loathsome contagious diseases, which every one else shunned. One day I was advising an application to a man's face for poison—he would not see one of the doctors, because, he said, the doctor did him no good—and I told him this remedy had cured a Sister who was poisoned. The man looked at me in perfect astonishment. "A Sister!" he exclaimed. I answered "Yes." "Why!" said he, "I didn't know the Sisters ever got anything like that." I told him "To be sure they did. They are liable to take disease as well as any one else." "To be sure *not!*" he said, "For the boys often say they must be different from other people, for they do for us what no other person would do. They are not afraid of fevers, small-pox or anything else." The physicians acknowledged that they would have lost many more patients, had it not been for the Sisters' watchful care and knowledge of medicine. The officers as well as the soldiers showed the greatest respect for the Sisters. The Surgeon in Charge, Dr. I. J. Hayes, often remarked with pleasure that the Sisters had such influence over the soldiers. No matter how rudely they might behave, as soon as the Sister of that ward or any other made her appearance, they became quiet and orderly. They have often refused to go on night-watch or detailed duty for the doctor, but never once when the Sister asked it of them. The Surgeon in Charge gave orders upon our first arrival at the Hospital that any want of obedience or respect should be severely punished, but, happily, there was not a single instance of either. One incident will show the good feeling of all towards the Sisters. One of the patients of Ward _____ had been in town on a pass, and had indulged too freely in liquor, but on his return he went quietly to bed. Sister—not knowing his condition—took him his medicine, touched the bed-clothes to rouse him, and the poor man, being stupid and sleepy, thought his comrades were teasing him. He gave a blow that sent Sister and the medicine across the room. Some of the convalescents seized him by the collar and would have choked him if Sister had not interfered. He was reported and sent under an escort to the guard-house, where the stocks were being prepared for him. Nothing could be done for his release, as the Surgeon in Charge was absent. As soon as he returned, the Sisters begged that the poor man might return to his ward, and be relieved from all punishment as well as from the guard-house. The Surgeon said, as he could refuse nothing to the Sisters, their request was granted, but in order to make a strong impression on the soldiers, he dispatched an order to each ward, which was read at roll-call, to the effect that this man was released only at the earnest entreaty of the Sister Superior and the Sister of the ward. Otherwise, he would have been severely dealt with. When the poor man came to himself and learned what he had done, he begged a thousand pardons of Sister, and promised never to touch liquor again. On Christmas, Easter, Thanksgiving Day, etc., at our request all the prisoners in the guard-house were liberated. The officers often came to us to solicit favors from Dr. Hayes for them, as they "knew he would not refuse the Sisters anything they asked him."

As to the visitors at the Hospital, in the beginning some of them were very much prejudiced, and one day asked Dr. Hayes why he had the Sisters of Charity to nurse in his Hospital, when there were "ever so many" ladies who would be happy to do that service? He answered, because he considered the Sisters of Charity the only women in the world capable of nursing the sick properly. . . .

Lewis Bruce was baptized on January 25, 1865. His conversion was brought about through reading Catholic books. He said he had been taught to believe everything bad of Catholics. As soon as he learned the truth, his faith was so strong that he had no difficulty in believing anything the Church proposes. Before he knew the catechism, as well as after, he reduced to practice the doctrines of the Church with the docility of a child. He showed the sincerity of his conversion by overcoming a naturally stubborn and ungovernable disposition. Everyone noticed the great change in him previous to making his First Communion on March 19th, not quite one month after his baptism. The hand of God is plainly evident in one circumstance relative to that baptism. On Saturday morning he told Sister that the invalid corps to which he belonged was going away on Monday, and he had not been baptized, nor received sufficient instruction. Sister told him to see Father McGrane and tell him the circumstances, which he did. But as Father had not met him before, he hesitated about baptizing him, and told him to return on the following Friday. The poor boy repeated this to Sister, and added that he would have to leave on the next morning. Sister went to the chapel, and kneeling before the Blessed Sacrament, placed the poor boy in the Sacred Heart of Jesus, as an assured place of refuge, earnestly beseeching our Lord not to let the poor boy go away until he had received Baptism. Sister received a speedy answer to her prayer. The company did not leave on Monday, but was delayed for some time. The young man not only was baptized, but made his First Communion, and a little later, his Easter Communion also.

Another patient—of Ward H—was Andrew Hopkins, whose baptism we had the consolation to witness in our chapel. He had been a sufferer for two months. As soon as he was able to go about, he became Sister's "extra diet boy" (that means the one who brings the extra diet from the kitchen and performs other little offices for the Sister. They are generally well disposed and simple, docile natures, and there are many such in every ward). From day to day, Andrew would ask Sister questions regarding our religion, to which he generally received brief answers, as his own and Sister's time was so occupied. He generally concluded with something like this: "I wish I was a Christian; but I think that God must never have intended me to become one, for I have tried it so often. There is so much to be done to be a good one, that I often think I could never go through the half of it. I never was baptized, and was always knocked about up to the time I came into the army." He lost his parents while very young, and had no relatives to take an interest in him. Still, he showed signs of a good disposition, and was attracted to the practice of virtue more than many who have had the advantages of a good education. Sister gave him "The Catholic Christian Instructed," telling him to read it, and he would find therein the way to know how to love and serve God, and become a good Christian. After reading it, he believed its teachings, and immediately applied to Father McGrane for Baptism, telling him that he wished to become a Christian, now that he had found out the way. After having a long conversation with him, Father admired his dispositions very much, and told him to come to him that same evening after Vespers, when he gave him an instruction, and immediately baptized him, fearing that he would soon be sent to his regiment. It was really providential, for the next day he received orders to be ready to leave for his regiment within twenty-four hours. He regretted having to leave without being better instructed, that he might be better able—as he said himself—to instruct others whom he might meet who were as he had been. However, he said, he could not complain, Our Lord had done so much for him, and with what different feelings he could now enter the battlefield! He felt he was a child of God, and had a right to his place in heaven. He went away cheerfully to perform any duty assigned him, offering all to Our Lord in thanksgiving for these favors. Sister gave him a medal, telling him to wear it always, and to place himself under the protection of our Blessed Mother, who would obtain all blessings for him. She also advised him, if his regiment should stop at any place for a considerable time, to apply to the nearest priest for instruction for his First Communion. He was quite delighted at this prospect, and so left for his regiment. Poor Andrew, in the bustle of hospital life, had been almost forgotten when there arrived a letter from the Rev. Mr. Butler, showing us that we were not forgotten by Andrew, and that he did not neglect to profit by Sister's advice, to be instructed in the religion which he had so happily embraced. The following is the letter:

"Covington, Ky.,
"Jan. 5, 1864.

"Sister N _____

"Dear Sister: _____

"By the earnest request of one of your good converts, Andrew J. Hopkins, I send these few lines to express his heartfelt gratitude for your kindness to him during his stay in the Hospital, and especially to thank you a thousand times, with your chaplain, who baptized him, for all the instruction and spiritual assistance you have given him. I find him a very earnest and pious young man. I gave him constant instruction until he was able to make his First Communion, since which he has been a second time admitted to that Divine Favor. He asks me to present his compliments to you and your zealous Pastor, and assure him that he has faithfully kept his promises to him. Indeed, I regard him as one of the most pious and sincere converts I have ever known. Be assured, that his gratitude to you will never fail. Such cases afford you the hundredfold reward here below, for it is a great happiness to have drawn a soul to the service of God, and to have taught it to seek the things which are above, and not those which are of the earth. And certainly we have great confidence in the prayers of such souls to obtain for us the grace necessary for our perseverance in these labors of charity by which we serve the Person of Our Saviour in the persons of his poor earthly children. Present my respectful regards to your good chaplain, and also Andrew's earnest thanks. He is quite troubled by forgetting the Reverend gentleman's name. Will you kindly reply to this letter and let me have his name. Andrew also begs me to inquire for John Hughes, a sick soldier in the same ward with him. He has been in daily expectation of being sent to his regiment in East Tennessee. He has been off once, but had to return for want of officers to direct the men. As he may go at any moment, he requests your reply may be sent to me. With the highest regards, kind Sister, I am

"Your very humble servant in Christ,
"T. R. Butler, V.G.,
"Pastor of the Cathedral,
"Covington, Ky. . . . "

September 27th.—Quite an excitement was created about 2 o'clock, caused by the visit of Generals Sigel and Hammond. The former lost a leg in one of the late battles of Gettysburg, and has been since that time under the care of the Sisters in Washington. He is now able to go about on crutches. Dr. Hayes, with the principal surgeons, accompanied them in making the circuit of the Hospital. The patients, who were all eager to see once more their good old generals, who had stood by them so valiantly in the terrible engagement, came out of the wards as best they could, many of them also on crutches, and crowded in the corridors to cheer and welcome them as they passed along. One poor young lad, who was very sick, who Sister thought would feel the privation of not being able to see them, replied to her words of consolation: "Do not feel sorry on my account. I would any time rather see a Sister than a general, for it was a Sister, who came to see me when I was unable to help myself, in an old barn near Gettysburg, where I was. She dressed my wounds and gave me a drink, and took care of me until I came here." The poor boy is a Protestant, and never saw a Sister before that time.

59 ▪ COMPLEX MARRIAGE IN THE ONEIDA COMMUNITY

Bible Communism, a systematic exposition of the religious and social theories of the Oneida Association, was published in 1853 in part to dispel false rumors about the group's sexual practices. The theories presented are acknowledged as those of John Humphrey Noyes (1811–1886) and the association from its beginning. Noyes contended that the kingdom of God had been ushered in when Jerusalem was finally destroyed, but only in its heavenly form. The church, therefore, had continued to sustain traditional institutions. It was time for this to change and for the earthly kingdom to begin to take shape. The old order had to give way to new forms of living, but Noyes pointed out that even at Oneida, this would occur gradually. Bible Communism *presents an ideal rather than a description of reality. The selection below incorporates a number of propositions from the book's chapter on social theory. They argue that the marriage of one man to one woman will give way in the kingdom to the marriage of a believer to all other believers. Sexual intercourse will have its amative or affectionate side exalted over the propagative as the discharge of semen is prevented. Women will be freed from the dangers and burdens of childbearing and labor will no longer be divided along gender lines.*

Source: *Bible Communism: A Compilation from the Annual Reports and Other Publications of the Oneida Association and Its Branches,* 26–27, 31–32, 40–42, 45–48, 61–62. Brooklyn, N.Y.: Office of the Circular, 1853.

PROPOSITION V.— In the kingdom of heaven, the institution of marriage which assigns the exclusive possession of one woman to one man, does not exist. Matt. 22:23-30. "In the resurrection they neither marry nor are given in marriage...."

PROPOSITION VI.— In the kingdom of heaven, the intimate union of life and interests, which in the world is limited to pairs, extends through the whole body of believers; i.e. *complex* marriage takes the place of simple. John 17:21. Christ prayed that *all* believers might be one, *even as* he and the Father are one. His unity with the Father is defined in the words, *"All mine are thine, and all thine are mine."* Ver. 10. This perfect community of interests, then, will be the condition of *all*, when his prayer is answered. The universal unity of the members of Christ, is described in the same terms that are used to describe marriage-unity. Compare 1 Cor. 12:12-27, with Gen. 2:24. See also 1 Cor. 6:15-17, and Eph. 5:30-32....

PROPOSITION IX.— The abolishment of sexual exclusiveness is involved in the love-relation required between all believers by the express injunction of Christ and the apostles, and by the whole tenor of the New Testament. "The new commandment is, that we love one another," and that, not by pairs, as in the world, but *en masse*. We are required to love one another *fervently* (1 Peter 1:22) or, as the original might be rendered, *burningly*. The fashion of the world forbids a man and woman who are otherwise appropriated, to love one another burningly—to flow into each other's hearts. But if they obey Christ they must do this; and whoever would allow them to do this, and yet would forbid them (on any other ground than that of present expediency) to express their unity of hearts by bodily unity, would "strain at a gnat and swallow a camel"; for unity of hearts is as much more important than the bodily expression of it, as a camel is bigger than a gnat....

PROPOSITION X.— The abolishment of worldly restrictions on sexual intercourse, is involved in the anti-legality of the gospel. It is incompatible with the state of perfected freedom towards which Paul's gospel of "grace without law" leads, that man should be allowed and required to *love* in all directions, and yet be forbidden to *express* love in its most natural and beautiful form, except in one direction. In fact, Paul says with direct reference to sexual intercourse—" 'All things are *lawful* for me,' but all things are not expedient; 'all things are lawful for me,' but I will not be brought under the power of any" (1 Cor. 6:12); thus placing the restrictions which were necessary in the transition period on the basis, not of law, but of expediency and the demands of spiritual freedom, and leaving it fairly to be inferred that in the final state, when hostile surroundings and powers of bondage cease, all restrictions also will cease....

PROPOSITION XVI.— The restoration of true relations between the sexes, is a matter second in importance only to the reconciliation of man to God.

The distinction of male and female is that which makes man the image of God, i.e. the image of the Father and the Son. Gen. 1:27. The relation of male and female was the first social relation. Gen. 2:22. It is therefore the root of all other social relations. The derangement of this relation was the first result of the original breach with God. Gen. 3:7; comp. 2:25. Adam and Eve were, at the beginning, in open, fearless, spiritual fellowship, first with God, and secondly, with each other. Their transgression produced two corresponding alienations, viz., first, an alienation from God, indicated by their fear of meeting him, and their hiding themselves among the trees of the garden; and, secondly, an alienation from each other, indicated by their shame at their nakedness, and their hiding themselves from each other by clothing. These were the two great manifestations of original sin—the only manifestations presented to notice in the inspired record of the apostasy. The first thing then to be done, in an attempt to redeem man and reörganize society, is to bring about reconciliation with God; and the second thing is to bring about a true union of the sexes. In other words, religion is the first subject of interest, and sexual morality the second, in the great enterprise of establishing the kingdom of God on earth. . . .

PROPOSITION XVII.— Dividing the sexual relation into two branches, the amative and propagative, the amative or love-relation is first in importance, as it is in the order of nature. God made woman because "he saw it was *not good for man to be alone*" (Gen. 2:18); i.e. for social, not primarily for propagative purposes. Eve was called Adam's "help-meet." In the whole of the specific account of the creation of woman, she is regarded as his companion, and her maternal office is not brought into view. Gen. 2:18-25. Amativeness was necessarily the first social affection developed in the garden of Eden. The second commandment of the eternal law of love,—"thou shalt love thy neighbor as thyself"—had amativeness for its first channel; for Eve was at first Adam's only neighbor.—Propagation, and the affections connected with it, did not commence their operation during the period of innocence.—After the fall, God said to the woman,— "I will greatly multiply thy sorrow and thy conception"; from which it is to be inferred that in the original state, conception would have been comparatively infrequent. . . .

PROPOSITION XIX.— The propagative part of the sexual relation is in its nature the *expensive* department. 1. While amativeness keeps the capital stock of life circulating between two, propagation introduces a third partner. 2. The propagative act, i.e. the emission of the seed, is a drain on the life of man, and when habitual, produces disease. 3. The infirmities and vital expenses of woman during the long period of pregnancy, waste her constitution. 4. The awful agonies of child-birth heavily tax the life of woman. 5. The cares of the nursing period bear heavily on woman. 6. The cares of both parents, through the period of the childhood of their offspring, are many and burdensome. 7. The labor of man is greatly increased by the necessity of providing for children. A portion of these expenses would undoubtedly have been curtailed, if human nature had remained in its original integrity, and will be, when it is restored. But it is still self-evident, that the birth of children, viewed either as a vital or a mechanical operation, is in its nature expensive; and the fact that multiplied conception was imposed as a curse, indicates that it was so regarded by the Creator. . . .

PROPOSITION XX.— The amative and propagative functions of the sexual organs are distinct from each other, and may be separated practically. They are confounded in the world, both in the theories of physiologists and in universal practice. The amative function is regarded merely as a bait to the propagative, and is merged in it. The sexual organs are called "organs of reproduction," or "organs of generation," but not organs of love or organs of union. But if amativeness is, as we have seen, the first and noblest of the social affections, and if the propagative part of the sexual relation was originally secondary, and became paramount by the subversion of order in the fall, we are bound to raise the amative office of the sexual organs into a distinct and paramount function. It is held in the world, that the sexual organs have two distinct functions, viz., the urinary and the propagative. We affirm that they have *three*—the urinary, the propagative, and the amative, i.e., they are conductors, first of the urine, secondly of the semen, and thirdly of the social magnetism. And the amative is as distinct from the propagative, as the propagative is from the urinary. In fact, strictly speaking, the organs of propagation are *physiologically* distinct from the organs of union in both sexes. The testicles are the organs of reproduction in the male, and the uterus in the female. These are distinct from the organs of union. The sexual conjunction of male and female, no more necessarily involves the discharge of the semen than of the urine. The discharge of the semen, instead of being the main act of sexual intercourse, properly so called, is really the sequel and termination of it. Sexual intercourse, pure and simple, is the conjunction of the organs of union, and the interchange of magnetic influences, or conversation of spirits, through the medium of that conjunction. The communication from the seminal vessels to the uterus, which constitutes the propagative act, is distinct from, subsequent to, and not necessarily connected with, this intercourse. (On the one hand, the seminal discharge can be voluntarily withheld in sexual connection; and on the other, it can be produced without sexual connection, as it is in masturbation. This latter fact demonstrates that the discharge of the semen and the pleasure connected with it, is not essentially social, since it can be produced in solitude; it is a personal and not a dual affair. This, indeed, is evident from a physiological analysis of it. The pleasure of the act is not produced by contact and interchange of life with the female, but by the action of the seminal fluid on certain internal nerves of the male organ. The appetite and that which satisfies it, are both within the man, and of course the pleasure is personal, and may be obtained without sexual intercourse.) We insist then that the amative function—that which consists in a simple union of persons, making "of twain one flesh," and giving a medium of magnetic and spiritual interchange—is a distinct and independent function, as superior to the reproductive as we have shown amativeness to be to propagation....

PROPOSITION XXIV.— In vital society, labor will become attractive. Loving companionship in labor, and especially the mingling of the sexes, makes labor attractive. The present division of labor between the sexes separates them entirely. The woman keeps house, and the man labors abroad. Men and women are married only after dark and during bed-time. Instead of this, in vital society men and women will mingle in both of their peculiar departments of work. It will be economically as well as spiritually profitable, to marry them indoors and out, by day as well as by night. When the partition between the sexes is taken away, and man ceases to make woman a propagative drudge, when love takes the place of shame, and fashion follows nature in dress and business, men and women will be able to mingle in all their employments, as boys and girls mingle in their sports; and then labor will be attractive....

PROPOSITION XXV.— We can now see our way to victory over death. Reconciliation with God opens the way for the reconciliation of the sexes. Reconciliation of the sexes emancipates woman, and opens the way for vital society. Vital society increases strength, diminishes work, and makes labor attractive, thus removing the antecedents of death. First, we abolish sin; then shame; then the curse on woman of exhausting child-bearing; then the curse on man of exhausting labor; and so we arrive regularly at the tree of life, (as per Gen. 3).

60 ▪ THE DUALITY OF GOD IN SHAKER BELIEF

A brother of social reformer George Henry Evans, Frederick William Evans (1808–1893) developed a keen interest in socialism along with causes such as land reform and abolition. In 1830 he joined the Shaker community at New Lebanon, New York. He rose to a position of prominence among the Shakers, writing and lecturing on many subjects pertaining to them. Evans tried to shape Shaker doctrine as well as describe it. In the Compendium *he responds to public desire to know more about the origins of the society, its beliefs, and its membership requirements. He claims that God is androgynous since humanity and the natural world, made in God's image, encompass both male and female. Christ, therefore, must also exhibit this duality. And as only the male aspect of Christ could be manifest in Jesus, Ann Lee appeared as an incarnation of the Mother Spirit.*

Source: Frederick W. Evans. *Compendium of the Origin, History, Principles, Rules and Regulations, Government, and Doctrines of the United Society of Believers in Christ's Second Appearing*, 103–9. 4th ed. New Lebanon, N.Y.: n.p., 1867.

An all-important, sublime, and foundational doctrine of the Shakers is the Existence of an Eternal Father and an Eternal Mother in Deity—the Heavenly Parents of all angelical and human beings. They claim that the *knowledge of God* has been *progressive*, from age to age, and from Dispensation to Dispensation.

In the *first* cycle, when spirituality in man was "as the waters to the ankles," God was known only as a great Spirit. In the *second* cycle, when spirituality was "as the waters to the knees," men began to inquire *who* and *what* God was, and received for answer, "I am that I am." You are not prepared to comprehend me further.

In the *third* cycle, when spirituality in the soul was "as the waters to the loins," God, for the first time, was revealed to man as *Father*.

And in the *fourth* cycle, when spirituality is becoming as a deep and broad expanse of waters, "that can not be measured" (see Ezek. 47), God is also revealed in the character of *Mother*—and Eternal Mother—the bearing Spirit of all the creation of God, to whom the Shakers think reference is made in the Scriptures, particularly in the following extracts from the book of "Proverbs," under the appellation of *Wisdom:*

"The Lord possessed me in the beginning of his way, before his works of old. I was set up from everlasting, from the beginning, or ever the earth was. When there were no depths I was brought forth: when there were no fountains abounding with water. Before the mountains were settled, before the hills was I brought forth: while as yet He had not made the earth, nor the fields, nor the highest part of the dust of the world.

"When He prepared the heavens, I was there: when He set a compass upon the face of the depth: when He established the clouds above: when He strengthened the fountains of the deep: when He gave to the sea his decree, that the waters should not pass his commandment: when He appointed the foundations of the earth: then I was by Him, as One brought up with Him; and I was daily his delight, rejoicing always before Him."

As *Father*, God is the infinite Fountain of intelligence, and the Source of all power—"the Almighty, great and terrible in majesty"; "the high and lofty One, that inhabiteth eternity, whose name is Holy, dwelling in the high and holy place"; and "a consuming fire."

But, as *Mother,* *"God is love"* and tenderness! If all the *maternal* affections of all the female or bearing spirits in animated nature were combined together, and then concentred in *one individual human female*, that person would be but as a type or image of our Eternal Heavenly *Mother*.

The *duality* of God is expressed in the book of "Genesis" as follows: "Let us make man in our image, after our likeness. So God created man in his own image; male and female created He them; and called their name Adam."

From which, the Shakers insist, that it is the male and female in man that is peculiarly the *"image of God."* In this conclusion they further strengthen themselves from the Apostle Paul, who affirms that the order of the "God-head," and the "eternal creative power of God," which would otherwise be invisible to man, are "clearly seen, by," through, and in, "the things that are made."

Consequently, if this be admitted, it follows, from the undeniable fact that all the things which God has "made" are *dual;* beginning with the *mineral* kingdom, which, from the "old red sandstone" to the very latest geological formation, exhibit the action of *two forces*, the positive and negative, which forms, in the *vegetable* kingdom, gradually resolve themselves into male and female types, from the fern to the polypus; and, in the *animal* kingdom, they are progressively developed from the polypus up to the simia tribes; and ultimately they culminate in *man* and *woman*, the image of God their Creator.

It seems scarcely possible to resist this evidence of a *dual order*, so "clearly seen" throughout all the domains of nature; or to admit it, without proving that *God also is* DUAL, Father and Mother, the image and likeness of man, whom He has made *male* and *female*.

"No carnal man hath seen God at any time," or witnessed an act of arbitrary, sovereign, creative power. The "eternal [creative] power" of God is only known to man through the perpetual operation of the originating and reproducing powers of male and female principles.

The Shakers believe that the distinction of sex is eternal; that it inheres in the soul itself; and that no angels or spirits exist who are not male and female.

From the fact that Adam (and Eve) "was the figure of him that was to come," they argue that the "second Adam, the Lord from heaven, a quickening Spirit," was also *dual*, male and female; and that they were the spiritual Father and Mother of Jesus, begetting, watching over, and bearing him in the regeneration, towards the *new birth*, into their own quickening spiritual element.

Every thing is begotten, travails, and is born into the elements of its parents. "That which is [begotten and] born of the flesh, is flesh; and that which is [begotten and] born of the Spirit, is spirit."

Jesus, being a male, could only reveal and manifest the *Father* in Christ and God. But when the *second* Adam appeared to Ann, and became her spiritual Parents, she, being a female, revealed and manifested the *Mother Spirit* in Christ and in Deity.

The affectional nature in man seeks its Source and Parent—the Maternal Spirit in Deity. Ignorance, or a perverted theology, may divert it into wrong channels, as in the worshipers of female gods in the heathen nations, which are known to be more numerous than all others; or the Roman Catholic adoration of the Virgin Mary—"the Mother of God." But nothing can destroy the intuitive reverence of the human soul for a *Heavenly Mother*. It is as innate and universal as is the belief in Deity.

61 ▪ SHAKER WOMEN IN COMMUNITY

Journalist Charles Nordhoff (1830–1901) provides a valuable account of Shaker life in his The Communistic Societies of the United States. *A newspaper assignment led him to visit a number of communal groups to observe among other things their daily routines, industries, systems of government, religious creeds and practices, and history. He weaves into his description of the Shakers some observations on the roles assumed by women. They were clearly included in the authoritative ministry that was to teach, guide, and direct on matters temporal and spiritual. They were appointed as ministers, elders, and deacons but were also delegated the more traditionally female tasks of mending clothing and cooking.*

Source: Charles Nordhoff. *The Communistic Societies of the United States from Personal Visit and Observation*, 137–41. New York: Schocken Books, 1965.

The government or administration of the Shaker societies is partly spiritual and partly temporal. "The visible Head of the Church of Christ on earth is vested in a Ministry, consisting of male and female, not less than three, and generally four in number, two of each sex. The first in the Ministry stands as the leading elder of the society. Those who compose the Ministry are selected from the Church, and appointed by the last preceding head or leading character; and their authority is confirmed and established by the spontaneous union of the whole body. Those of the United Society who are selected and called to the important work of the Ministry, to lead and direct the Church of Christ, must be blameless characters, faithful, honest, and upright, clothed with the spirit of meekness and humility, gifted with wisdom and understanding, and of great experience in the things of God. As faithful embassadors of Christ, they are invested with wisdom and authority, by the revelation of God, to guide, teach, and direct his Church on earth in its spiritual travel, and to counsel and advise in other matters of importance, whether spiritual or temporal.

"To the Ministry appertains, therefore, the power to appoint ministers, elders, and deacons, and with the elders to assign offices of care and trust to such brethren and sisters as they shall judge to be best qualified for the several offices to which they may be assigned. Such appointments, being communicated to the members of the Church concerned, and having received the mutual approbation of the Church, or the family concerned, are thereby confirmed and established until altered or repealed by the same authority.

"Although the society at New Lebanon is the centre of union to all the other societies, yet the more immediate duties of the Ministry in this place extend only to the two societies of New Lebanon and Watervliet. [Groveland has since been added to this circle.] Other societies are under the direction of a ministry appointed to preside over them; and in most instances two or more societies constitute a bishopric, being united under the superintendence of the same ministry."

Each society has ministers, in the Novitiate family, to instruct and train neophytes, and to go out into the world to preach when it may be desirable. Each family has two elders, male and female, to teach, exhort, and lead the family in spiritual concerns. It has also deacons and deaconesses, who provide for the support and convenience of the family, and regulate the various branches of industry in which the members are employed, and transact business with those without. Under the deacons are "care-takers," who are the foremen and forewomen in the different pursuits.

It will be seen that this is a complete and judicious system of administration. It has worked well for a long time. A notable feature of the system is that the members do not appoint their rulers, nor are they consulted openly or directly about such appointments. The Ministry are self-perpetuating; and they select and appoint all subordinates, being morally, but it seems not otherwise, responsible to the members.

Finally, "all the members are equally holden, according to their several abilities, to maintain one united interest, and therefore all labor *with their hands*, in some useful occupation, for the mutual comfort and benefit of themselves and each other, and for the general good of the society or family to which they belong. Ministers, elders, and deacons, all without exception, are industriously employed in some *manual* occupation, except in the time taken up in the necessary duties of their respective callings." So carefully is this rule observed that even the supreme heads of the Shaker Church—the four who constitute the Ministry at Mount Lebanon, Daniel Boler, Giles B. Avery, Ann Taylor, and Polly Reed—labor at basket-making in the intervals of their travels and ministrations, and have a separate little "shop" for this purpose near the church. They live in a house built against the church, and eat in a separate room in the family of the first order; and, I believe, generally keep themselves somewhat apart from the people.

The property of each society, no matter of how many families it is composed, is for convenience held in the name of the trustees, who are usually members of the Church family, or first order; but each family or commune keeps its own accounts and transacts its business separately.

The Shaker family rises at half-past four in the summer, and five o'clock in the winter; breakfasts at six or half-past six; dines at twelve; sups at six; and by nine or half-past are all in bed and the lights are out.

They eat in a general hall. The tables have no cloth, or rather are covered with oil-cloth; the men eat at one table, women at another, and children at a third; and the meal is eaten in silence, no conversation being held at table. When all are assembled for a meal they kneel in silence for a moment; and this is repeated on rising from the table, and on rising in the morning and before going to bed.

When they get up in the morning, each person takes two chairs, and, setting them back to back, takes off the bedclothing, piece by piece, and folding each neatly once, lays it across the backs of the chairs, the pillows being first laid on the seats of the chairs. In the men's rooms the slops are also carried out of the house by one of them; and the room is then left to the women, who sweep, make the beds, and put every thing to rights. All this is done before breakfast; and by breakfast time what New-Englanders call "chores" are all finished, and the day's work in the shops or in the fields may begin.

Each brother is assigned to a sister, who takes care of his clothing, mends when it is needed, looks after his washing, tells him when he requires a new garment, reproves him if he is not orderly, and keeps a general sisterly oversight over his habits and temporal needs.

In cooking, and the general labor of the dining-room and kitchen, the sisters take turns; a certain number, sufficient to make the work light, serving a month at a time. The younger sisters do the washing and ironing; and the clothes which are washed on Monday are not ironed till the following week.

62 ▪ PUBLIC ROLES FOR WOMEN IN CHRISTIAN SCIENCE

Although controversy and dissension surrounded her later relationship with Christian Science, Augusta Stetson (1842–1928) had an enormous influence over the development of the movement in her role as pastor of the First Church of Christ, Scientist, in New York City. While trying to support herself and her ailing husband in 1884 as a public lecturer, she heard Mary Baker Eddy speak. She was persuaded to take a three-week course at Eddy's Massachusetts Metaphysical College and subsequently began to practice Christian Science healing in Maine. Reports of her success as well as her strong personality and oratorical skills led Eddy to choose her first as one of five preachers in Boston and then as organizer for the fledgling church in New York. The passages from Stetson's Reminiscences *show her in official roles as practitioner and preacher. She uses the principles of Christian Science to overcome her fear that she would prove an inadequate communicator of truth.*

Source: Augusta E. Stetson. *Reminiscences, Sermons, and Correspondence Proving Adherence to the Principle of Christian Science as Taught by Mary Baker Eddy*, 8–10, 12–16. New York: G. P. Putnam's Sons, 1913.

Another case was one of dropsy. A woman had been wheeled about in her chair for thirteen months and had so increased in size that she was a monstrosity. Her weight was so burdensome that she was a great sufferer. Her husband with much difficulty got her into a sleigh and brought her to me, at a farm house, where I was treating another case. I told the man that I could not treat his wife, as I was about to return to Boston, and that the case might require more time than I had to give. The woman begged me to give her just one treatment. I did and they went away. On the way home, driving through the woods, she asked her husband, "What makes it so light?" He replied, "It is not light," but she exclaimed again, "What makes it so light?" He thought then that she was suffering from some hallucination and, as he told me afterwards, he tried to calm her, but once more she cried, "What makes it so light?" In relating this experience, he told me that he asked himself, "Why did I take her to that woman? I would rather have my wife in her old condition than in this state." He said that he reproached himself for having brought this awful condition upon her, but that he pacified her and hurried home. When she got out of the sleigh, about eleven o'clock at night, she exclaimed, "John, I am healed!" and added, "I can go into the house as fast as you!" She ran into the house and upon taking off her gloves found that her hands and her body were of normal size. The bloat had entirely disappeared. The husband and wife together fell on their knees and thanked God for His wonderful power to heal. I heard from the woman several years afterward that she was perfectly healthy. At the time when Christian Science restored her to health, she dismissed her household help, did her own work, and "took in" sewing, and I learned that she became a good Christian Scientist. . . .

In all these cases to which I have referred I taught my patients the Science of being, and put into their hands *Science and Health with Key to the Scriptures* and our Leader's, Mrs. Eddy's, other writings, giving them some explanation of how to apply the Principle of Christian Science. . . .

To resume my reminiscences, Mrs. Eddy called me to her home in Columbus Avenue, Boston, and asked me if I would take the pulpit and preach at Chickering Hall on Sunday. I was startled, and told her that I did not think I could do it,—that I had never preached a sermon. Mrs. Eddy said, "God will give you the words and enable you to speak." I asked, "What shall I take for a text?" She replied, "God will tell you—go to Him." I asked, "Will you look over my sermon after I have written it?" She said, "You can bring it to me." I went home burdened with the responsibility that she had imposed upon me. However, I went to work and selected my text which was from 2 Timothy 1:7, "For God hath not given us the spirit of fear; but of power, and of love, and of a sound mind."

I struggled over that sermon during the week. Finally, I wrote it and took it to Mrs. Eddy. She glanced over it and said, "This is all right; I will be with you in the pulpit to-morrow."

When I arrived at the Hall on Sunday morning, Mrs. Eddy met me in the dressing-room, went upon the platform with me, listened to the sermon, and when it was over, took me in her carriage to the street car. She seemed greatly pleased with my work and highly commended it. After that she appointed me, with four others, to preach in her pulpit—a position which I held until she sent me to New York City. . . .

I called upon Mrs. Eddy one day and was told to go to her room. Half way up the stairs I met her coming down, and as we stood for a moment, talking, she said to me, "I want you to go to New York City." Thinking that she desired me to go to a patient, I asked, "When do you wish me to go?" She saw that I did not understand what she meant, and said, "Well, some time this autumn." Then I understood that it was not to a patient and I said, "But I do not know any one in New York. Do you want me to see a patient?" She replied, "No, I want you to go there to help establish the Christianity of Christian Science. There will be plenty of people who will attempt to work in Christian Science, but will only pervert it, and the result will be mental relief on a material basis, and faith cure. I want the *Christianity* of Christian Science established." I said, "Mrs. Eddy, I do not know any one there." She asked, "Is not God there?" I replied, "Oh, yes,

God is there,—He is everywhere," and added, "but I have my work to do here—my husband, my patients, my classes, and my home. I do not know about going to New York. I know nothing of it, although I am familiar with foreign cities. I do not know how I can take care of myself in that great expensive place, where I should be required to represent properly our Cause." Mrs. Eddy answered, "If the Astors or the Vanderbilts should send for you, would you be afraid that they would not supply your needs while you were doing their work?" I answered, "Oh no!" Then she asked, "Have you not as much faith in God as you have in man?" I hesitated, then replied, "I will go." I had then been practising Christian Science in Boston for two years, teaching classes and preaching (with others) in Mrs. Eddy's pulpit.

At that time I had many patients in Reading, Massachusetts, and had done some instantaneous healing there, of which Mrs. Eddy knew. One day when I was calling upon her she asked me if I would secure a hall or church in Reading and get an audience for her, including as many of the clergymen as I could. She said she would come and address them.

I immediately went to work and with the help of my patients engaged the Congregational Church. Four ministers were invited, and when the evening came the assembled audience occupied every seat. The four clergymen sat at the foot of the platform, but Mrs. Eddy was not there. I had gone to three trains in the afternoon to meet her and at last in despair I entered the church. I was in a dilemma. I was embarrassed because Mrs. Eddy did not appear and I felt that I ought to apologize to the audience for her non-appearance. I had made no preparation to address this large assembly, including four clergymen, and, as I had never lectured on Christian Science, I was desperate. I called on God to give me wisdom to know whether to apologize and dismiss the congregation or to do the best I could to give them some idea of the Science of being. Finally I decided that I must speak the Word. I addressed them for an hour and a half, prefacing my remarks with the statement that Mrs. Eddy must have been detained, but if they desired to hear me I would do the best I could to impart to them the little that I had learned during my short experience in the demonstration of Christian Science.

The next morning I went directly to Mrs. Eddy and told her that I thought it was most unkind for her to put me in that position. There was the audience assembled, expecting to be addressed by a great woman, and there was I with very little knowledge and no preparation. I asked her, "Why did you not come?" She answered, "I was there." I did not know at that time what she meant and thought that her *personal* presence was necessary. She smiled at my innocence, and ignorance of her methods of testing her students. She said, "But you stood, Augusta. You stood, you did not run." She referred to this nearly every time I saw her after that event, and in these words, "You stood, did you not? You did not run," or "Do you remember the lecture at Reading, and how you stood? You did not run—did you?" I saw later that this was one of the tests that she had given me on the journey from sense to Soul.

Chapter 9

THE MOVE TOWARD
FULL PARTICIPATION

63 ▪ THE LICENSING AND ORDINATION
OF METHODIST WOMEN

Despite the efforts of women such as Anna Howard Shaw and Anna Oliver, the Methodist Episcopal Church, North, refused to ordain women or grant them licenses to preach. When the general conference met in 1920, the Kansas conference submitted a memorial supporting the licensing and ordination of women. The 1920 conference agreed to the former, but referred the question of ordination to a seven-member commission. Their report does not question the belief that women can be called to preach and does recommend that they be ordained as local preachers. They should not, however, be admitted to membership in the annual conferences. The issue, thus, was not whether women should preach and offer the sacraments but whether the denomination was willing to guarantee positions to ordained women, a right accompanying admission to the annual conference. The church was urged to use caution here. The report, which was adopted at the 1924 general conference, did not precipitate a debate over female ordination although it was challenged by a substitute motion, "That to women be granted the same ministerial rights and privileges as are granted to men."

Source: Raymond J. Wade, ed. "Report of the Commission on Licensing and Ordaining Women." In *Journal of the Twenty-ninth Delegated General Conference of the Methodist Episcopal Church Held at Springfield, Massachusetts,* 1697–98. New York: Methodist Book Concern, 1924.

On May 25, 1920, the General Conference of that year adopted a report of the Committee on Itinerancy, referring to a commission of seven, the expediency of granting to women ordination and admission to the Annual Conference. After careful individual study and common discussion, your Commission found itself with three definite convictions:

First—That the validity of a woman's call to preach is not involved in any action which the General Conference may take in respect of the ordination of women and their admission into the Annual Conference;

191

Second—That, inasmuch as the ordination of women and their admission into the Annual Conference would inaugurate far-reaching social and spiritual issues, such action ought not to be undertaken either as an administrative expedient to meet the emergency created by a temporary decrease in ministerial supply, or as an economic expedient to adjust ministerial supply to inadequate financial support;

Third—That in the connectional polity of Methodism, the ordination of women and their admission to the Annual Conference would introduce peculiar and embarrassing difficulties. In non-connectional churches, in which, alone, ordained women have been admitted to settled pastorates, the relation can be terminated at will by either party to the contract. In Methodism our connectional polity guarantees to every effective minister a church and to every self-supporting church a minister; and the pastoral relation is established by appointment of constituted authority, and properly terminated only with the consent of constituted authority.

Your Commission, also, after wise and careful exploration of both the mind of our own Church and the experiences of other Churches, has been led to conclude that the indifference of the Church at large to the matter of the ordination of women and their admission to the Annual Conference, is in itself evidence that no imperative demand for such ordination and admission exists; that Methodism had had altogether too limited experience in licensing of women as preachers to provide a basis upon which a final decision ought to be reached, and furthermore, that the knowledge and experience of other churches, in which women have served and are still serving as settled pastors, are too fragmentary and insufficient to justify the Commission in offering a final decision.

However, the very evident and acute need for an effective sacramental ministry on the part of women, in certain home and particularly in the foreign fields, has seemed to your Commission to indicate clearly an expansion of service which the Church, with reason and propriety, can open to them.

Your Commission, accordingly, taking into consideration these and other factors of significance, unanimously recommends that the General Conference enact such measures as shall provide for the ordination of women as local preachers under the conditions and satisfactory to the requirements which the Discipline has determined and maintains for ordained local preachers.

64 · UNREST AMONG PRESBYTERIAN WOMEN

In an attempt to deal with numerous divisive issues that threatened the unity of the Presbyterian Church in the U.S.A., the church's general assembly appointed a committee to draw up a list of the causes of unrest. Last on the list was the status of women. In the spring of 1926 the assembly responded by appointing Margaret E. Hodge and Katharine Bennett, both prominent leaders in the women's missionary movement, to investigate the matter further. In November 1927 the women presented their report, later described as "thoughtful and disturbing," to the general council of the assembly. The report was based on a careful study of letters, official documents, and personal consultations with church women. The authors concluded that there was a group of women, "not large but intellectually keen," who were dissatisfied with their exclusion from policy-making bodies in general and from the 1923 process that led to the elimination of separate women's mission boards in particular. Making matters worse was the fact that the reorganization made it possible for local ministers and judicatories to divert the money collected by women to projects they had not chosen.

Source: Katharine Bennett and Margaret E. Hodge. *Causes of Unrest among the Women of the Church*, 10–13, 16–19. Philadelphia: n.p., 1927.

The new national missionary organizations seized the imagination of Presbyterian women and in the first decade after they were formed their resources and their service grew amazingly. Each decade saw increasing gifts and greatly augmented interest until today women's local missionary organizations in the Presbyterian Church number 6554 and their annual gifts are in the neighborhood of $3,000,000—the sum total of their gifts during half a century having amounted to about $45,000,000. But this has not been the only contribution made. Women have placed much stress on education and knowledge of the task as a basis for giving. As their specific knowledge of need increased, so their zeal to meet that need grew. For years hundreds of thousands of women have been studying the National and Foreign Mission fields in monthly meetings of their societies, through literature especially prepared for them, and of late years through the Mission text-books. Knowledge has begotten interest, interest has begotten love and love has begotten deep, devoted, understanding prayer. The woman's organization in the church has called for a great body of volunteer workers at mission headquarters, in synodical and presbyterial and local societies,—a group avidly loyal both to the mission field and to the organization which had come into being to support the mission fields.

No small impetus to this service was the fact that women of other churches were similarly organized and working along the same lines. The various national denominational women's organizations before consolidation spread, numbered about seventy-five, representing both Home and Foreign Missions, with about 60,000 auxiliary missionary societies in which over 2,000,000 women are enrolled, the gifts of these groups

amounting to eight to ten million dollars annually. When the era of reorganization of Boards and Agencies of the churches came, facts which were
recognized but which were not seriously disturbing became important. So
long as there was a service into which they could put their strength and affection, the women were willing to ignore the disabilities that faced them
in general church work, although similar disabilities had been removed in
other activities. But when the church, by action taken by the men of the
church with but the slightest consultation with the women, and then only
as to methods, decided to absorb these agencies which had been built up
by the women, the by-product of such decision was to open the whole
question of the status of women in the church. Then women faced the fact
that their sex constitute about *60 per cent of the membership of the Presbyterian Church*, but that a woman as an individual has no status beyond a
congregational meeting in her local church, and that the long developed
and carefully erected agencies which she had cherished could be absorbed
without a question being seriously asked of her as to her wishes in this
matter. The women looked about into business and professional life and
saw women rapidly taking their place side by side with men, with full freedom to serve in any position for which they had the qualifications. They
saw the church, which affirmed spiritual equality, lagging far behind in the
practical expression of it; they saw democracy in civic work, autocracy in
church administrations.

It should not surprise anyone that among thinking women there arose a
serious question as to whether their place of service could longer be found
in the church when a great organization which they had built could be
autocratically destroyed by vote of male members of the church without
there seeming to arise in the mind of the latter any question as to the justice,
wisdom or fairness of their actions.

Unless we speak most frankly of the conditions as they exist in our own
denomination we cannot hope to see eye to eye in this matter. The women
of our church, notoriously one of the most conservative, have been placed
on the Boards of the church, and it is certain that many of the men in the
church have felt that this was a real promotion and that the women should
be grateful for this recognition. A prominent clergyman of our denomination said to the writer that there had been a real desire "to be generous to
the ladies!" But in facing this situation it must be recalled that the women of
the Presbyterian Church had carefully and painstakingly built up large and
flourishing organizations, that these organizations were taken from them
without their consent, and in some cases in opposition to their wishes,
by a purely masculine vote, and that when the new Boards were organized the proportion of women upon them was definitely named. Women
were not to be placed there on their merits as are men, but plans were so

made that however valuable they might be they should never in the voting outnumber the men of the Boards.

A number of denominations have united their general and women's boards of missions; so far as we know each one that has done this has taken action only after the fullest and freest discussion wherein women both spoke and voted and in some cases a fifty-fifty membership of men and women was provided for. In the Presbyterian Church the women, although they constitute the majority of church members, are allocated to a minority which has apparently no relation to ability to render service but is based entirely on sex.

Where in other than church service women have been denied equal opportunity with men, they have organized separately, but the Presbyterian Church, because of its ecclesiastical plan and its rigidity, having refused her equality of opportunity, also has denied to her the right of separate expression. Within the denomination no compensatory achievements are possible to her.

It has been commented that when women are placed on various church bodies men will no longer remain on them. If there be any truth in this statement then it should be recognized and woman be given the opportunity to move forward alone. "Men and women," said Edward S. Martin, "never work together on a great scale on equal terms on the same employment. When the women come in the men go out, or else lose standing and character." If Mr. Martin voices a common male point of view the sooner it is acknowledged the sooner will some problems be cleared.

The experience of many denominations has seemed to indicate that women are ready to work and can work with men, but that men do not work well with women, and very seldom desire to do so. Is not this position a bit illogical, that the men refuse to allow the women to work alone, but are not prepared to work with them? . . .

To many women all over the country who have striven for the accomplishment of their undertakings for the mission field and who have largely considered these gifts as "extras," the "single budget" has brought perplexities, and in some cases "unrest"; they wish to aid the church loyally, they wish to do the thing that will be for the ultimate good, but when as in many cases a session without consultation with those concerned *orders* that all agencies within the church shall come into the new plan of a "single budget" unrest of a serious kind is often stirred.

Methods of apportioning the money under the single budget vary: in some cases the Woman's Missionary Society is promised its full quota irrespective of whether the church's quota is all secured; this is bad; in other cases the Woman's Missionary Society receives an amount which is the per cent of its apportionment to the church's apportionment. One great difficulty has arisen because so often the church is not so keen about raising its full apportionment as is the Society. We can let a few typical cases speak for themselves as to some results that cause "unrest"; these are quotes from letters from active women workers:

> "Before our Church used the Budget system, our Missionary Society sent in as its apportionment about $770.—Then the budget system was put in, and the Session asked us to desist from soliciting with them at the time of the every member canvass. The Session agreed to give us $500. in four quarterly payments. They gave us $450. the first year, $375. the second year and now they feel that we should be pro-rated."

> "Shall we take just what we can get and remain under the budget plan, as the Session feels we should? This is the problem. We are trying to find some way out and so we are writing to you for advice in the matter. We want to do our 'bit' but we also realize that a church divided in itself cannot stand."

We are ready to grant that there have been and are cases where the gifts of the women through the Woman's Missionary Society are out of proportion to the Church offerings, but there may be two sides even to this. Cases have been known where the women have prosecuted their task with zeal and the church has lagged.

The frequent efforts of pastors, sessions, trustees, Board representatives and others to supplement deficits in funds by the use of the funds raised by the women for the specific work entrusted to them leads to one of the most often repeated expressions: "Why do not the men promote the work and the securing of funds in the church itself, instead of trying to make up deficits out of the women's designated funds[?]"

A recent report from an active Presbyterian center in which a Conference had been held, sent by an intelligent woman, contained the following words: "They (the men) lost no opportunity to promote the single budget—or to covertly knock the Woman's Missionary Society as a parasite sapping the life of the Church benevolence."

Since reorganization, activities of various kinds on the part of the men have called forth similar comments again and again, and "unrest" has increased. Or should this be noted as due to "uncertainty"—the women do not know where they stand. They were instructed to continue as before, but how can they? Every agency of the church has turned jealous eyes toward their activities and in one way or another many strive to destroy their organization, to utilize their funds,—and yet to ignore them. Among all these distracting influences the women, with no power to enforce decisions, are troubled and wonder more and more if their best service cannot be given outside of the church. The ignoring that existed before consolidation was infinitely more simple than the confusion of today.

Are not the women part of the church? They are indeed.

Then should they not be interested in all phases of the church's work? Yes, indeed, and they are to a remarkable degree, as shown by their giving to the Church budget, but they see keen injustice in the constant pressure to place on 25 per cent of the women of the church heavier financial responsibilities, while at the same time there exists a latent antagonism to the very organization that makes these gifts possible.

Are the women unwilling to accept the control prescribed by Presbyterian law?

Yes and *No*. A good many women were most sympathetic to the statements in the petition referred to before; as follows:

1. The women have no part in determining the policy or defining the faith of the Presbyterian Church. This is contrary to the spirit of both justice and democracy.

2. The biological fact of sex excludes women from a seat in the General Assembly and the other courts of the Church. Intelligence and spirituality should be the determining qualities for a seat in these bodies.

And many women who were not, and are not, ready to subscribe to statements they felt to be radical, nevertheless are of the opinion that the autocratic methods in vogue fail to secure real cooperation, and believe that much of the present confusion could have been avoided had men and women thought together on equal terms in the church's planning.

As women have advanced from "Womanly Woman to Intelligent Being," as Mr. Langdon-Davies says, they are having too many opportunities for service to be content to be relegated to the group which prepares suppers, cares for flowers, does deaconess work and deals with details. They are glad to share in the doing of these and other things which come naturally within the scope of their activities, but they desire to share likewise in the opportunities for larger service. One woman, nationally known, called to lead large undertakings outside of the church, and a devoted member of the Presbyterian Church, wrote that "the Presbyterian church does little less than insult the intelligence of its womanhood; that when she was in the Congregational Church in a prayer meeting she felt that she had to be using her mind to see if she could not make a contribution to the meeting, but that in the Presbyterian Church, all that was expected of her was just to sit. She was never expected to speak in any regular church service, even of the informal prayer meeting type." It is true that this is not today true of all Presbyterian churches, but it does represent much of Presbyterian habit.

What harm has resulted and may result to the church from the autocratic control by one sex?

Men's methods and women's differ, but both types should be valuable and each support the work of the other. Men generalize; women particularize. Such generalizations commonly accepted are not always true as they sound, but if they be true, both forms of service must be valuable. Men "view with alarm." Women "want to do something about it." Each should supplement the other.

But the chief harm is that women's forward looking has been largely stopped in the Presbyterian Church. Their Boards, and the organizations that stood back of those Boards, were always under careful scrutiny by the women of the Church as to aims and methods and the mission field itself received loving but critical interest that it might always measure to the highest standard. At the time of reorganization these women were recognizing the great new life open to the women of the church and were thinking in terms of larger plans, new forms of service and new emphasis that should embrace more of the activities of the church and enlist more women actively in the service of the church.

65 ▪ INVESTIGATING THE STATUS OF WOMEN IN THE CHURCHES

The modification of traditional gender roles caused by World War II, particularly in Europe, prompted the World Council of Churches to hold a discussion on the "Life and Work of Women in the Church" at its 1948 meeting. Material gathered for the discussion was then used by Kathleen Bliss in the preparation of her 1952 study, The Service and Status of Women in the Churches. *Part of her work is a detailed examination of the role women were currently playing on local and national governing bodies. She points out that while legal barriers to such participation were generally gone, tradition and custom continued to exclude women. She also notes that women usually appeared first on national religious bodies and only more slowly in local positions. In her concluding chapter on "Change and Opportunity," she makes it clear that women who had experienced success in the secular work world were finding the church, which relegated them to institutional kitchens and nurseries, increasingly unattractive.*

Source: Kathleen Bliss. *The Service and Status of Women in the Churches,* 172–75, 184–87, 197–99. London: SCM Press, 1952.

The great majority of the Churches in the United States are of European origin: a minority of Churches are American in origin and have a separate existence from Europe, and divisions and mergers have made for variations.

In the Baptist and Congregational Churches women may share in the work of governing the Church locally (though this varies between local churches) and denominationally. In the Southern Baptist Convention, a very large and in many respects conservative Church, there seems to be no place for women locally although they sit in the highest assembly of the Church. The larger of the Congregational bodies has a ruling that one third of the members of national boards and of the biennial meetings of the General Council must be women. This Church reports that about one-tenth of its local churches have women deacons. But "for Congregational, Disciple and American Baptist Churches, the question whether deaconesses are equal to deacons can only be answered by a person knowing a given local church. They may meet with the deacons and share in certain of their tasks; again they may not. Rarely, certainly, do deaconesses serve the Lord's Supper as the deacons do" (by serving the Lord's Supper is meant carrying the elements from the minister's hands to the people, who remain in their seats). Two women have held the office of President of the American Baptist Convention. The Congregational Christian General Council elected a woman moderator in 1948. Seven Presbyterian Churches are listed. The largest of these, the Presbyterian U.S.A., admits women both as deacons and as elders, but their functions differ from church to church; in some they are allowed to serve the Lord's Supper and in others they are not. One of the matters of church order in which the Presbyterian churches are divided is the admission of women to the diaconate and eldership. The Presbyterian Church U.S., the second largest body, will not admit women either as deacons or as elders, though women have served on national boards since 1924. Thirty per cent of the Presbyterian U.S.A. churches which replied said that they had women deacons. The proportion of women among the elders is much smaller, and for this reason there are very few women in the General Assembly (of which the Moderator in 1947 was a woman).

In the Reformed Church of America and in the Evangelical and Reformed Church the government of the local church rests in the Consistory, composed of elders and deacons. The Consistory (called in some Evangelical and Reformed Churches the Church Council) takes responsibility, with the minister, for the spiritual work of the church and also looks after the property and the church charitable work. The Reformed Church of America does not allow women to be members of consistories, and although they have the right to vote, tradition still prevents it in many churches. In the Evangelical and Reformed Church there has been a gradual increase in the number of women in the consistories, some congregations have had them for as long as twenty years, but most of the minority of churches which have them at all have done so only recently, and very few women serve on the higher boards of the Church.

The Churches of the Disciples of Christ closely resemble both Congregational and Presbyterian Churches in church order. Women are admitted as elders and deacons, but the report adds, "The eldership is the point at which the strong tradition of sex equality in the Disciple Churches breaks down. Only 1.1 per cent. of Disciple Churches reported women elders—a total of five women in three churches out of 277 reporting. This, however, may be in excess of the proportion in the country as a whole. An exceptionally well informed Disciples minister was surprised to hear that there were any. The reason may probably be that the elders administer the Lord's Supper: the minister does not ordinarily do so."

In the Methodist Churches of the United States women have equal rights with men. About three-quarters of the Churches reported that they had both men and women stewards. Stewards correspond somewhat in function to congregational deacons, but are elected after nomination by the minister. The American report voices the complaint of some Methodist women that older women with means are usually chosen, and the younger, trained woman tends to be passed over. A Methodist Status of Women Commission has been working to get women to accept responsibility and Churches to appoint them as stewards. A higher proportion of local congregations appoint women to local boards in the Methodist than in any other Church. Class leaders, who played and still play in Great Britain so large a share in the development of Methodism as a Church, are not mentioned in the American report, though it is added that most Methodist Churches have "a lay leader who takes a special responsibility with the minister for the spiritual welfare of the Church. Women are eligible but apparently only serve in smaller churches. At the Annual Conference level women have been lay leaders in extremely few cases." The Evangelical United Brethren Churches have class leaders and a small number of Churches have women among them.

The position of women in the Protestant Episcopal Church of America differs markedly from their position in the Church of England. They serve on parish vestries if their diocesan convention decides that they may, and dioceses which permit them to serve appear to be in a minority. There are no examples of women serving as churchwardens, although in some dioceses they are allowed to do so. In 1946 the Episcopal General Convention had a woman delegate for the first time, but later two women were elected as lay representatives by their dioceses and by a majority vote the National Convention refused to allow them to be seated.

Lutheranism in America is divided into a number of Churches, some of them regional, others of them national according to the country of Europe from which their original founders came. The governing body of most Lutheran congregations is the Church Council. In most Lutheran Churches women are not allowed to serve on the Church Council (the governing body of the local church), but in the United Lutheran Church, the largest Lutheran group in the United States, they are allowed to serve unless the constitution of the local church forbids it. In Lutheran, as in Churches of the Congregational type, a meeting of all church members is held once a year, or failing that, such a meeting is summoned when a new minister is to be called or some important decision has to be taken. Women are, as church members, eligible to take part in these meetings and on the whole are taking a growing share in them. It is interesting that one of the smaller Churches, the Augustana Synod, has no women participating in church government at the local level, but a fair proportion of women are found on the regional and national boards of the Church.

Most of the Churches which took part in the American survey replied, in answer to a question, that they thought women were playing a larger part in the affairs of the Churches now than they were in 1940. The question was sent to local churches as well as to denominational headquarters. Tradition against their participation is often far stronger than any legal barrier, and many women reported that it is often enough for the minister to invite all men to be present, or for the leading laymen to make it known that they would not welcome the presence of women for women to forgo their legal rights in the interest of peace and harmony. The custom in many churches of appointing officers for life makes changes difficult. One new trend in the manner in which the government of the local church is carried on is making for the easy participation of women in places where they were before excluded. In a number of denominations it is customary for local churches to set up a church council or executive consisting of representatives of the major organizations in the church. In some denominations the function of such a body is advisory, but in others it is a standing committee, responsible for executive decisions in the congregation, and the trustees of the property, empowered to act for the local church, are appointed from this body. Women are to be found with fair frequency among the trustees of local churches of most denominations. The powers of such a council vary from one local church to another. Women's organizations are represented on the councils by women. The American report draws an interesting comparison between the position which women occupy in the Church and in civic life in the United States. "By and large, in church life women's participation in governing bodies is likely to begin with token representation on national boards or committees. Gradually this is extended to local church committees and then to local church boards. In civic life women are most active at the lower rungs of the ladder. . . . "

There are perhaps two main questions which are implicit in the comments made in the reports. The first is the question whether at this moment in the history of a distracted world the Churches are really making the fullest uses of all their resources of personnel in order to fulfil their mission in the world. Are the gifts and willingness of women being used to the best advantage by the Churches? This book is an attempt to answer that question. By showing what women have done in places where they have been given, or have created, opportunity, it may suggest ways in which the service of women could be enlarged, the life of the Church enriched and its message strengthened. There is no other answer than "Look and judge."

Behind this question lies another, far more difficult to define, let alone to answer. It can perhaps be put partially in this way. Are women, married or not, being helped by the Church to understand the problems of the age as they affect women, to play their part in modern life as Christians and as women? But this question cannot be answered unless there is an understanding of what women are, and what their place in society is. What is needed is that there should start within the Churches, among those who care about this matter, a process of thought about women in modern society, an imaginative act of understanding, and entering into, a total experience. For there has been a revolutionary change in the place of women in society. Women not only live a very different life from that of their grandparents, but—and this is even more important—they think differently about themselves. It has been left on the whole to secular thinkers and writers to try to understand this revolution and such books as *Male and Female* by Margaret Mead, who writes as an anthropologist, and *Le deuxième Sexe* by the French existentialist philosopher, Simone de Beauvoir, are eagerly read because they seek to enter into the total experience of women in the modern world and to provide some signposts in a bewildering scene. But Christian writers are silent except for the quantities of practical little books, many of them valuable within their limited range on Christian marriage and Christian home life. Except for Professor Karl Barth's exegesis of the creation story in the third volume of his *Dogmatik*, there is nothing to put beside the books here mentioned.

The reason for this lack of prophetic imaginative writing from the Christian side is at least in part that the Churches are deeply divided in what they think about the place of women in the modern world and in the Church. The woman who accepts the judgment of men on most subjects, who is happy in the small practical tasks to be found in every congregation and seeks protection from the harsh problems of the modern world, will certainly find a niche for herself in the Church and feel that she belongs. And it is quite right that she should do so. Thousands of women the world over expect the Church to be a place where, free for a short period from the continuous demands of families which look to them for everything, they can find rest and refreshment for the soul, friendship and a simple outlet for their desire to help others. One of the reports summarizes the activities of women in many congregations in the following words. "Serving meals at religious gatherings and social functions, raising money by bazaars and fêtes and devices of all kinds; touring as choirs, concert parties, entertainments and competitions; individual church women hold house functions and afternoon parties, musical luncheons, children's concerts, puppet shows, etc. In many Churches women prepare the Sacramental bread and wine for the communion service." To get the picture quite right one must add that this report also describes other activities, such as organizing the Women's World Day of Prayer and work for the United Nations Association. But none the less, it is true that in a great many Churches women work at projects of the kind quoted with immense energy and organizing power but with decreasing conviction, at least among some. "We rather wonder whether the endless cups of tea which women do and are expected to prepare are the only or even the chief contribution which women have to make to the Church." Here speaks another voice, the voice of the woman who is not caught into the busy round of the life of a vigorous congregation with more than half her self. Beyond her is the woman who simply cannot imagine herself ever being able, whatever her goodwill, to throw herself into the kind of social life which is the *sine qua non* of so many successful congregations. "If women take an active part in the life and work of the Church it very often demands so much time that they have no energy left for friendships and family relationships," says one report. There are large numbers of women who are Christians and members of their Churches, but their share in the life of the Church is limited by their feeling that their main work for Christ lies outside the actual walls of the church in society where they work. Often they feel that their situation is not understood in the Church and they do not get from it the spiritual nourishment which they know themselves to need. They also mark the contrast between the workaday world in which, in very many walks of life, it is true, as one report puts it, that "contributions are judged on their merits and not by whether they come from a man or a woman," and the Church where this is often not the case, where "women are seldom stimulated to use their varied gifts" and where "it is doubtful whether the variety of their gifts is recognized." The woman of an independent cast of mind who has earned her own living and perhaps that of dependents and is accustomed to taking her share in decisions without diffidence usually finds it difficult to be at home in the church. . . .

Such an acceptance of the fact that woman is a worker would cause a very big change in the treatment of women in the Churches. The Churches are most successful with married women, especially older married women: they hardly touch that 30 per cent of women who are economically employed, and this 30 per cent contains a high proportion of women in the prime of life and a significant proportion of women who are more than unskilled labor—skilled responsible workers and potential leaders. Basically women are kept out of certain offices in the Church, and operate mainly in groups with other women, because a certain picture of what a woman is prevails in many church circles. Though few would admit as much, many Christians believe that the woman is a secondary being, an agent enabling and completing man: probing will uncover the existence of ancient taboos about women's impurity, still lurking in most unexpected places. Many of the women who have written in the reports quoted in this book feel a sense of despair about the way in which Bible texts are used to justify and support already held opinions about the place of women in the Church. When Churches are in a desperate position for lack of man-power, all sorts of service is gladly accepted from women: when the situation is eased, theological reasons against women doing this kind of work are at once raised. Some women feel quite as strongly the debasement of theology involved in this procedure as true injustice to women! Other reports speak of gifted women who have gained qualifications in divinity, for whom the Church finds no place. Very many reports refer to the low pay and status accorded to full time women workers in the Church and to the uncertainty which surrounds their position. There is something of a vicious circle in regard to this: many able women do not enter the direct service of the Church because they know that they will find themselves committed to what one report describes as "a collection of good works" or even to all the odd jobs in a congregation, some of them doubtfully valuable, many of them easily performed by those without training. Therefore among those offering to serve in the Church there are, if the truth be told, a fair sprinkling who are not capable of carrying larger responsibility than is at present given to them, and they supply in some Churches an excuse for not enlarging the sphere of service for women.

If there is one thing more than another that these reports show quite clearly it is the uselessness of theoretical argument about what women can, may or ought to do. Such arguments quickly lead into the quagmire of discussing what woman is, as though she were a given and finalized collection of attributes and limitations. As Simone de Beauvoir points out in the book already cited, man is a continuous becoming, constantly exhibiting new and surprising powers of controlling and indeed creating his environment; and the same is true of woman, that she is not a biologically determined creature, so that one can say what she is because one knows what she has been in the past, when she has had to relate herself to particular social conditions and to live within the sphere that man allowed her. She, like man, is a creature with unrealized resources, and she is far behind man in this historical process of showing what she is, because of centuries in which her life was dominated by the necessity of preserving the race. Therefore, says Simone de Beauvoir, she must "display her possibilities," not stand and argue. Karl Barth has said something much the same, that in this question of women in the Church it is for women to "show what they can do."

66 · PRESBYTERIAN WOMEN AS MINISTERS

Margaret E. Towner, a director of Christian education in a Pennsylvania church, was ordained into the ministry of the Presbyterian Church U.S.A. on October 24, 1956. The first woman to be granted ordination by this major denomination, Towner had completed a Bachelor of Divinity degree at Union Theological Seminary, New York, in order to become a more skilled Christian educator and not to secure a pulpit. Her educational preparation and vocational interests typified those of most Presbyterian women who entered the ministry in the late 1950s and 1960s. Although she later became an advocate of sole pastorates for women, Towner, in this interview for Presbyterian Life, *sees a role for ordained women in smaller churches that could not afford to hire both an assistant pastor and a director of Christian education.*

Source: "Presbyterian Church U.S.A. Ordains First Woman Minister." *Presbyterian Life* (October 27, 1956): 18.

At a service this month in the First Presbyterian Church of Syracuse, New York, a young woman stood before representatives of the presbytery to take the vows by which she became an ordained minister in the Presbyterian Church U.S.A. Miss Margaret E. Towner, thirty-one-year-old minister of Christian education at the First Presbyterian Church, Allentown, Pennsylvania, is, as far as is known, the first woman in the church's history to receive the title "the Reverend."

Ordination for Miss Towner and other women became possible last spring when the General Assembly voted final approval to a change in the church's Constitution. Already at least one young woman has been taken under care of presbytery preparatory to entering seminary (P.L., Sept. 29), but Miss Towner's ordination is the first to be reported.

Miss Towner was well established as a medical photographer at the famous Mayo Clinic when she first began to think seriously of church work.

To give her thoughts time to develop, she began taking courses in education at the Syracuse University audio-visual center. For experience Miss Towner volunteered to fulfill the duties of director of Christian education at the East Genesee Presbyterian Church. "It was then," she says, "that I learned how much churches, especially smaller ones, need guidance in present methods of teaching children and training adults."

Once her mind was made up, Miss Towner promptly enrolled at Union Theological Seminary, New York. She took the full three-year theological course and was graduated in 1953 with the degree of Bachelor of Divinity. "I felt that only by taking the same courses as a future pastor would I receive adequate training as a Christian educator."

Miss Towner came to the large (1,600 members) church in Allentown two years ago, following a year as director of Christian education at the Takoma Park Presbyterian Church, just outside Washington, D.C.

Miss Towner considers herself a poor preacher, and has not sought ordination to have a pulpit. In the Presbyterian Church, she explains, persons can be called to a church to perform many functions besides preaching. "There are ministers of youth, ministers of parish visiting, in addition to ministers of Christian education. All these functions are becoming increasingly important in the multiple ministries of churches today."

Her concern for the educational programs of smaller churches is shared by Dr. Walter H. Eastwood, pastor of the Allentown church. He preached the sermon for Miss Towner's ordination in her home church at Syracuse. Dr. Eastwood has also helped the new minister find time to plan courses and schedule training conferences for small churches in the Lehigh Presbytery, of which she now becomes a member. In addition she directs a church school of 150 children at the Lock Ridge Memorial Church of Alburtis, some ten miles from Allentown. For several years Dr. Eastwood has been moderator of the Lock Ridge session, and ruling elders from Allentown have helped the fifty-member church function. A student from Princeton Seminary preaches there.

In the future, Miss Towner believes, ordained women will be asked to serve as assistant pastors of moderate-size churches. "These congregations can't afford both an assistant pastor and a director of Christian education. After they have gained sufficient experience, the young assistant ministers often are quick to leave to become pastors of their own churches. Ordained women may prove the solution to the smaller churches' problem. A woman minister could help with pastoral duties and guide the educational program, too."

At first the news that Miss Towner was to become an ordained minister perplexed some members of the Allentown congregation. "After church they approached me with worried looks and asked whether I was leaving. I assured them I wasn't and would continue doing the same jobs."

No one has seemed disturbed about the change in Miss Towner's ecclesiastical status. She has received hearty congratulations from everyone, including the session, all of whom are men.

67 · RAISING THE CONSCIOUSNESS OF BAPTIST WOMEN

In 1971 The American Baptist Woman, *a magazine for denominational leaders, published an article urging women to take an honest look at their role in church and society. The author, Lois Blankenship, was one of many women in the 1970s who had grown increasingly frustrated with the way in which women were bound to passive, subservient, domestic roles regardless of their interests and abilities. She chides Christian women for their complicity in this cultural stereotyping, reminding them that every person is called to achieve his or her God-given potential. Role models of women who had broken stereotypical patterns were essential. The women of the church could help with this by coming out of the kitchens and becoming deacons, trustees, and ordained ministers.*

Source: Lois Blankenship. "Woman Looks at Herself." *The American Baptist Woman* 15 (January 1971): 2, 14.

On a national TV commercial a harassed-looking housewife is shown trying to sort pieces of laundry. She is confused about which pieces to place in the cold water wash and which in hot water. A comforting man's voice comes on and gently rescues her with the one detergent which he assures her is for all laundry. She smiles, relieved, and says, "Oh, thank you, sir! Now I don't have to *think* anymore."

Was that woman you? Have you, unthinkingly, "bought" the ad-men's bait that women are naive and gullible, which philosophy goes out over the air day after day? Do you ever stop to look at yourself and discover who you are and what you think? Do you really know yourself? Have you reflected about what it means to be a unique person—the only one like you in existence? Do you truly comprehend and appreciate the fact that you are created by God in his own image?

Of course, you know that never in all creation has there been another person with fingerprints like yours, no one else with thoughts like yours nor feelings like yours, and no one else can stand where you stand in your unique relationship to God. He created you to respond to him in your own unique way. He created you for your unique mission in his world. He has created, loved, and called you into full-time service for him.

It is a tenet of the Christian faith that every person is called to achieve his God-given potential in service to his Creator. Sadly, however, numerous women have sold out to traditional society's concepts of persons. Instead of magnifying personhood, that is, love and respect for oneself and for every other person as one's peer, with each called to develop his own unique capacities, our culture tends to dehumanize persons.

This is done in myriad and subtle ways, chief of which is to designate life roles by sex rather than ability and interest. Both men and women are caught in this bondage, but more women tend to accept their bondage and try to convince themselves that it is right and normal. Such conditioning starts almost at birth so that by the time they finish college most women accept the limited alternatives offered them and have lost all motivation to choose others.

A recent child's book illustrates the insidious indoctrination which begins at an early age: "Boys are doctors, girls are nurses; boys are pilots, girls are stewardesses; boys invent things, girls use what boys invent; boys are presidents, girls are first ladies."

No wonder women for years have been willing to consider themselves appendages to their husbands, with their lives lived through their husbands, their futures experienced through their children. Those in the work world have seemed content to receive much less pay for their work than that received by men in the same jobs, and to take the less significant jobs, leaving men all the executive, decision-making opportunities. At an early age they completely swallowed the culture's doctrine that to get along in society a woman must play a passive, subservient role, no matter with what desires, interests, and abilities God may have endowed her. What wife would feel free to speak out as did Nora in Ibsen's *A Doll's House?*

HELMER: Before all else you are a wife and mother.

NORA: That I no longer believe. I believe that before all else I am a human being, just as much as you are—or at least that I should try to become one.

Why do women permit the "dumb" image of themselves which TV commercials consistently portray, such as the one described in the opening paragraph? Is it that women have been so brainwashed that they actually see themselves as the maimed persons the ad-men describe? Take another example: the suave man's voice to the housewife, "We all know how it feels to cook something new—it's scary....Let us bring you rice dinners."

Even family life is programmed. Marriage is a property relationship, and children are the products we produce. People exist only as consumers, victims of advertisements which create bigger and bigger appetites for things. Since women handle most of the family's money, they become the prey of the system and sell their souls to the promises of the money gods.

Children begin very young to adopt a philosophy about life and sex roles and begin to shape their own self-images. We are concerned, as Christians, that they develop a healthy, positive sense of their own worth which is necessary if they are to be able to accept God's demands that they strive to achieve their full potential.

It is very important for them to have adults in their experience who are models of such faithfulness. This need includes both men and women, but at this particular period in history it is important for children to break out of the old stereotypes that women are wives, mothers, teachers, nurses, secretaries, and that men are ministers, doctors, lawyers, scientists, politicians.

We need to expose our children to women who are successful in the fields which previously have been thought of as appropriate only for men, and to women who are engaged in important work in the community. We need also to let them know women who, no matter what their occupation, know what is going on in the world, who are able to discuss issues and are not afraid to express their views.

This means some real changes in the church, and already some are coming. In many churches women have declared their unwillingness to continue to provide offerings while the men decide how to spend them. In large numbers women are coming out of the church kitchens to help make the decisions at the tables. Women trustees and deacons are becoming more numerous.

The time is ripe for women to seek ordination and pulpits. If today's children are to overthrow the traditional stereotypes, then women must accept their status of personhood and stand alongside men to shoulder the responsibilities God places on his people.

The noted author, Pearl Buck, states that men have changed in their expectations of women but most women seem to be unaware of contemporary views of men. She thinks that men have a new estimate of what women can be and should be in relationship to themselves as men. "He has discovered that he likes to talk with intelligent women. Never before has the intelligent and educated woman had so much good male companionship as now."

Fortunately, many women are sensitive to God's call to develop themselves and are assuming new roles to meet today's needs, which are quite different than those our mothers and grandmothers faced. The average

American woman now lives to age seventy-four and has her last child at about age twenty-six. When she is thirty-two or thirty-three all her children are in school. Before she is forty her youngest child is out of high school and she is left with nearly thirty-five years of life, ten years of it as a widow.

What she does with these years is significantly vital. They tell much about her image of herself, whether she knows herself as a person of worth apart from what she has done for others or they have done for her. She can, as many women are now doing, go back to school and retrain for useful service.

She can enter politics and give much needed support and status in this field which is all-crucial to our world survival. She can call other women together to change the system which puts women down, and she can help everyone she meets to consider himself or herself a creation of God who can stand up and be counted, who can look every other person in the eye as his or her peer.

In the novel *The Chosen*, the boy Reuven is worried about his father's health. The father tells his son, "We live less than the time it takes to blink an eye, if we measure our lives against eternity. I learned a long time ago that a blink of an eye in itself is nothing. But the *eye* that blinks, *that* is something. A span of life is nothing, but the *person* who lives that span is something. He can fill that tiny span with meaning so its quality is immeasurable though its quantity be insignificant."

Look at yourself, American Baptist woman. What good will you be? What truth will you do?

68 · THE PATRIARCHAL CHURCH

Mary Daly's The Church and the Second Sex *captured the attention of the public with its forthright condemnation of sexist attitudes and practices in the Christian tradition and threatened Daly's job as a professor at Boston College. Inspired by philosopher Rosemary Lauer's writing on the Catholic church's treatment of women and angered by the passive, subservient role of Catholic sisters at the Second Vatican Council, Daly in 1965 accepted a challenge to write a book on women in the church. She clearly exposed antifeminism, arguing that the traditional notion of God as immutable inhibits social change and reinforces the idea that revelation has been given once and for all in the Bible. Like many Catholics in the wake of the Second Vatican Council, she was hopeful that the church would correct past injustices. A few years later, however, Daly was identifying herself as a post-Christian feminist, urging women to reject rather than attempt to reform such a patriarchal institution.*

Source: Mary Daly. *The Church and the Second Sex*, with the "Feminist Post-Christian Introduction" and "New Archaic After Words," 179–84. 1968, 1975; Boston: Beacon Press, 1985.

If the change of atmosphere which is so badly needed is really to come about, the best talents and concerted efforts of many persons working in different areas will be required. In this chapter we shall indicate some theological inadequacies which are at the source of Catholic androcentrism. To become aware of the scope and context of the work of ridding theology of its ancient bias is of first importance, not only for theologians but for all who are interested in the women-Church problem.

Once having taken note of the more obvious misogynistic notions which have become embedded in Christian tradition, one begins to see that the roots of these are profound and that they are interrelated. Theology is comparable to an organism: a disease affecting one part quickly spreads to another part. Moreover, it is not enough to cure a symptom. In fact, instant cures of surface manifestations might simply disguise the fact that the disease is still present at a deeper level, ready to manifest itself in other forms.

From one point of view, antifeminism in Christian thought can be looked upon as a symptom. We shall consider it here from this aspect. This is by no means to deny that misogynism can be and is a psychological origin of the very doctrinal disorders which, in turn, serve to perpetuate it. The cause-effect relationship is not one-way. It is more accurate to describe it as a vicious circle. We are now approaching that circle from the point of view of the internal structure of theology itself. That is, we shall examine those inadequacies in the conceptualizations of basic doctrines which sustain and perpetuate androcentric theological teachings.

Ideas about God

In theology, at the root of such distortions as antifeminism is the problem of conceptualizations, images, and attitudes concerning God. Many intelligent people are not aware of the depth and far-reaching consequences of this problem. It appears to such persons that an image of God as "an old man with a beard" who lives "up in heaven" is too childish to be taken seriously by any adult. They feel certain their own belief is on a level far above these notions, and that the same is true of every educated adult. In actuality their confidence in themselves and in others like them is groundless. They fail to realize what a powerful grip such images have upon the imagination even after they have been consciously rejected as primitive and inadequate. Indeed, shades of "the old man with a beard"—his various metaphysical equivalents—continue to appear even in the most learned speculations of theologians. They appear even more obviously and frequently in the watered-down, popularized versions of these speculations, for example, in text books, religion classes, and sermons.

What does the abiding presence of such images have to do with the problem with which this book is concerned? On one level the answer to this question may be glimpsed when one considers that the image in question is, obviously, of a person of the male sex. Of course, no theologian or biblical scholar believes that God literally belongs to the male sex. However, there are bits of evidence that the absurd idea that God is male lingers on in the minds of theologians, preachers and simple believers, on a level which is not entirely explicit or conscious. One has only to think of the predictable and spontaneous reaction of shock and embarrassment if a speaker were to stand before a group and refer to God as "she." Indeed, many would find it unfitting, not quite "normal" to refer to God as "she," and chances are that if forced to choose between "she" and "it" to refer to the divinity, many would prefer the latter pronoun, which, although unsatisfactory, would appear to them less blasphemous than the feminine.

Even the best theological writing can occasionally reflect the confusion over God and sex, even when a conscious effort is being made to avoid confusion. The following passage, from a well-known scholar, is an interesting specimen:

> We have already noticed that in the Mesopotamian myths sex was as primeval as nature itself. The Hebrews could not accept this view, for there was no sex in the God they worshipped. God is, of course, masculine, but not in the sense of sexual distinction, and the Hebrew found it necessary to state expressly, in the form of a story, that sex was introduced into the world by the creative Deity, who is above sex as he is above all the things which he made.[1]

What is fascinating here is that in a passage which patently explains that the God of the Old Testament is above sex, in which the author goes to great pains to make this clear, we find the bland assertion that "God is, of course, masculine." The meaning is, of course, not clear. In fact, this is the sort of nonsense statement which philosophers of the linguistic analysis school delight in dissecting. What can "masculine" mean if predicated of a Being in which there is no sex? Is this a statement about God or is it rather a statement of the author's and/or the Hebrews' opinion of the male sex? In any case, the subtle conditioning effected by the widespread opinion that God is masculine, whatever that may mean, is unlikely to engender much self-esteem in women, or much esteem for women.

---

1. John L. McKenzie, *The Two-edged Sword: An Interpretation of the Old Testament* (Milwaukee: Bruce, 1956), 93–94.

There are other distortions in traditional notions of the divinity which are quite distinct from vague identifications of God with the male sex, although they may very well be connected with these identifications. Many of these distortions have recently come under criticism by some theologians, who attribute them to an exaggerated influence of Greek philosophy upon Christian thought, and who now advocate a "de-hellenization" of Christian doctrine.[2] It is important to be aware of these perverted notions and of their bearing upon the problems with which we are concerned in this book.

Among the misleading and harmful notions about God which the modern "de-hellenizing" theologians have in mind are certain concepts which occur in connection with "divine omnipotence," "divine immutability," and "divine providence." The classical formulations of the doctrine that God is omnipotent bear with them associations and images which modern man tends to find alienating. This is especially the case because these formulations involve the idea that God is immutable. The picture which comes through is of an all-powerful, all-just God who evidently wills or, at least, permits oppressive conditions to exist. Moreover, this God is said to be changeless. In the face of such a God, man is despairing and helpless. He wonders why he should commit himself to attempting to improve his lot or trying to bring about social justice, if such a God exists.

In fact, then, such notions can and do have the effect of paralyzing the human will to change evil conditions and can inspire callousness and insensitivity. This effect upon attitudes is reinforced by certain ideas of divine providence as a fixed plan being copied out in history. With such a frame of reference, there is a temptation to glorify the *status quo*, to assume that the social conditions peculiar to any given time and place are right simply because they exist. Evidently, if one wishes to arouse theological awareness concerning problems of social justice, such as those which concern women, he should take into account the built-in resistance arising from such thought-patterns.

Scholastic theologians can argue that this is a caricature of the traditional doctrines of divine immutability, omnipotence, and providence. They can point out that classical theology has always stressed charity, that it has always insisted upon man's free-will, which is not destroyed by divine omnipotence. They can point to the thousand refinements in scholastic thought which are ignored in such a representation as we have given. The difficulty, is, however, that these efforts to "save" man's freedom have never been particularly convincing, despite their subtle and elaborate logic. What comes through to modern man is a picture of God and of man's situation which is paralyzing and alienating.

---

2. See Leslie Dewart, *The Future of Belief* (New York: Herder and Herder, 1966).

The Static World-view

The central characteristic of the world-view which results is changelessness. The frame of mind which it engenders is hardly open to theological development and social change. It is therefore not sympathetic to the problem that women and other disadvantaged groups face in relation to the Church and to other cultural institutions. Consistent with this static view is a limited conception of biological nature and of the "natural law"—interpreted as God's will. A mentality conditioned by such ideas instinctively opposes radical efforts to control and transcend the limits imposed by biological nature. The typical conservative theologians who have opposed change in the Catholic Church's position on birth control have this frame of reference. And, of course, it is consistent with this line of thinking that the myth of "immutable feminine nature and masculine nature," which is in reality a pattern of images derived in large measure from social conditioning, be set up as normative.

The resistance which the static world-view presents to ideas of social change is fortified by another idea which must be considered inimical to healthy development. This is the idea that divine revelation was given to man in the past, once and for all, and that it was "closed" at the end of the apostolic age. There can easily follow from this the idea that certain statements in the Bible represent descriptions of an unalterable divine plan, and that these statements must be accepted now and forcibly applied even though the social context in which we find ourselves is vastly different from the situation in biblical times. We have seen in a previous chapter how disastrous this attitude has been in relation to the texts of Paul and to the opening chapters of Genesis concerning women.

Contemporary theologians are beginning to take account of the inadequacies of the old notion of revelation as closed. Of course, there has always been some awareness of these inadequacies since, in fact, there has been doctrinal development in every age. Traditional theologians have tried to reconcile this undeniable fact of development with the doctrine that revelation is "closed" by arguing that content which was implicitly contained in revelation becomes, in the course of time, more explicit. Complex theories have been developed elaborating upon this, but these have been less than completely satisfactory. They tend to overemphasize the need for justification of every change in terms of the past. Some contemporary Catholic theologians, notably Gabriel Moran, are beginning to insist that revelation is an event, and that it exists today as a present event.[3] This implies a radical openness to the

<hr>

3. Gabriel Moran, "The God of Revelation," *Commonweal* 85 (10 February 1967): 499–503.

facts of contemporary experience. We are in need of such a concept of revelation, which will help to create the atmosphere needed for honest re-examination of contemporary issues, such as the Church's attitude concerning women.

Chapter 10

AGENTS OF TRANSFORMATION

69 ▪ ADMISSION OF WOMEN
TO THE PRIESTHOOD

The Vatican's "Declaration on the Question of the Admission of Women to the Ministerial Priesthood" was published in January 1977. It was a response more to ferment within the Catholic Church than to the external forces of the women's liberation movement and Protestant ordination policies. The Second Vatican Council defined the church as the people of God and called for lay involvement in all aspects of church life. A flood of books and articles calling for the ordination of women to the priesthood resulted. The declaration, which presents new reasons to justify existing legislation, concludes that the church "does not consider herself authorized to admit women to priestly ordination." As we see in sections one and two, the basis for this is that Jesus did not call a woman to be one of the Twelve, despite his willingness to break with cultural norms on many occasions. We are reminded by some scholars, however, that the declaration contains hints of indecisiveness and ambiguity. We read, for example, that the facts of Jesus' life "do not make the matter immediately obvious."

Source: "Declaration on the Question of the Admission of Women to the Ministerial Priesthood." In *Women Priests: A Catholic Commentary on the Vatican Declaration*, edited by Leonard Swidler and Arlene Swidler, 38–40. New York: Paulist Press, 1977.

The Church's Constant Tradition

The Catholic Church has never felt that priestly or episcopal ordination can be validly conferred on women. A few heretical sects in the first centuries, especially Gnostic ones, entrusted the exercise of the priestly ministry to women: this innovation was immediately noted and condemned by the Fathers, who considered it as unacceptable in the Church. It is true that in the writings of the Fathers one will find the undeniable influence of prejudices unfavorable to women, but nevertheless, it should be noted that these prejudices had hardly any influence on their pastoral activity, and still less on their spiritual direction. But over and above considerations inspired by the spirit of the times, one finds expressed—especially in the canonical documents of the Antiochian and Egyptian traditions—this essential reason, namely, that by calling only men to the priestly Order and ministry in its true sense, the Church intends to remain faithful to the type of ordained ministry willed by the Lord Jesus Christ and carefully maintained by the Apostles.

The same conviction animates mediaeval theology, even if the Scholastic doctors, in their desire to clarify by reason the data of faith, often present arguments on this point that modern thought would have difficulty in admitting or would even rightly reject. Since that period and up to our own time, it can be said that the question has not been raised again, for the practice has enjoyed peaceful and universal acceptance.

The Church's tradition in the matter has thus been so firm in the course of the centuries that the Magisterium has not felt the need to intervene in order to formulate a principle which was not attacked, or to defend a law which was not challenged. But each time that this tradition had the occasion to manifest itself, it witnessed to the Church's desire to conform to the model left to her by the Lord.

The same tradition has been faithfully safeguarded by the Churches of the East. Their unanimity on this point is all the more remarkable since in many other questions their discipline admits of a great diversity. At the present time these same Churches refuse to associate themselves with requests directed towards securing the accession of women to priestly ordination.

The Attitude of Christ

Jesus did not call any woman to become part of the Twelve. If he acted in this way, it was not in order to conform to the customs of his time, for his attitude towards women was quite different from that of his milieu, and he deliberately and courageously broke with it.

For example, to the great astonishment of his own disciples Jesus converses publicly with the Samaritan woman (cf. John 4:27); he takes no notice of the state of legal impurity of the woman who had suffered from haemorrhages (cf. Matt. 9:20-22); he allows a sinful woman to approach him in the house of Simon the Pharisee (cf. Luke 7:37ff.); and by pardoning the woman taken in adultery, he means to show that one must not be more severe towards the fault of a woman than towards that of man (cf. John 8:11). He does not hesitate to depart from the Mosaic Law in order to affirm the equality of the rights and duties of men and women with regard to the marriage bond (cf. Mark 10:2-11; Matt. 19:3-9).

In his itinerant ministry Jesus was accompanied not only by the Twelve but also by a group of women: "Mary, surnamed the Magdalene, from whom seven demons had gone out, Joanna the wife of Herod's steward Chuza, Susanna, and several others who provided for them out of their own resources" (Luke 8:2-3). Contrary to the Jewish mentality, which did not accord great value to the testimony of women, as Jewish law attests, it was nevertheless women who were the first to have the privilege of seeing the risen Lord, and it was they who were charged by Jesus to take the first paschal message to the Apostles themselves (cf. Matt. 28:7-10; Luke 24:9-10; John 20:11-18), in order to prepare the latter to become the official witnesses to the Resurrection.

It is true that these facts do not make the matter immediately obvious. This is no surprise, for the questions that the Word of God brings before us go beyond the obvious. In order to reach the ultimate meaning of the mission of Jesus and the ultimate meaning of Scripture, a purely historical exegesis of the texts cannot suffice. But it must be recognized that we have here a number of convergent indications that make all the more remarkable the fact that Jesus did not entrust the apostolic charge to women. Even his Mother, who was so closely associated with the mystery of her Son, and whose incomparable role is emphasized by the Gospels of Luke and John, was not invested with the apostolic ministry. This fact was to lead the Fathers to present her as the example of Christ's will in this domain; as Pope Innocent III repeated later, at the beginning of the thirteenth century, "Although the Blessed Virgin Mary surpassed in dignity and in excellence all the Apostles, nevertheless it was not to her but to them that the Lord entrusted the keys of the Kingdom of Heaven."

70 · TRANSFORMATION OF THE CATHOLIC SISTERHOOD

The author of this document discusses the Catholic sisterhood in the late twentieth century in the context of individual life stories and the framework or world view in which they unfold. For American nuns, the stories were once homogeneous and their framework (God's "blueprint") both clear and certain. The Second Vatican Council changed this, introducing diversity and ambiguity into their lives. The concepts of poverty and obedience have faded as useful ways to determine what it means to be a nun. The life-styles espoused by many sisters, including their dress and choice of occupation, differ little from women in the world. Celibacy remains their only distinguishing feature, and its value is persistently questioned. The author, in conclusion, has to face the possibility that as women in religious orders lose their uniqueness, this ancient institution in the church may disappear.

Source: Joanmarie Smith. "The Nun's Story." In *Women and Religion: A Reader for the Clergy*, edited by Regina Coll, 61–67. New York: Paulist Press, 1982.

God's plan was that I become a Sister of St. Joseph. He called me, held out a vocation to me. And I answered that call. In the novitiate I was educated to what being a nun involved. One became a bride of Christ. The rule provided such a detailed blueprint for living out that title that lay persons could only envy us. "You keep the holy rule and the holy rule will keep you" was a frequently heard adage that made eminent sense to me then—in that framework; in fact, it still does—in that framework.

It is my impression that priests who entered the seminary at this same time were similarly educated—that they saw themselves in analogous terms and that their framework was characterized (as was ours) by stability, simplicity, and certitude. The framework was God-given and, therefore, changeless. They would be "priests forever." And there was no complexity about what that involved. Moreover, one could be certain that in obeying one's pastor or bishop one could do no wrong—even if the pastor's or bishop's orders were wrong (Shades of "You keep the rule and the rule will keep you"). Then a funny thing happened on the way from Vatican Council II.

Vatican II, of course, did not usher in the shift in framework; it simply crystallized the shift as a possibility. The question could now at least be posed: After the Galileo case, we no longer think that our act of faith commits us to a particular physics; must we still think that our faith commits us to a particular metaphysics? Theoretically, the jury is still out on that one. But, more and more, nuns have consciously or unconsciously changed their framework. For priests, the change has not been so easy or so widespread. It is my contention that the clash in frameworks has been the source of much of any conflict which exists between nuns and priests who must work together. . . .

The nuns' story began to change to a myriad of stories in the late 1960s. From 1965 to 1970, I taught in a sister formation college. Setting up these intercongregational institutions had the effect, first of all, of fostering relationships across congregational lines. It was simultaneously discovered that the differences among congregations were minuscule. In fact, any differences stemmed more from the different personalities at the helm of the order than from differing philosophies or theologies informing them. An even more important effect was the focused inquiry that was promoted among these young women. During a council when the Church was questioning its own identity, no area was beyond the pale of investigation. In the fall-out from that period, nuns' stories changed radically. Among those who entered the convent from 1960 to 1975, approximately two-thirds have left. The median age of my own congregation is, at this time, fifty-six and rising! Those who stayed began to live a different story-framework—a story now characterized by uncertainty, complexity, and instability. . . .

One of the most prominent features of this new story-framework is that it lacks a neat theology of what it is to be a nun. The bride of Christ theology, except in the most conservative congregations, disappeared somewhat in the way the ideology of indulgences did. People just stopped using the term and the trappings that reinforced it. There were no more wedding gowns at the reception of postulants into the novitiate, no more books or hymns about "sponsae Christi." The vows themselves became problematic.

Poverty is an evil. The dilemma is obvious. To embrace what is universally seen to be an evil smacks of masochism. On the other hand, to call the relatively middle-class security that most congregations enjoy "poverty" smacks of obscenity. In the old context, fidelity to the vow had hinged on permission. Poverty was equated with dependence. The ideal of dependence was subverted by studies into the psychology of maturity. Independence and interdependence are the values pursued by actualizing adults. Simultaneously, the incongruity of a situation where one thinks oneself poor yet could study abroad, take trips, have a car for personal use, etc., as long as one had permission, became apparent. The new interpretation of poverty is simplicity. Members of congregations are enjoined to simplify their lives as much as possible—an ideal, it must be noted, enjoined not only on all Christians but upon everyone as the world's population increases and its resources decrease. That left obedience and chastity as the defining notes of women in religious orders.

I sometimes mark the unraveling of the theology of sisterhood in my religious congregation with a letter from the motherhouse saying that a sister could take a walk around the block without asking the superior. We had been taught that obedience was the linchpin of our religious vocation. Obviously the other two vows could be absorbed by it. We heard that, in fact, there were some congregations who "took" only the vow of obedience. If the bell calling us to prayer or work or recreation was considered "the voice of God," how much more so were the superior's words. God spoke through her so that anything she enjoined was God's will for us. Moreover, anything we asked to do and were permitted to do then became blessed by the assurance that it, too, was God's will. In that context, then, it was not at all absurd that in my congregation, once a month, the sisters would gather in their convents to ask permission "to pass from one part of the house to another, to wash and mend our clothes. . . ." Such an exercise ever more closely allied our lives with our "calling." But if one could walk around the block without permission, why couldn't one go home to visit the family without permission? Or, for that matter, why couldn't one go to Europe? With that letter from the motherhouse, therefore, the toothpaste started coming out of the tube, as it were. And it became impossible to put back—at least it would not go back into the same tube.

The period from the change that this letter presaged to its verbalization in the documents of the congregation seemed endless at the time. In retrospect, however, the shift occurred with marvelous speed. Our temporary "rule" (an interesting juxtaposition of terms) still speaks of discerning God's will (there's still a blueprint somewhere), but now describes this will being made known "in a multiplicity of ways—in prayer, Scripture, personal events, the needs of our time, dialogue with the sisters with whom we live, with those in authority and the people to whom we minister." In addition, in the section where the rule treats of obedience, the emphasis is on personal decisions, responsibility and dialogue. The rule no longer "keeps us." The certitude is gone. What is left, then, to mark off the vocation? Chastity?

But chastity is also a human value. To be respectful and modest—in the richest senses of those terms—toward oneself and others is, again, a value of personhood, not specifically of persons in religious orders. Not so celibacy. The Jews remind us that the *very* first commandment is to increase and multiply (Gen. 1:28)—a commandment most people are happy to obey. To forgo fulfilling this commandment is unique in the universe. Such a stance remarkably specifies a group who embraces it. It is not surprising, then, that "chastity" like "bride of Christ" has disappeared from our vocabulary. Celibacy has replaced it. At this critical point our lives overlap those of priests. There is a crucial difference, however. Celibacy is not an essential note of priesthood. It is grounded in an historical necessity. As such, it is recognized as purely disciplinary, and most theologians agree that the celibacy requirement in the Roman rite will, in the future, become as optional as it has always been in the Eastern rite. With nuns, however, a paradox has arisen. More and more, celibacy has become the specifying note of their vocation. This has the effect of having one's identity based on a sexual anomaly. Of course, there is nothing wrong with that if you can ground the value of the situation in a compelling framework. My constitutions speak of celibacy freeing the sister "to respond to God and his people with her entire sensitivity and affectivity." At first reading this seems obvious enough. Yet, it seems to me, there is an unfortunate implication embedded in such thinking. It overlooks the fact that most of the most dramatic service to humanity is rendered by married persons— doctors, statesmen, religious missionaries of other communions, among them. Such oversight neglects the common wisdom that their service is energized and enhanced in and by their marriage. Another form of the implication might go: If celibacy is freeing, sex must be a drag—literally and figuratively.

Not all the theory of celibacy is in that bag, however. There is also the thesis that celibacy acts as a sign in this world of the eschaton. "By the consecration of her entire humanity, with all that this implies for her as a woman, she is a sign of the transcendence of God calling her and all people to the fullness of life—total union with him." This may, of course, be the case, but it does seem that a radical commitment to justice could serve similarly, if not so uniquely, as that sign. But if celibacy were no longer held as a specifying note of what it means to be a nun, what would be left? That question anguishes many of us today. But some have learned not simply to live with the ambiguity of our situation, but to embrace it as the human condition because they have completely abandoned the old framework or paradigm against which they previously lived out their stories. Ambiguity has replaced certitude as the primary color of their lives. However, an even more fascinating characteristic of life in religious orders today is that sisters with different contexts can live in the same congregation and even, at times, side by side....

A different context changes not only the text of a story but also its texture. The different frameworks that brace the various members' stories produce a complex living situation. The dress of the members is a dramatic signal of more profound diversity within religious orders. I imagine that my own congregation is similar to many others in having within its ranks women who still wear a habit whose fundamentals can be traced back centuries. Other women wear what is termed "the modified habit." (An interesting aside on the modified habit: they are, for the most part, indistinguishable congregationally; that is, the dress that was once so distinctive for each religious order has been replaced by a uniform that simply signals "nun" with no further qualifications. In this our garb resembles the Roman collar.) Still other women are in various renditions of contemporary dress variously secured from such disparate places as thrift shops and Bonwit Teller.

Such diversity dramatically reflects the multiplicity of stories being lived simultaneously. Most of the communities in my congregation operate without a superior. The buck of responsibility for these communities stops at each sister. The style and content of our prayer life is also the responsibility of the local community, and each sister shapes her spirituality in the light of the local decision. We group and determine how the money which comes into the house will be dispersed after we pay our tax to the larger congregation. We also choose our work, our living situation. The complexity that such variety introduces into the congregation as a whole and into each local community, potentially at least, enriches the texture of our lives or, to use Whitehead's term, the intensity. Harmony in music provides a fruitful analogy. The texture and richness of a harmony depends upon the quality and spread of the notes. Any single note that becomes another or is not "true" to its identity diminishes the entire harmony.

But nuns must now face the dawning realization that with such ambiguity in defining ourselves and with such an assortment of lifestyles (with the exception of celibacy) we may not really be a unique entity after all. The question is endemic to nuns' meetings: "What is the essence of religious life?" The anguish of the question is exacerbated by those persons (especially those women who have left religious orders) who justifiably take umbrage at our equating *religious* life with life in a religious order. It seems that whatever we are doing as nuns we could readily do as "women in the world." We know this to be so because, more often than not, we are already doing whatever we are doing with "women in the world." In the light of these realities, and faced with the statistics of decreasing numbers and an increasing median age, members of religious order are having to learn to live with an instability more profound than economic anxiety. It is the instability introduced in the face of ultimately losing one's identity—of dying. . . .

People die, and institutions die, of course, but they are other people, other institutions. In the past ten years, nuns have had to confront, with varying degrees of consciousness and with varying degrees of success, the possible (some would say "imminent") death of nunhood as an institution. In a way, it's easier to accept the inevitability that one's own life will end than the inevitability that the institution in which one has lived this life will end. A frequently heard comment on this situation goes: "Well, religious life as we know it may change, but it will survive in some form." This may, in fact, be the case, or it may be an advanced form of denial, the first stage of the response to dying.

Then there is the danger of self-fulfilling prophecy. We may not be dying, but sounding the death knell will certainly discourage any vibrant young women from joining us. It is an especially acute sorrow to think of the possible death of an institution which can now, more than ever, offer both its members and those it serves such a maturing and rich existence. And so it goes.

71 ▪ A NEW LEADERSHIP STYLE

A graduate of Colgate Rochester Divinity School, Janet Gifford-Thorne was called to be the pastor of the struggling Plumbrook Baptist Church in Michigan in 1975, a time when few Protestant churches were considering women to fill their vacant pulpits. In this essay she describes the vision of ministry and concept of leadership that she put into practice to transform the Plumbrook congregation. All Christians, she believes, are called to ministry, and her task is to help those in her congregation to discover their gifts and be empowered to use them. She acted upon this vision by preparing thirty members of Plumbrook to assume her worship, pastoral care, and administrative responsibilities while she was on maternity leave. Men, she claims, are expected to assume most of the workload in a church in a domineering and authoritative manner. Because pastoral patterns for women have not been established, however, they have an opportunity to bring a collaborative style of leadership to Protestant life.

Source: Janet Gifford-Thorne. "Expression of a Vision." In *Women as Pastors,* edited by Lyle E. Schaller, 86–92. Creative Leadership Series. Nashville: Abingdon, 1982.

Plumbrook Church was at a low point in its history when I began. It had been organized twelve years previously, in 1963, as a new church in the suburban area north of Detroit. Even in the best of circumstances, the founding years of a new congregation require hard work and determination. The Plumbrook congregation had persevered when many other new churches had folded, but it was barely surviving.

The highly mobile population in the surrounding area had an impact on church involvement. Looking at the membership was like standing in one place and watching a passing parade. Without persistent efforts in church growth the congregation had dwindled severely as it entered its second decade of life. Worship attendance ranged from thirty to forty. There were only fifty-six active resident members. To many it appeared Plumbrook Church was dying.

Churches located in areas like Plumbrook, where there is a highly mobile population, face a great challenge in their growth. They must develop ways of inviting new people into their midst continually. If they do not concentrate energy and imagination on this ministry of outreach and receptivity toward others, simple attrition will result in a diminishing congregation, unable to carry on a vigorous ministry.

I sensed the qualities of grit and determination in the people. They were survivors. The question that hovered over the people's minds and surfaced often in conversation during the early days of my pastorate was this: "Will we be able to keep the doors of the church open?" The unanswered question I faced as a newly installed pastor was this: "Will we be able to change from a 'survivor's' church where survival is the consuming goal to a 'ministry' church where we live out a vital Christian ministry?"

I worked to instill a sense of purpose and direction among the members.

I was convinced that when people have a vision of who they are, of what they represent, of where they are heading, then they will achieve more than they ever dreamed possible. That conviction has been borne out in my experience at Plumbrook.

I hold a particular vision that motivates my ministry. My understanding is that all Christians are called by Christ into ministry. The ministries differ according to the gifts we possess. My ministry is to help others discover their gifts and their particular callings.

The meaning of the term *laity* comes from the Greek *laos*, which translates as "the whole people of God." This informs my understanding that the ministry of Christ belongs to the whole people. I see my responsibility as pastor to empower others for ministry.

The location of ministry has no restrictive boundaries. Ministry, i.e., acting on behalf of Christ, happens wherever we are, in the church and in the world. For purposes of clarity I speak of the ministry of the gathered church and the ministry of the scattered church. The church gathers for worship, study, and nurture, then scatters so that its members will incarnate the presence of Christ in their jobs, at home, at school, and in community pursuits.

From the beginning of my pastorate, I made it clear that the people of Plumbrook Church were ministers and that the destiny of the congregation belonged to us all. This sense of ownership which the congregation holds about their church has been one of the prime factors in moving out of a period of decay and hopelessness into a time of growth and vision.

I perceive the ministry of empowerment to be one of releasing people for responsible action. A mental image I carry with me that illustrates this point is one of a juggler juggling a set of oranges. The task of the pastor is not to juggle oranges as an enjoyable demonstration for others to watch, but rather to hand the oranges, i.e., the ministry, on to people for them to handle.

Through my experience as the pastor at Plumbrook, the congregation and I and the wider church are gaining important knowledge about the role of women in the pastoral ministry. A positive contribution that women are making to the whole church has to do with a new style of leadership. Growing within me is the conviction that women clergy are often gifted for a style of sharing in mutual ministry with the laity. We are not perceived in as authoritarian a light as male clergy are. We do not have to overcome generations of expectation that the pastor is a go-it-alone juggler, or a dominating figure. The women's liberation movement has reminded us to celebrate the collaborative style of shared leadership. A man who is a member of Plumbrook Church observed, "The reason the church does what it does the way it does it, is partially because of a talent of Jan's for getting people to do this and partially because she is a woman. The fact that she is a woman, people don't look at her as much as an authority figure, so they feel freer to do things and less like she's dominating."

I have met with some resistance in my empowering the ministry of others. Often, after reaching some new stage of responsible ministry, a woman or man will look back and reveal, "When I brought that problem to you and you wouldn't let me drop it in your lap or take it away from me, I was so angry. When you suggested that I had the resources to solve that dilemma or try that new venture in life, I was so frightened." But in almost every instance the people do venture forth and grow exceedingly in ability and self-concept as Christ's ministers.

I heard a member of Plumbrook Church describe my style of ministry by saying, "Jan's style of pastoring is that she holds you with one arm while pushing you to self-confident independent ministry with the other. Her habit of repressing her own insights and asking, 'What do we do now?' causes others to take charge." I really love the thousands of opportunities the pastoral ministry affords for sparking creativity in people. Creative people become active people.

A leave of absence is an opportunity for the pastor to step back and let those active people take charge. There are so many situations in which a leave of absence may occur that the learning coming out of our direct experience at Plumbrook has universal application to diverse settings. A planned leave of absence may be undertaken for obtaining specialized training, as a time for research and writing, for surgical purposes, or for vacation.

One question that intrigues the mind when consideration is given having a woman as pastor is, "What would be the experience for congregation and pastor if she were to become pregnant?" My story includes this experience of pregnancy and subsequent planned leave of absence.

The news of my pregnancy was received with delight by the congregation. We agreed that I would be away from the job for six weeks following the birth of my baby. The leave of absence was a combination of three weeks paid maternity leave, followed by three weeks of my regular vacation time.

Over a period of five months, the leaders of the congregation and I planned for the leave. Our goal was that, during my absence, the ministry of the gathered church would not skip a beat in being carried out completely by the laity. We accomplished our goal.

We concentrated our energies on preparing people to lead the church in three major areas of the pastoral role: worship, pastoral care, and administration. Thirty people secured training or were otherwise prepared to minister in these areas. Sermons were written, worship celebrations planned, training in hospital and prospective-new-member calling accomplished, administrative duties to be delegated were outlined. As the due date drew near, the congregation commissioned the thirty for their particular ministries within the church at a worship celebration. We were ready.

My daughter Elizabeth was born in the early hours of Friday, May 26, 1978. Her birth signaled the beginning of two very important new identities; mine as a mother, and the congregation's as a people equipped to do the ministry within the church.

Without exception, the laity described the maternity leave as a thoroughly positive experience for Plumbrook Baptist Church. My planned leave was a very significant chapter in the life of the church. For a short, intensive time period, a large number of laity concentrated their ministry within the structure of the church. When I returned to work, they were released from this focus of ministry. We could then return to the ongoing rhythm of shared ministry.

Today my energies are devoted primarily to ministry within the church. A group of gifted and capable laity share in this arena with me. For many of the laity, their primary ministries are found in the places of their vocations, including job and home.

The reason we have energy for both church and world ministry in a congregation that numbers around 120 members is that we keep the operation of the church "clean and lean." The structure of the church is simple.

In my opinion, one of the greatest wastes of human energy on behalf of the Church is the way in which so many congregations are structured to gobble up the laity's time and energy in meaningless activity instead of purposeful action. I have learned that organizational structure can serve to either block or empower the ministries of people.

An important part of my ministry is the mobilization of precious and limited human resources. At Plumbrook we designed a new organizational structure. A single Council of nine people serves as the center of the design. It, along with two standing committees, is the only fixed part of our structure. The rest is totally flexible. The result of our having reshaped the structure allows us to mobilize people around particular needs. When a certain number of people are needed to handle a given task, they join forces. When the task is accomplished, they are free to rest or go on to another ministry task. People are able to choose the areas of the church's life that interest them.

We have come a long way, the congregation and I, since I began my pastorate. Decay has given way to growth. Hopelessness has been transformed into vision. Depression has been converted into optimism. Plumbrook Baptist Church is now a many-faceted center of Christian ministry.

72 · A FEMINIST CRITIQUE
OF THEOLOGICAL EDUCATION

This document is not the work of a single author but rather the product of collaborative reflection and writing by nineteen women committed to religion and feminism. Their complete work, Your Daughters Shall Prophesy, *is an attempt to address sexism in American theological education by advocating alternative structures and models of leadership. Here they present some of their working assumptions that inform their evaluation of existing programs and their vision for the future. They point out that theological education is fragmented, involving subordinate students who passively receive knowledge from experts. Women are outsiders in this process. They are not physically present on seminary staffs, and their history and experiences are only marginal to the core curriculum in which much has been invested. Women desire theological education that is wholistic. The writers are convinced that such education would lead to a more collaborative style of ministry that would, in turn, benefit the churches.*

Source: The Cornwall Collective. *Your Daughters Shall Prophesy: Feminist Alternatives in Theological Education*, 2–8. New York: Pilgrim Press, 1980.

Women seminarians in the United States today enter a system of theological education that has its roots in the early nineteenth century. Within a few years of the founding of Andover Theological Seminary (Congregational), in 1809, the Andover curriculum became the model for theological education: it remained the model until the early twentieth century and is influential even today. That first curriculum included courses in Sacred Literature, Christian Theology, Sacred Rhetoric, and Ecclesiastical History. Early in this century there was a significant modification of the curriculum, with the introduction of "practical" courses in religious education, psychology and sociology of religion, liturgics, and preaching. Contemporary curricula conventionally offer "practical" courses, along with three "academic" areas—scripture, church history, and theology. The division between practical and academic disciplines remains in force, although there has been some renaming and revaluation; for example, psychology and sociology of religion, and social ethics may be regarded as academic and offered under the rubric of "Church and Society." Ancient assumptions about what constitutes the "core" curriculum have been canonized.

Organized around disciplines, each with its specialized language and methodology, seminaries have adopted the university model of education, claiming "objectivity" as the rationale for a supposedly value-free approach to scholarship. In fact, of course, scholarship is never value-free, and in the schools under discussion it reflects the attitudes and stance of white, middle-class men. Furthermore, the university model itself, derived from nineteenth-century Tübingen (and before that from thirteenth-century Paris), is hierarchical, competitive, and heavily weighted with class, race, and gender bias. Each professor, working alone and usually in competition with his (*sic*) colleagues, imparts to students those bits and pieces of a discipline that he and the school (in the modified Andover curriculum) feel the student should learn. When the student has collected enough pieces, she/he graduates and, in the case of doctoral students, proceeds to pass on the slightly used pieces in another classroom. Despite a few attempts at integration—mostly in the form of doctoral exams in which the burden of integration is on the student—the pieces are seldom gathered into a pattern meaningful to the student.

In the present system of promotion and tenure, young scholars are trapped into the self-perpetuating disciplines of the traditional curriculum. Publication is emphasized over teaching as the criterion for reward. Students in turn learn to do research that fits the specialized, departmentalized models of "scholarly" work, and those who attempt to do research that integrates the theory and practice of ministry must rely on their own resources. Too often they are told that their interests are peripheral to the essential tasks of theological education. Consistent with this approach to research, the teaching/learning models typically adhere to what Paulo Freire calls a "banking" concept of education: the professor holds a certain body of knowledge, which he deposits in the brain of the student; the student holds it there until the professor calls for it, when it is returned—perhaps with a little interest, perhaps without, for the student's own ideas are add-ons. In this model, required courses ensure that the student acquires what the white, male, middle-class decision-makers of the school regard as basic preparation for ministry. There is little provision for assisting the student to define learning goals, and little recognition of the resources students bring to the educational process. In such a setting, the perspectives of racial minorities, of the poor, and of women are seen as marginal or are totally excluded....

As feminists, we have become increasingly aware of the ways in which women are outsiders to the process of theological education. We are not only physically outside, excluded from positions of power such as faculty appointments and top administrative positions; we are psychically outside, because our history and experience are not taken seriously. Women generally are confined to minor, supportive roles, usually low-level administrative or junior faculty positions, serving at the pleasure of white males who do not hesitate to replace women who "cause trouble." This system reflects and perpetuates the sexism that prevails throughout the life of the church. Theological schools acknowledge, record, and interpret the experience of a minority of people in the Christian tradition, claiming that experience as valid for everyone. We do not reject the entire tradition of theological education, but we do insist that it presents only one perspective on a complex reality. Like every other field, theology has become "professional"; it has its own requirements for acquiring credentials and certification. As people invest time, money, and energy in this process, their livelihood and self-esteem come to depend upon maintaining control of a "certain territory on the knowledge map." Powerful territorial imperatives emerge, and methods are soon developed to discredit those outside. When women challenge the basic assumptions in which these imperatives are rooted, they enter the arena of power politics.

The white male perspective is assumed in theological education to define the totality of Judeo-Christian understandings about God. That perspective is universalized as the norm against which all other "talk about God" is evaluated. Such other talk has been called interesting, relevant, even "liberating" by some liberals, but it is not acknowledged as "theology." Questions raised by women, blacks, Hispanics, Native Americans, and the poor are seen as peripheral. New courses may be invented and added to the core curriculum to deal with the interests of current students, but such courses do not alter the structures or assumptions of the disciplines. There are courses in "New Testament" and in "Women in the New Testament," in "Church History" and in "Women in Church History," but basic educational questions are not addressed.

In introductory courses the works of feminist or liberation theologians still appear at the end of the syllabus as optional choices for papers. However, the perceptions of these theologians have not modified the study or the interpretation of Paul or Aquinas, nor are they regarded as integral to the intellectual and spiritual formation of the minister. The Research/Resource Associates Program (R/RA) at Harvard Divinity School provides excellent examples of this phenomenon. The program was designed to bring women from across the country to do research and to provide Harvard with resources to be used in implementing changes in the core curriculum. Although there have been many positive effects of the program, including courses designed and taught by associates that have served women well, the purpose for which the program was designed has *not* been fulfilled. Not one course designed by an associate has been incorporated into the core curriculum, nor is there any evidence that research done by associates has found its way into the main body of course work offered by other faculty in the various disciplines.

Refusing to acquiesce quietly in the system of traditional theological education, feminists have begun to bring to collective consciousness the history, creativity, insights, and experiences of women in faith communities. Believing that the barriers between disciplines are for the most part arbitrary, that clinical pastoral education is not usefully separated from theology and ethics, that church history is neither teachable nor meaningful without social and economic analysis, and that most of the dissertations stacked in theological libraries were written by, for, and about an elite, feminists have articulated a new set of assumptions, which grow out of women's experience of reality. . . .

Basic to a feminist approach to theological education is the understanding of education as a wholistic process. The word wholistic is in danger of becoming a cliche, but it is still a convenient shorthand for many of the values feminists want to embody. As we attempt to give specific content to the word, its meaning is clarified. Wholistic learning involves both cognitive and affective aspects, and can be expressed in part by such phrases as "knowledge is total experience," or "knowing embraces theory and practice." Dualisms of thought and feeling, being and doing, contemplating and acting, personal and public, sacred and profane create their own demons. Rather than define these aspects of reality as though each had a life of its own, feminists struggle to discover the web of interconnectedness that leads to the formation of images of wholeness. Without such images, fruitless discussions about the relative merits of one side or the other of a dichotomy (for example, the primacy of the academic over the practical fields of theological education) continue to blunt the energy and creativity of both women and men. A call to wholeness affirms that human beings learn through multiple avenues—through the senses, feelings, intuitions—and that learnings can be expressed in many ways—through image and symbol, poetry, dance, and story, as well as through analytical prose. The collection of prose, poetry, and drawings called "The Lady Who Used to Be a Strawberry" is just one example of the work accomplished in courses based on a wholistic approach to theological education. The collection was developed by participants in a course offered through the Graduate Theological Union by the Center for Women and Religion (at that time, 1974, called the Office of Women's Affairs). The course, entitled "Women/Yoga/Creativity," combined the reading and discussion of works by feminist writers, the body movement and reflective discipline of yoga, and the creative expression of participants.

In the context of a wholistic approach, theological education can most effectively attend to its primary task: the preparation of women and men for ministry. In such a context, intellectual understanding is integrated with the development of skills. Instead of the hierarchical, fragmented, departmentalized, competitive approach derived from university models, wholistic approaches are learner-centered, experience-based, open-access, and cooperatively oriented. When students learn only in a setting in which one man (usually the case) is "in charge" and has all the knowledge to be given out as he chooses to those over whom he holds power, they are learning a style of ministry. This style is replicated in the ministry when the one person "in charge" transmits to the church the values represented by hierarchy, fragmentation, and competition. Basic to a feminist understanding of ministry, however, is the assumption that it requires a setting of mutuality in which persons are enabled to value and to name their own experiences, learn from them, and move toward new understandings in the light of their own authority and of cooperative power relations.

Mobilized by our critique of the present system of theological education, and energized by our vision of the possibilities of alternative approaches, women around the country have attempted to develop programs based on feminist assumptions and through them to affect the larger system of theological education.

73 · INCLUSIVE LANGUAGE FOR WORSHIP

In 1980 the Division of Education and Ministry of the National Council of Churches of Christ appointed a committee of six men and six women to prepare lectionary readings for public worship using inclusive language. Working with Greek and Hebrew texts, other translations, and commentaries, the committee produced three one-year cycles of readings that recast some of the wording of the Revised Standard Version of the Bible. Specifically, the committee worked to change the male bias in language for God, Jesus, and human beings. In the excerpts here, which come from the second cycle of readings, "Lord" is changed to "Sovereign" to avoid the common understanding of "lord" as a man with power and authority. In two instances names have been added to the text. Women's names are included where the generation of offspring is discussed, and God is described as "Father and Mother," the one who both begat and gave birth to Jesus. As the humanity of Jesus is what is crucial to salvation, Jesus becomes the "Child of God" in the revised text.

Source: *An Inclusive Language Lectionary: Readings for Year B*. Prepared by the Inclusive Language Lectionary Committee appointed by the Division of Education and Ministry, National Council of the Churches of Christ in the U.S.A., 40, 74, 82. Philadelphia: Westminster Press, 1984.

Ephesians 1:3-6, 15-18

The writer of the letter to the Ephesians begins by praising God's glorious grace in Jesus Christ.

Blessed be God the Father [*and Mother*] of our Sovereign Jesus Christ, who has blessed us in Christ with every spiritual blessing in the heavenly places, even as God chose us in Christ before the foundation of the world, that we should be holy and blameless before God, who destined us in love to be God's children through Jesus Christ, according to the purpose of God's will, to the praise of God's glorious grace freely bestowed on us in the Beloved.

For this reason, because I have heard of your faith in the Sovereign Jesus and your love toward all the saints, I do not cease to give thanks for you, remembering you in my prayers, that the God of our Sovereign Jesus Christ, the Father [*and Mother*] of glory, may give you a spirit of wisdom and of revelation in the knowledge of God, having the eyes of your hearts enlightened, that you may know what is the hope to which you have been called, what are the riches of God's glorious inheritance in the saints.

Psalm 105:1-11

O give thanks to God, call on God's name,
  make known God's deeds among the peoples!
Sing to God, sing praises to God,
  tell of all God's wonderful works!
Glory in God's holy name;
  let the hearts of those who seek God rejoice!
Seek God and God's strength,
  seek God's presence continually!
Remember the wonderful works that God has done,
  God's miracles, and the judgments God uttered,
O offspring of Abraham [*and Sarah,*] God's servants,
  children of Jacob, [*Rachel, and Leah,*] God's chosen ones!

This is the Sovereign One our God,
  whose judgments are in all the earth.
God is mindful of the covenant for ever,
  of the word that God commanded, for a thousand generations,
the covenant which God made with Abraham,
  God's sworn promise to Isaac,
confirmed to Jacob as a statute,
  to Israel as an everlasting covenant,

saying, "To you I will give the land of Canaan
as your portion for an inheritance."

John 3:14-21

Acceptance or rejection of God's love in Jesus Christ brings its own consequence.

And as Moses lifted up the serpent in the wilderness, so must the
Human One be lifted up, that whoever believes in the Human One may
have eternal life.

For God so loved the world that God gave God's only Child, that whoever believes in that Child should not perish but have eternal life. For God
sent that Child into the world, not to condemn the world, but that through
that Child the world might be saved. Whoever believes in the Child [*of God*]
is not condemned; whoever does not believe is condemned already, for not
having believed in the name of the only Child of God. And this is the judgment, that the light has come into the world, and people loved the shadows
rather than the light, because their deeds were evil. For all who do evil hate
the light, and do not come to the light, lest their deeds should be exposed.
But all who do what is true come to the light, that it may be clearly seen
that their deeds have been wrought in God.

74 · FEMINIST VIEWS OF SIN AND SALVATION

In this section of Human Liberation in a Feminist Perspective, *feminist
theologian Letty Russell discusses the willingness of contemporary religious seekers
to be flexible in their definitions of sin and salvation. Firmly rooted in the biblical
concept of* shalom, *liberation theologians, for example, assert that salvation is
much more than individual deliverance from sin and death. It is personal and
social well-being, the transformation of economic, political, social, and mental
structures. Women, Russell points out, are particularly interested in moving
beyond the definition of sin as aggression and lust, which has been emphasized by
male theologians, to an understanding of sin as underdevelopment or negation
of the self. Women, in their quest for liberation, also find it important to define
sin as "the refusal to give others room to breathe and live as human beings."*

Source: Letty M. Russell. *Human Liberation in a Feminist Perspective—A Theology*,
109–13. Philadelphia: Westminster Press, 1974.

One of the interesting things that has happened to the understanding of
salvation today is that, in a world of diversity and change, people feel free
to use a variety of definitions of salvation. In the search for meaning every
religion and ideology is explored for its offer of liberation, wholeness, and

blessing.[1] There is a growing awareness of the wholeness of human beings in their body, mind, and spirit and in their social relationship in today's world. For some this has led to a renewed stress on *shalom* as a gift of total wholeness and well-being in community.[2] The search for peace in a wartorn world where each new outbreak of fighting brings not only untold suffering but the threat of total destruction has led others to speak of *shalom* as the symbol of peace and harmony for which they long and work. Others see *shalom* as an expression of wholeness and harmony between humanity and the environment which is being destroyed by a technological society.[3]

Nowhere is the stress on salvation as seen in the motifs of *shalom* clearer than among those searching for ways of expressing the good news of God's traditioning action in situations of oppression, hunger, and alienation in our sorry world. Liberation theologies, which seek to reflect on the praxis of God's liberation in the light of particular circumstances of oppression, are returning to the motifs of liberation and blessing as they are found in the biblical tradition. Without denying that salvation includes the message of individual deliverance from sin and death (Rom. 5–7) they, nevertheless, place emphasis on the total goal of salvation (Rom. 8), which is the gift of *shalom* (complete social and physical wholeness and harmony). Gutiérrez says:

> Salvation is not something otherworldly, in regard to which the present life is merely a test. Salvation—the communion of . . . [people] with God and the communion of . . . [people] among themselves—is something which embraces all human reality, transforms it, and leads it to its fullness in Christ.[4]

In these emerging liberation theologies the two overlapping motifs of *shalom* appear again as a description of the usable future. The first motif of *liberation* is seen as the gift of God's action in history, as well as the agenda of those who join together in community to transform the world. For Third World and Fourth World people the motif of liberation expresses an important aspect of the *shalom* for which they seek. Speaking about "The Dialectic of Theology and Life," James Cone reminds us that "Jesus is not

1. *Salvation Today and Contemporary Experience: A Collection of Texts for Critical Study and Reflection* (Geneva: World Council of Churches, 1972).

2. Gabriel Fackre, *Do and Tell: Engagement Evangelism in the 70's* (Grand Rapids, Mich.: Wm. B. Eerdmans Publishing Company, 1973), 34; Letty M. Russell, "Shalom in Postmodern Society," in *A Colloquy on Christian Education*, ed. John A. Westerhoff III (United Church Press, 1972), 97–105; *Colloquy*, National Shalom Conference Issue 6 (March 1973).

3. Fackre, *Do and Tell*, 86; *Colloquy, A Curriculum for Peace* 5 (July/August 1972).

4. Gustavo Gutiérrez, *A Theology of Liberation*, trans. and ed. Caridad Inda and John Eagleson (Maryknoll, N.Y.: Orbis Books, 1972), 151; cf. A. Schoors, *I Am God Your Savior* (Leiden: E. J. Brill, 1973).

a doctrine" but an eternal event of liberation who makes freedom possible. From this context of Christ as Liberator emerges a life of interdependence in the lives of black people. He is the Word of truth in their lives.[5] In the area of justice and economic development, those at work to bring about an evolutionary process for transforming economic, social, political, and mental structures point to a connection with salvation in its implication of freedom. Thus in *Liberation, Development, and Salvation*, René Laurentin says that "development presupposes a liberation from systems in which any development is impossible."[6]

Writers such as Rosemary Ruether and Dorothee Sölle emphasize the same theme. Ruether, in her book *Liberation Theology*, speaks of the destructive character of dualisms such as that between the individual and the collective, and the body and the soul, and sets out to analyze various polarities which are barriers to the theology and praxis of liberation. Sölle speaks of the gospel's business as "liberation of all human beings. Its concern rests with the oppressed, the poor, the crying."[7]

The second motif that overlaps with liberation is the meaning and experience of *shalom* as *blessing*. In the writers concerned with liberation theology this is usually interpreted as *humanization:* the setting free of all humanity to have a future and a hope. The blessings of the Patriarchs are now interpreted in modern contexts as the need for full personal and social well-being, as well as the need for the power to participate in shaping the world.

For those who experience *shalom* as new wholeness and liberation as human beings, *sin* is also viewed as a collective reality. The social as well as the individual responsibility for sin is stressed so that *oppression* is itself viewed as a symbol of the social reality of sin. Dorothee Sölle writes:

> Sin to us is eminently political, a social term: the sins of which Jesus reminds me and which he puts before my eyes are the sins of my own people, of my own white race, of my own bourgeois and propertied class.[8]

---

5. James Cone, "The Dialectic of Theology and Life" (inaugural lecture as professor of theology, Union Theological Seminary, New York City, Oct. 11, 1973); and cf. "Black Theology and Reconciliation," *Christianity and Crisis* 32 (January 22, 1973): 303–8.

6. René Laurentin, *Liberation, Development, and Salvation* (Maryknoll, N.Y.: Orbis Books, 1972), 53.

7. Rosemary Radford Ruether, *Liberation Theology* (New York: Paulist Press, 1973), 7–9, 16–22; Dorothee Sölle, "The Gospel and Liberation," *Commonweal* (December 22, 1972): 270.

8. Sölle, "The Gospel and Liberation," 273–74; cf. Gordon D. Kaufman, "The Imago Dei as Man's Historicity," *The Journal of Religion* 36 (July 1956): 165–67.

Going back to the root meaning of one word for salvation (*yeshu'ah*, from a root meaning "to be broad, or spacious"; "to have room"), sin is interpreted as the denial of this room or space in which to live.[9] Just as Isaiah 49:19-20 symbolizes the oppression of Israel as a land "too narrow for your inhabitants" and Psalm 4:1 speaks of salvation as the gift of "room when I was in distress," liberation theologies point to sin as the refusal to give others room to breathe and live as human beings. According to Gutiérrez:

> Sin is regarded as a social, historical fact, the absence of . . . [human-hood] and love in relationships among . . . [people], the breach of friendship with God and with other . . . [people], and, therefore, an interior, personal fracture. When it is considered in this way, the collective dimensions of sin are rediscovered.[10]

Women are very much interested in the reinterpretation of the meaning of sin in a feminist perspective. In church traditions sin has been interpreted not only individualistically but also as associated with sex and with women. A forthright rejection of such misogyny, including the misinterpretations of the Adam and Eve story which flow from this perspective, can be seen in many feminist writers. For instance, Mary Daly writes:

> In the mentality of the Fathers, woman and sexuality were identified. Their horror of sex was also a horror of woman. There is no evidence that they realized the projected mechanisms involved in this misogynistic attitude. In fact, male guilt feelings over sex and hyper-susceptibility to sexual stimulation and suggestion were transferred to "the other," the guilty sex.[11]

Another area of reinterpretation of the traditions concerning sin which interests feminist writers is the male perspective on what constitutes human sin and temptation. Aggression, lust, and hybris may not be at the top of the list for women who have been enculturated to be submissive. Valarie Saiving Goldstein writes:

> The temptations of woman *as woman* are not the same as the temptations of man *as man*, and the specifically feminine forms of sin— "feminine" not because they are confined to women or because women are incapable of sinning in other ways but because they are

---

9. A. Richardson, "Salvation, Savior," *Interpreter's Dictionary of the Bible*, vol. 4 (Nashville: Abingdon, 1962), 169; J. Verkuyl, *The Message of Liberation in Our Age* (Grand Rapids, Mich.: Wm. B. Eerdmans Publishing Company, 1970), 17–18.

10. Gutiérrez, *Theology of Liberation*, 175; Ruether, *Liberation*, 8.

11. Mary Daly, *The Church and the Second Sex* (New York: Harper & Row, 1968), 46–47; cf. Ruether, *Liberation*, 95–113.

outgrowths of the basic feminine character structure—have a quality which can never be encompassed by such terms as "pride," and
"will-to-power." They are better suggested by such items as triviality,
distractibility, and diffuseness; lack of an organizing center or focus;
dependence on others for one's own self-definition; tolerance at the
expense of standards of excellence; . . . in short, underdevelopment or
negation of self.[12]

In various liberation theologies sin is viewed not only as the opposite
of liberation or the oppression of others but also as the opposite of humanization or the *dehumanization* of others by means of excluding their
perspectives from the meaning of human reality and wholeness.

In summary we can say that salvation today, as well as the understanding of sin today, has regained its social and communal emphasis in writings
on liberation theology. Not denying individual responsibility and accountability, they still drive us also to see the dimension of responsibility and
accountability in terms of the liberation and blessing for all oppressed and
defuturized persons. For many people today, liberation is understood as a
gift of God at once personal and social which is only ours as it is constantly
shared with others.

---

12. Valarie Saiving Goldstein, "The Human Situation: A Feminine View," *The Journal of
Religion* 40 (April 1960): 108–9.